Greenhouse—Place of Magic

DUTTON GARDEN GUIDES

Carol Woodward, Consulting Editor

Gertrude S. Wister
HARDY GARDEN BULBS

Dr. Louis Pyenson
KEEP YOUR GARDEN HEALTHY

Alys Sutcliffe
HOUSE PLANTS FOR CITY DWELLERS

Harold O. Perkins
ORNAMENTAL TREES FOR HOME GROUNDS

Edwin F. Steffek, Consulting Editor

Gertrude B. Foster
HERBS FOR EVERY GARDEN

Charles H. Potter
GREENHOUSE—PLACE OF MAGIC

GREENHOUSE—

Place of Magic
REVISED EDITION

by Charles H. Potter

A Sunrise Book
E. P. Dutton & Co., Inc.
New York   1976

Published simultaneously in Canada by Clarke, Irwin & Company Limited, Toronto and Vancouver

ISBN: 0-87690-199-2(p)
Library of Congress Catalog Card Number: 66–21304

Dutton-Sunrise, Inc., a subsidiary of E. P. Dutton & Co., Inc.

To my wife, Neva,
who did the hard work

Table of Contents

Illustrations

Preface

Growing flowers and plants in a greenhouse is the ultimate refinement of the greatest of all hobbies—gardening.

For many years I have been an avid gardener both as an amateur and as a commercial grower. During those years my experience has run the gamut from pruning a tree on a winter's day, warding off the cold wind with warm gloves and tightly zippered jacket, to tending my little greenhouse on an equally cold day while in my shirtsleeves. My greenhouse experience has been tempered by the commercial grower's aspect where every nickel must count, and heightened by the amateur grower's enthusiastic viewpoint, which is curbed only by the money which the family budget will allow for a greenhouse hobby and the time which can be spent to enjoy it.

The two-way viewpoint made it possible for me to store up a great deal of knowledge which would otherwise not have been possible. My practical experience has been augmented by regular attendance for many years at grower meetings where I have listened to U.S.D.A. plant research men from Beltsville, Maryland and other places; expert growers, specialists in their respective fields; county agents, and others. My notes have been voluminous.

If I were to set forth here acknowledgments to all those who made this book possible, I would have a book of names alone, for I would have to start with the ancients who first gardened in Babylon, Egypt, Greece, and Rome, ending with the last gardener with whom I talked most recently, my neighbor across the street. For such is the ancient, yet modern, occupation and hobby of gardening, be it indoors or under a greenhouse roof. Each one who has ever gardened for profit or for fun or has indulged in horticultural research has a share in this book, for all have contributed somewhere along the line. Come, read ahead, and let's see what I have to say about what all these thousands of people have done and said which applies to gardening under glass.

CHAPTER I
Why a Home Greenhouse?

There is one thing that you will find practically impossible to carry into your own greenhouse and that is tension. Every gardener is aware of the tonic of the feel of moist, warm earth, the sight of lush green foliage and colorful flowers, and the delicious fragrances. The gardener with a greenhouse is keenly aware of the intensification of these delights. Everything becomes more intimate—i.e., those gardening joys which are pleasing and exhilarating.

And along with relaxation, the greenhouse offers the whole family a shared hobby. It can be a place in which plants and cut flowers are produced both for your home and your friends. The women of the household can go there to snip a flower to wear. And the man of the house can take pride in growing plants for all purposes—indoors and out.

If you are new to this hobby of greenhouse-growing, and if you are the wage earner or the budget-minder, the matter of cost is bound to be in your thoughts. Then there are two other matters of equal importance when you consider a home greenhouse: (1) how much time will you have to devote to the hobby of greenhouse growing? (2) will the home greenhouse tie you down so that you can never get away when you want to?

How much *will* a home greenhouse cost? That depends upon a number of things. For one thing, the cost will be in direct proportion to the style you choose. It will also depend upon the size of the greenhouse you build. Greenhouses can be extremely simple, made of inexpensive materials, and with manual heat and ventilation controls, or they can be of the finest construction materials and have everything from heating, ventilating, cooling, to watering controlled automatically. Usually the home greenhouse is in between. Avoid if possible using the cheapest wood framework; it is actually less expensive in the long run to use better materials, for the maintenance is less and the greenhouse will last much longer. Redwood is the finest wood used in the Pacific Northwest or in California for greenhouse construction, and Number One heart cypress is the best wood for greenhouse construction in many other parts of the country. Either of these materials will outlast fir and pine by many years. Cedar is often used and is quite long-lasting.

A prefabricated greenhouse will cost you a little more to erect, but it assures you a finer, tighter-fitting greenhouse, as a rule, with a

Prefab, sectional greenhouses are quickly assembled.

minimum of effort on your part. Still, if you have the time, and if you are handy with tools, you should not hesitate to build your own greenhouse from scratch. But when you do, pay close attention to the kind of materials you use.

The size of your greenhouse and the time you will be able to devote to your hobby are important considerations. No matter how carefully you may think you have judged both, it is a safe bet that you will find your greenhouse will fill up with plants faster than guinea pigs fill up a pen. The best advice is to fit your greenhouse hobby to a size which will give you a feeling of satisfaction without frustration.

Does a greenhouse tie one down? In almost every neighborhood there are dozens of people who would like to get their hands in a greenhouse at least once in a while. If you can ferret out such persons in your neighborhood, and, perhaps, share a bit of your greenhouse hobby with them by way of a gift plant now and then or frequent peeks at what you are doing, you should have no problem whatsoever finding a good greenhouse-minder when you want to be away. A good outdoor gardener can quickly be taught the essentials concerning the regulation of your greenhouse and the care of your plants when you are absent.

CHAPTER II
Build It in the Sun

"Where will I put it?" Greenhouse manufacturers are way ahead of anyone who asks that question today, for they have greenhouses that will fit any situation. There are free-standing greenhouses; lean-to and breezeway types of greenhouses; and end-attached greenhouses—even those for inside a home! It is possible to perch a greenhouse atop a garage or other building, but only if the garage or building is strong enough: there is considerable weight in a home greenhouse, especially if it is a steel one, by the time you add benches, soil, heating equipment, etc. Don't take a chance with an ordinary roof which has not been reinforced.

The free-standing greenhouse offers the best way to achieve ideal growing conditions for your flowers and plants. It affords maximum light; every corner is available for growing space. This type of greenhouse, however, is more costly to heat than one which is attached to the home, for the loss of heat through glass is greater than it is through a wall of a house, and a certain amount of warmth comes from the home.

The end-attached greenhouse has the advantage that if it is attached to a back or side door, it will be easily accessible from the home or yard. The end-attached greenhouse is usually of even span —with equal-length rafters on both sides—similar to the free-standing greenhouse. It is easy to add to its length, just as it is with a free-standing greenhouse.

Far more lean-to greenhouses are seen than any other type, because they are usually easier to erect and very often they may be made part of the architecture of the home. Done properly, they enhance the beauty of the home. The lean-to greenhouse can fit onto the home at a doorway or over a window area. The latter can be enlarged so that access to the greenhouse is easy from the home.

A site for a home greenhouse should have good drainage, but if it does not exist, it can be provided. A serious situation can be corrected with tile, and gravel can be used to correct a minor drainage problem.

And your home greenhouse must set level. If you do not have a level site for it, level the area before you build. This will aid your construction, and give you level places beneath the benches for placement of plants which use less light.

But the single, most important consideration when choosing a site for a greenhouse is the matter of natural light. It is always best to place your greenhouse where your plants will get maximum sunlight. Shade may always be added. Beware of shade trees, because they can create problems. Heavy shade created by the foliage during the summer months will limit production to certain plants. Furthermore, there is always the messiness of leaves falling on the greenhouse and into the troughs, and the danger of limbs falling on the glass.

For an attached greenhouse, a southwest exposure provides the maximum of light, but if you must choose between an east or west exposure, take the former. The morning hours for a plant are the most productive. By afternoon, the energy of a plant has started to slow down; hence, the afternoon sunlight is of less good to the plant than morning sunlight. Nevertheless, if you must place your attached greenhouse on the west side of the house, do so; you *can* grow flowers and plants in a west-attached greenhouse.

The greenhouse which is easily accessible to both home and garden is the ideal. It is handy for work—and readily available for pleasure.

CHAPTER III
Greenhouse Materials

If you are a real dyed-in-the-wool, do-it-yourself person with a good knowledge of construction, no doubt you will want to build your greenhouse from scratch. The plans you need can be obtained from most of the state agricultural colleges or from county agents. If you are a semi do-it-yourselfer, you might find it a bit easier to erect one of the prefab greenhouses which are manufactured by several companies. You will find a list of such manufacturers at the end of this chapter.

There are new building materials available today which insure easy erection of the greenhouse and provide longer life for the structure. If you can afford the finest materials, you will be able to do away with most maintenance and, therefore, save money in the long run. Even without investing a large amount, however, you can erect a durable greenhouse and an attractive one which will be an asset to your property.

The Foundation

There are some prefab houses nowadays and even some do-it-yourself greenhouses which eliminate a foundation, as such, altogether except for that portion which is below the soil line. If you plan to use space beneath the bench or grow certain plants which will not get by on a minimum of light, then you certainly will want a greenhouse without a true foundation. Where the weather is mild enough, as in the south or in California, there are prefab types of greenhouse which set right on the ground itself, requiring no foundation.

There was a time when greenhouses were built mainly with a double-wood foundation with an air space between the two layers of wood. It was cheap, not difficult to erect, and, therefore, popular. Today, wood is being used less and less for the foundation, since other materials offer greater stability, more protection from the elements, and make maintenance easier.

A combination of wood (for the framework) and Transite (asbestos sheeting) is often used for the sides. Transite costs more than wood but is more durable and requires only limited maintenance, providing the wood members are resting on cement blocks or a low cement foundation.

The stability of a greenhouse is important, especially in areas where wind may be a problem. If you live in such an area, you should have a good solid masonry foundation or submerged concrete or metal posts to which you may anchor the framework of the greenhouse. And regardless of the wind factor, a solid foundation is necessary where winters are cold. Remember that the temperature is lowest at the ground level.

Masonry foundations afford the finest type of foundation possible. Their cost is greater, but they solve the problems of durability and protection from cold. A first-class masonry foundation—which should be extended three or four feet beneath the surface in cold climates and two feet or more above the surface—can be constructed of stone, brick, concrete or pumice blocks, or of poured concrete. If you are searching for the maximum in beauty, you might choose a fancy-type stone or an attractive brick for the foundation. Concrete or pumice blocks, properly installed, can also provide a greenhouse with a good husky foundation. Stuccoed attractively on the outside, either can look quite rich. Most gardeners, however, prefer to use concrete. It is easily poured, economical, and durable. A good mixture of concrete for a greenhouse foundation is that of 1 part cement, 3 parts sand, and 5 parts gravel. A good waterproof mixture is one consisting of 1 part cement, 2½ parts sand, and 3½ parts gravel.

THE FRAME AND ITS COMPONENTS

For the frame, too, the major points are economy and durability—along with the additional factor of heat transmission.

Earlier greenhouses were built almost entirely of wood, usually cedar or fir, but this was strictly a matter of economy and availability. Even steel greenhouses were pretty much out of the picture at first because of their cost. Then came the idea of using iron or steel framework and wood components for a greater amount of light, greater strength, and longer-lasting construction. Next was the all-steel greenhouse, then the structural-steel greenhouse, and, most recently, the all-aluminum greenhouse. Here are the prime factors to consider concerning each of these materials:

The biggest objection to the use of cedar or fir is that it will rot too quickly, but if you apply wood preservatives, plus a good under-coat and at least two coats of a high-quality greenhouse paint at the time of erection, you can insure a long-lasting greenhouse, with proper maintenance. But you should use only good, well-seasoned straight-grained wood; in a dry climate, unseasoned wood cracks and twists when used for greenhouse rafters. The best of soft woods is first-grade red cedar.

As noted, redwood is one of the best woods to use for greenhouse construction. Rafters should be of clear heart California redwood, for this is strong, dense-grained lumber that mills smoothly and is free from ragged surfaces and furry edges which can be collection places for the moisture and dirt that will encourage rot or fungus growth. Redwood for greenhouses should be cut from inside the sap ring and not from the sapwood. Shake or knotty core redwood should not be used. Redwood lumber for greenhouse construction should be purchased from a greenhouse supply company to insure getting redwood that has been properly kiln-dried for this particular use.

Note that the acid preservative which makes redwood so long-lasting is corrosive to iron and steel, and so for the nails, bolts, screws, etc., you must use those which have been galvanized by a hot-dip process—electroplating steel or iron does not give the necessary protection. Never use black iron and steel nails, screws, etc., with redwood, as the acid in the wood will erode them.

Even though redwood is noted for its long-lasting quality, it should also be treated with a wood preservative (copper naphthenate solution), just as the fir or cedar, to give it added life. Redwood, as any other wood, should be properly joined or fastened to other parts of the greenhouse so that points where fungus or rot may lodge are eliminated.

Cypress is the best-lasting of all the wood used for greenhouse rafters and gutters—*provided* it is the right kind of cypress: clear heartwood of swamp-grown cypress. It is more expensive than other grades of cypress and much more expensive than the other woods, but well worth it. Never use upland cypress or the kinds containing sapwood, for they will rot within five years. Highland cypress trees, which are firmly rooted in the ground, develop "shake" in them from the wind, while the swamp-grown trees "give" when the wind blows and hence are unaffected

Cypress will remain maintenance-free longer than other woods, but it should still be painted to add to its life and attractiveness; also to provide a greater amount of light reflection into the greenhouse. Because cypress is porous, paint will sink into the wood and not go on smoothly, but this will be to your advantage for the paint is not easily dislodged and therefore lasts longer.

Wooden bars will transmit less heat to the outside than will metal ones. Also, wood has less inclination to sweat than has metal, though aluminum bars that will carry off condensation have been designed. Bar caps (preformed aluminum covers for the rafters) can be used to protect the sash bars, eliminate upkeep, and prevent slippage of glass.

An iron or steel frame is preferable, unless economy is of prime importance. Iron or steel frame construction provides extra strength and more light transmission because the structural parts are thinner and less numerous than those of wood. The iron or steel frame does of course require a certain amount of maintenance and must be kept covered with paint to prevent rust. To begin with, it should have two or three coats of a good rust-preventive paint.

Most home greenhouses are not wide enough to need posts to support the framework. If you are planning a wide greenhouse, consider one of structural steel. Then you won't need posts and cross braces; you will have less maintenance and greater light.

Steel gives strength not afforded by any other material and, if properly maintained, is certainly permanent. Its cost is greater than that of wood but less than that of aluminum. It is easy to err with steel by not giving it enough protection from rust at the start. Steel members should be painted with rust-inhibiting paint before erection of the greenhouse and then at least two more coats are advisable after completion. Pay strict attention to those places where the original coats of paint may have been scuffed or scratched and to the places where the members are joined together. These are the places where rust, the chief enemy of steel and iron, gets in its dirty work. Use stainless steel or galvanized bolts and fastenings with steel; otherwise rust is given an open invitation to get started.

The big clamor the past few years has been toward all-aluminum greenhouse construction. Most certainly, aluminum offers the permanent features you want in a greenhouse and also brings down the cost of maintenance. But it does cost considerably more at the start.

Aluminum sash bars are now made of extruded aluminum alloy, and structural members of the "all" aluminum house are made of aluminum alloy or hot-dip galvanized steel. Doors are aluminum alloy and the hardware is aluminum alloy, stainless steel, or hot-galvanized steel. Combined, these materials really do add up to a relatively maintenance-free greenhouse. No painting of bars is required because, as the bars age, they become a dull silver color, and aluminum does not deteriorate with the weather to any extent.

Another advantage with aluminum is that wider spans can be used, and so it is possible to use wider panes of glass, thereby admitting more light into the greenhouse than in greenhouses built with wood sash bars. This can be a distinct advantage in the growing of some plants.

Manufacturers have overcome the problem of aluminum sash bars which drip from condensation of moisture. Aluminum bars are now available so that the condensation which forms on them is carried off to the side instead of below. But aluminum retains one main objection: its heat loss is considerably greater than is wood's, and you will have a larger fuel bill.

Ideal, of course, would be a material embodying features of metals and woods and providing for greenhouse construction at a low cost. As of now there is no such material. Perhaps the age of plastics will provide one.

Benches and Aisles

Construct your benches of good durable material, preferably a good cedar or cypress, and be sure to treat the benches with copper naphthenate; this will add considerable life to them. Place the benches on a framework of galvanized pipe and you will do away with a great deal of maintenance. Use galvanized nails in joining the wood members of the benches together.

Make your benches the right height for you, though if two or more persons are to use the greenhouse, some sort of compromise in bench height may be necessary. Leave space between your benches and the sides of your greenhouse so that air may circulate around the benches and thereby help to prevent fungus diseases from getting established. Side benches should not be wider than 36 inches; anything wider will make it difficult for you to water and care for your plants. But center benches in the greenhouse may be as wide as 72 inches.

The aisles of the greenhouse should be a *minimum* of 18 inches wide. If you plan to use a wheelbarrow in the greenhouse, you may want them wider. Cement walks make the finest of aisles. Next best are those covered with flagstone, gravel, sand, or other materials which will not become muddy each time you water.

Plastic vs. Glass

Glass was once the only material used to cover a greenhouse; it is still the most universally used material. Now, though, glass and plastic can be used as partners: glass for the principal or outer covering of the greenhouse and polyethylene plastic on the inside of the rafters, so that there is an air space beween the glass and the plastic; this layer of air makes heating the greenhouse more economical.

Don't be fooled into thinking that any sort of glass is suitable for a greenhouse. The ordinary window type of glass used in a home is not the sort you want for a greenhouse. Also, don't be fooled into buying cheap imported glass: the panes often contain imperfections which interfere with good light transmission. You need first-grade double-strength glass with large panes to provide the light that will enable your plants to grow well. Double-strength glass will also withstand breakage from hail better.

The manner in which glass is fastened and calked is very important in a glass-covered greenhouse. Calking must be done as tightly as possible and with a minimum of overlap on the glass. Prefab greenhouses come equipped with special clips for fastening the glass to the sash bars.

All glazing compounds are certainly not of equal quality. The mastic sorts are good but the plastic glazing compounds are excellent. The tape or bead form of glazing compound is easiest to use, and it stays soft and pliable for years with no shrinkage.

This seems a good place to mention the importance of properly

Low-built Quonset-type plastic greenhouse. Plastic tape on roof gives extra protection from wind.

securing any of the plastic materials which you may use on your greenhouse. Flexible sorts are properly secured in various ways. Wire mesh is usually required beneath or above polyethylene or polyvinyl plastics. And wooden strips should be nailed on where the plastic crosses each sash bar. Additional stability can be assured by using plastic tape or plastic rope at intervals, stretched tightly over the plastic roof of the greenhouse.

The polyester plastic also requires that the structure be well built and secure enough to prevent swaying during a heavy wind. You need not use wire mesh with polyester plastic. The nails should be not more than 5 inches apart on the cap strip, and the film should be nailed from ½ to ¾ inch from the edge of the film. If nailed closer to the edge than this, there is too much danger of tearing.

There are five types of plastics which may be used for greenhouses:

(1) POLYETHYLENE. Polyethylene film comes in 2, 4, and 6-mil thicknesses. The heavier the polyethylene, the longer life it has. Two-mil poly used on the inside of the greenhouse can cut heating costs up to 40 per cent. Four-mil is available in 3, 4, 10, 12, 14, and 16-foot widths in flat sheet form. Avoid folded-over polyethylene wherever possible: folding somewhat weakens polyethylene plastic. Ordinary polyethylene has a life expectancy of but 3 to 8 months, depending upon the individual circumstances, and so it is best to use it only for a temporary situation, such as for bedding plants for the spring.

(2) ULTRA-VIOLET POLYETHYLENE. This type of polyethylene is used exclusively for greenhouses and is available in 4-mil and 6-mil thicknesses only. The 4-mil comes in 3-foot, 8-foot, 10-foot, 12-foot,

and 14-foot widths—and in 32-foot widths with one fold. The 6-mil comes in widths of 10, 12, 14, and 16 feet. Ultra-violet polyethylene tends to absorb the ultra-violet rays of the sun and it has a 6-to-14 months life. Its cost is 40 per cent greater than that of regular polyethylene. Although ultra-violet polyethylene has a slight cloudiness, this does not affect the light transmission.

(3) VINYL PLASTIC. This type of plastic is used mostly in the 8-mil thickness and it comes in 36-inch, 48-inch, and 60-inch widths. It lasts from one to two years and costs 4½ times as much as ordinary polyethylene. After years of exposure—the time depends on climate conditions—the plastic will be attacked by a fungus which causes it to cloud. Now, however, at least one company is putting out a vinyl plastic which resists the fungus attacks. But vinyl plastic is not recommended in areas where temperatures run as cold as 5 degrees F. below zero, because it becomes brittle at low temperatures.

(4) POLYESTER PLASTIC (MYLAR). This type of plastic comes in 3-mil and 5-mil thicknesses, the former used for the sides and walls of greenhouses and the latter for the roofs. It is a highly satisfactory form of flexible plastic. It lasts three years for the 3-mil and five years for the 5-mil. It requires an overlap and a stronger framework than the other plastic films used for greenhouse construction. If you stretch the mylar as tightly as possible, noise will be eliminated and your mylar will last longer. Besides, the greenhouse will look much neater.

(5) FIBERGLASS. This type of plastic comes in weights of 5 and 6 ounces per square foot. It comes in 26-inch, 34-inch, and 40-inch widths and lengths of 7 feet, 8 feet, and 12 feet. It is longer-lasting than the other plastics and gives adequate light transmission for good plant growth. At least one firm guarantees this type of plastic for 17 years.

Some of the earlier problems which arose in connection with the use of rigid plastics on greenhouses have been overcome or modified. The rigid plastics, of course, do away with the breakage factor accompanied by glass, but they do have a tendency to scar and weather with age. A refinishing process now available, however, does restore some of the rigid plastics to their former maximum usefulness. Newer-type greenhouse construction has been devised which makes it possible to install rigid-type plastic with greater speed than before. Manufacturers say that rigid plastics prevent heat loss better than do other kinds of plastics and even glass. Another claim for the rigid plastics is that they provide better use of sunlight: they are constructed so that the light rays will bend and strike the plants at various angles rather than from a single direction.

If speed of erection is important, remember that the pliable plastics are the fastest to apply. But if permanence and less maintenance are the most important factors to you, then by all means consider the rigid plastics or glass.

Home Greenhouse Manufacturers and Suppliers

Almando Greenhouses, 432 Estudillo Ave., San Leandro, California

Aluminum Greenhouses, Inc., 14615 Lorain Ave., Cleveland, Ohio 44111

American-Moniger Greenhouse Mfg. Corp., 1820 Flushing Ave., Brooklyn, New York 11237

Lord & Burnham, Irvington, New York, and Des Plaines, Illinois

Metropolitan Greenhouse Mfg. Co., 1851 Flushing Ave., Brooklyn, New York 11237

The Modern Greenhouse Mfg. Co., 2511 Jackson St. N.E., Minneapolis, Minnesota 55418

National Greenhouse Company, Pana, Illinois

J. A. Nearing Co. Inc., 4229 Bladensburg Rd., Brentwood, Maryland

R. J. Nolan & Associates, 1309 Center St., Des Plaines, Illinois

Pacific Coast Greenhouse Mfg. Co., 650 Bayshort Highway, Redwood City, California

Redfern's Prefab Greenhouse Mfg. Co., 3482 Scotts Valley Drive, Santa Cruz, California

Rough Brothers, 4229 Spring Grove Ave., Cincinnati, Ohio 45223

W. S. Rough Sales Co., 115 Conley Circle, Bloomington, Illinois

Stearns Greenhouses, 98 Taylor St., Neponset, Boston, Massachusetts 02122

Sturdi-Built Mfg. Co., 11304 S. W. Boones Ferry Road, Portland, Oregon

Texas Greenhouse Co., 2717 St. Louis Ave., Fort Worth, Texas

Trox Mfg. Co., 18-20 Angell St., Battle Creek, Michigan

Turner Greenhouses, Div. Turner Equip. Co., Inc., P.O. Box 1260, Goldsboro, North Carolina

Yoho and Hooker, 523 Williamson St., Youngstown, Ohio

CHAPTER IV
Modern Greenhouse Heating

What about heat? How much will I need? How much will it cost? First of all, the size of your greenhouse will have a great deal to do with the size of the heating equipment which you should install. And at this point you should consider how much you intend to expand your greenhouse eventually. It will save you time and money to install a large enough heating system at the start to fit your maximum goal.

If your plans are for a small greenhouse and you know you are not going to add to it, you can heat it with a portable electric heater, or even with an electric cable, if the temperature required is not too great. A soil-cable heating system may be all that you need, if you plan to grow only those things which take a minimum of heat. A soil-cable heating system can also be used as supplementary heat. It requires 10 watts for each square foot of space to be heated. Use lead-covered cable. One 40-foot unit will handle 36 square feet. When the cables are placed, be sure never to cross the wires: that would burn and short-circuit the cable. Two inches of sand should be placed beneath the cable and 1 inch on top. Best heating occurs when the sand is damp. Heat is retarded by dry sand which tends to insulate the cable.

In addition to the size of your greenhouse and the kinds of plants you intend to grow, there are five other major considerations which have a bearing upon your choice of heat. Ask yourself these questions: (1) What do the various kinds of heating systems cost? (2)

What space is available for installation and how convenient will the various types be for my particular greenhouse? (3) Are there existing facilities which I might put to good use? (4) Is there a margin of safety in the heating system I am considering? (5) What fuels are available in the area and what are their respective costs?

If you are in the same category as most of us, cost will be an important consideration. If an elaborate heating system is planned, it may require an expert to install it—probably the most that a good handyman will attempt is the installation of one of the packaged heating systems. You can get complete plans from greenhouse manufacturing concerns if you wish to go into larger-type installations. The kinds of plants you wish to grow will have a bearing upon the type of heating installation you make. The temperatures recommended for plants refer to nighttime conditions. Daytime temperature should run from 10° to 15° F. warmer. If the controlled climate of your greenhouse is to be cool (45° to 50° F. night temperature) for azaleas, camellias, alpine flowers, etc., you will obviously need considerably less heat than if you intend to run a warm greenhouse (60° to 65° F. night temperature) in order to accommodate the needs of orchids, African violets, anthuriums, etc. When the temperature outside is 0 degrees, if you wish to maintain a greenhouse at 60° you will need about twice as much fuel as you would for a 50° temperature.

It takes a good deal more space to install a complete hot-water or steam system than a gas-fired or electric heater. If the space problem is acute, a suspended heater can be the answer to your problem. And convenience ties in closely with space. It may be that the space available is not a convenient spot to place your heating equipment. When you consider space, too, you will need to think of fuel storage, if you use something besides electricity or gas. Another "space" problem to be considered has to do with the location of a stack or chimney. Oil and bottled gas, such as butane or propane, require that the chimney be tall so that harmful fumes will be dissipated safely outside the greenhouse. Because of the danger to plants from manufactured gas, do not install a gas-fired heater within the greenhouse. And to protect yourself and your property from fire, have your electrical work done by an expert.

If you have a hot-water, steam, or even a hot-air heating system in your home, and you plan to place the greenhouse close to your house, you might consider hooking in with your home heating system, provided, of course, that it is large enough. You can do so by installing a gravity system or an aquastat and a circulating pump. About five rows of 2-inch pipe around the perimeter of the greenhouse are needed to heat it properly whether the hot water is coming from the home heating system or a separate greenhouse boiler, unless finned pipes are used.

I do not recommend heating your home greenhouse with warm air from your hot-air furnace, but it can be done. You will need to place the greenhouse discharge vent so that the warm air is not blown directly on the plants. And you will need to make sure the greenhouse does not become too dry, by providing needed humidity.

For small attached greenhouses, the heating problem is solved sometimes simply by leaving a basement window or a doorway of the home open to supply warm air from the home to the greenhouse; a small fan should be used to make sure that the warm air circulates about the greenhouse. Here again there will be the matter of adding extra humidity to compensate for what is lost.

Avoid overloading the heating system. It should be large enough to allow a margin of safety in case of colder than usual weather. Again, keep in mind the possibility that you may want to increase the greenhouse size someday; you can save yourself money by installing a heating system now which will handle the increased space you may have later.

The costs of fuel vary throughout the country. In some places, such as the Pacific Northwest, electricity is quite reasonable; hence, electric heat is often used for home greenhouses in that part of the country. In other places oil or gas may offer the greatest economy. Coal, briquettes, or artificial gas are not usually considered unless there is a large or unique installation, seldom the case with a home greenhouse.

The heating equipment must provide good air circulation to assure even heat distribution. With hot-water and steam systems, air circulation is achieved generally by locating the pipes around the sides of the greenhouse or beneath the benches; the pipes should be far enough from the foundation to allow the warm air to rise. And it is a good idea to check, by means of thermometers, to make sure temperatures are even in all parts of the greenhouse; if not, a circulating fan should be installed.

If you are planning a larger greenhouse or a future major expansion, perhaps with an eye toward a commercial venture, by all means consider a hot-water or steam system. A hot-water system which uses a boiler with an aquastat control assures you of even heat at all times. When a thermostat located in the greenhouse calls for heat, a ready switch opens the valve on the line, and a circulating pump sends the water—already hot—through the heating pipes.

Finned tubing considerably increases the amount of heat given off by the hot water. One line of 2-inch finned tubing is equal in heat radiation to five lines of regular 2-inch piping. To equalize the heat in your greenhouse, install the greatest amount of finned tubing in the coldest part. Piping must, otherwise, be evenly distributed throughout the greenhouse and the pipes should be placed low. Ten-per-cent heat loss is incurred with high placement.

Always use black pipe instead of galvanized. More heat is possible with black pipe. If structural factors make it necessary to install the pipe at a higher level than it should be, small fans can be used to help overcome the heat loss.

Steam provides quicker heat than hot water and makes steam sterilization of the soil simple. Nevertheless, hot water rather than steam is generally used for small home greenhouses. Should you decide on steam, use a low-pressure system rather than a high, for there is less maintenance with the former. Have an expert install the system—he knows how to grade the pipes properly to eliminate cold-water pockets. The system may also need a condensate pump to return the water to tank or boiler.

One of the most popular types of heating systems being used for both commercial and amateur greenhouses today is the Modine hot-water system. It eliminates the installation of costly coils, and it is suspended from the roof. The unit heats its own water, which then goes through air-heating coils. The warm air is blown downward or horizontally, being deflected by a baffle that hangs beneath the unit, thereby eliminating the danger of drafts over the plants. The heat is evenly distributed throughout the greenhouse and hot air is not wasted at the greenhouse peak.

Some of the ordinary household space heaters are suitable for heating a small home greenhouse. These burn natural gas, kerosene, or light fuel oil. Among the better makes are Coleman, Mayflower, and Duo-Therm. Be sure to select one with sufficient capacity to heat a greenhouse of the size you have. Also be sure that the chimney extends high enough above the roof to insure an adequate draft. Note that with this type of heater care must be taken when the roof ventilators are open: a down-draft may extinguish the pilot light.

Far superior, however, are the NoVent and Saf-Aire, two of the most satisfactory types of gas heaters for the home greenhouse. The gas is burned in a sealed chamber and does not require a chimney.

Today the unit or space heaters are becoming more and more popular. They use steam or hot water and are fired with gas or electricity.

A horizontal-throw unit heater is better than one with a vertical throw of air, because it blows less directly on the plants. The vertical type is satisfactory in higher greenhouses. To provide good air circulation with electric heaters, try putting two in the greenhouse, in opposite corners and placed so that they blow toward one another. The air streams will meet and circulate upward and around to their places of origin. If you use a single electric heater, place it beneath the bench at one end of the greenhouse so that it will blow toward the door, setting up a circular motion of air from bottom to top and back again.

The fine packaged heating units which are designed for small greenhouses have adequate safety features and are easily installed.

Do not use a radiant heater in a greenhouse. A radiant heater warms the objects directly in line with its heat rays but it does not warm the air. Trying to grow plants this way is highly unsatisfactory.

How can you have varied temperature zones within one greenhouse? This is not as difficult as it sounds. It is accomplished by partitioning the greenhouse. (Different degrees of humidity can also be arranged in this manner.) A partitioned section can be given additional heat from a space heater or from an extra heating pipe or finned tubing.

Unfortunately, most home greenhouses are not equipped with any sort of auxiliary heat for emergencies. If you have valuable plants in your greenhouse, you should consider a stand-by electric heater. It can be used also to supply extra heat when temperatures outside are very low. If your plants are valuable enough, it is also wise to have a stand-by generator operated by a gasoline motor. In case of a power failure, it will supply the electrical energy needed to operate your heating plant.

Where additional heat is required for the entire greenhouse during cold weather, in a "hot-water" greenhouse a supplementary stand-by heating pipe can be used.

There are boilers which supply not only the hot water needed to heat the greenhouse but also the steam for steam sterilization. This type of boiler has a steam trim which carries 5 pounds of steam pressure in the dome. Hot water is removed just below the water line and the hot water circulated by centrifugal pumps.

Automatic Controls

At the top of the list of automatic controls are thermostats. They may be used to control both heat and cold. They control the temperature of the water, steam, or air and its delivery to the greenhouse. They also control the ventilators and other cooling devices used in greenhouses today. (See Chapter V on greenhouse cooling.) The better makes of automatic controls are sensitive to ½ to 1 degree F. The better the controls you install, the happier you will be. But have an expert do the installation for you; the average do-it-yourselfer is not sufficiently trained in these matters.

In order to prevent confusion and to make sure that your plants are getting exactly the temperature you want, be absolutely certain that each thermometer you use is accurate. Check the one in doubt against one of known accuracy by placing the two together in a shaded spot and comparing. Or, better yet, place the thermometers in a bucket of melted ice: the readings on the thermometers should be exactly 32 degrees.

Good thermostats for greenhouses use contact points which are sealed in mercury tubes so that they are moisture-proof, dust-proof, dirt-proof, and unaffected by fumes. This eliminates danger of corrosion or oxidation of the points. The thermostat for heat control in the greenhouse should be centrally located so that heat will be as uniform as possible throughout the greenhouse. Also be sure that the thermostat is protected from the direct rays of the sun.

There are line voltage thermostats and low voltage thermostats. The low voltage type is usually recommended, because it can be operated from storage batteries and so will work even during a power failure.

It is possible to have a single thermostat which will ring an alarm bell in your home when the greenhouse is either too hot or too cold. And, of course, there are soil thermometers and automatic thermostatic controls for the propagating-bed cables.

Hot water is fed to the greenhouse upon demand by the thermostat in the greenhouse which activates a circulating pump. (It's a good idea to have a manually operated wheel valve as well. This can be used to bypass the circulating pump and convert the system to a gravity feed, should an emergency arise.)

An aquastat is used to regulate the temperature of the water in the boiler. It keeps the water hot, and when the demand comes for heat, it pumps the water through the pipes. During the summer, the aquastat can be set to provide water of a lower temperature. This provides some economy.

Heating Controls

The greenhouse operator with an elaborate heating system, such as a steam boiler or a hot-water system which is also used for steam sterilization, needs a water-line regulator to keep the water in the boiler at the correct level. It automatically feeds water to the boiler when needed, and if a bad leak develops or the water supply fails, it stops the automatic firing of the burner and rings an alarm. Thus, there is no danger of cracking or burning out a boiler due to improper water supply.

Such a device, too, stops the automatic firing and sounds an alarm if something goes wrong. An automatic relief valve attached to the water line entering the boiler allows the water into the boiler as demand arises and also releases surplus water into a waste line as the water in the boiler expands. This relief valve is cut off when the water in the boiler is lowered to give a head of steam for the steam sterilization process. Also, the valve on the return line to the boiler is closed and the arm on the supply-line valve is disconnected to let the steam through. The supply line in the greenhouse can be fitted with "T's" where the steaming hose may be attached.

Important gauges needed on the boiler are those registering the temperature of the water in the boiler and the pressure when steam is used. A pop-off safety valve is needed to relieve too-high pressure. A very important instrument for a boiler heating system is the automatic stack switch. This is another safety device designed to shut off the burner operation and the flow of oil or gas should the fuel fail to ignite.

CHAPTER V

Greenhouse Cooling and Ventilation

Greenhouse cooling is just as practical for the amateur as for the commercial grower. And when a greenhouse is cooled properly, the quality of the plants and flowers improves; the growth becomes more lush and vigorous, the flowers larger and of better color and quality; plants mature on schedule. The moist air reduces the need for watering by as much as 50 per cent. Stagnant air is eliminated and shading need be used only for light control, not for cooling as well. And, most important from the human standpoint, working conditions are far more comfortable in an air-cooled greenhouse.

How is a greenhouse cooled? The process actually is an adaptation of the canvas-bag method of cooling water. At one end of the greenhouse is a large pad on which water is dripped. At the far end of the greenhouse is an exhaust fan (or fans) which literally pulls the air into the greenhouse through the pad.

When this is done, ventilators are closed and plastic baffles, which run from the inside ridge of the greenhouse to about halfway down the house's interior, force the air down low near the crops. The system provides a smooth, even flow of cooled, moist air which is well distributed over the growing area.

The filler used in the pads is usually made of aspen wood fiber, which has been found to be superior to any other material for this purpose. The fibers are covered with a wide mesh cloth on either side, and the 2-inch-thick pads are held in place by strong galvanized wire with a 1-by-2-inch mesh.

It takes 1 square foot of pad for every 150 cubic feet of air exhausted per minute to cool a greenhouse properly. That's an air velocity of 150 feet per minute, a rather rapid change of air.

Approximately ⅓ gallon of water per minute is required for every linear foot of pad, and this water is recirculated with less than 2-per-cent loss to evaporation each time. The amount of air to be exhausted is determined by the square feet of floor space in the greenhouse. For each square foot, 7 cubic feet of air should be exhausted per minute.

Naturally, because the air is drawn through the pad, you will need an exhaust fan of greater capacity than one which moves free air. For example, a 24-inch fan which moves 5,800 cubic feet of free air moves only 4,900 feet of air through the pad. Obviously, a tight greenhouse is essential.

There is still a problem with the fan and pad system, for along with the air some insects gain entry. The worst offenders are thrips and red spiders.

To prevent this, keep the area around the greenhouse free of weeds and keep the plants outdoors well sprayed or dusted. Use dieldrin (2 pints per 100 gallons of water) or other chemicals in the water you use for circulation through the pads. This kills the thrips and other insects as they are drawn into the pads. The evaporation makes it necessary to add additional dieldrin every two weeks. Warning: keep the pads tightly together and patch any holes which appear in them or insects will be drawn through the holes and will not come into contact with the insecticide.

Convection-tube Ventilation System

One of the big problems of ventilating plants in a greenhouse during the winter months when fresh air is needed is that of keeping cold-air drafts off plants. During the winter months, the conventional glass-covered greenhouse can usually provide enough ventilation with exhaust fans, unless sub-freezing weather has sealed them over. But when the weather is warm, more air is required and the exhaust fans alone will not do the job. And for plastic-covered greenhouses, which are virtually airtight, the exhaust fan cannot provide the air needed.

A convection tube is a thin translucent plastic tube, pierced with small openings, which extends the full length of the greenhouse and is attached to a fresh-air inlet located in the gable wall. The tube is fastened to the greenhouse by wires which run from the tube wire to rafters above. Exhaust fans at the opposite ends of the greenhouse, but not connected to the convection tube, are activated automatically with a thermostat. When a fan is turned on by the thermostat, a slight vacuum is created in the greenhouse. This causes fresh air to rush into the plastic convection tube, thereby inflating it. There are holes through the entire length of the tube through which the air drawn in is emitted. The jets of air projected into the greenhouse on a horizontal plane have time to be warmed by the existing air in the greenhouse before reaching the plants. When the desired temperature has been reached, the thermostat turns the fan off and the tube collapses.

The convection tube does not take the place of fan-and-pad cooling but the fans used for the cooling system can also be used for the convection-tube system.

Ventilation

Good ventilation is necessary in the greenhouse to provide: (1) a more accurately controlled temperature when it is warm during the day; (2) help in the control of disease problems such as mildew; (3) fresh air containing the all-important carbon dioxide; and (4) good humidity control.

Ventilation in the greenhouse was also once a strictly manual job. Now powered ventilators are available for all sorts of greenhouses, from the smallest amateur one to the largest of commercial installations.

Most home greenhouse operators use manually controlled vent sash for airing their houses either for economy of construction or because they have not as yet realized how convenient and important automatic ventilation can be to the growing of indoor plants. The simplest ventilating equipment consists of either push-up vent sash at the peak of the roof or push-up vent sash on the sides of the greenhouse. The roof type is best. A notched stick or one with holes in it is attached to each sash. As the sash is raised to the proper height the hole or notch on the stick is pushed over a protruding spike or rod fastened to the greenhouse to hold the vent open.

The best manually operated ventilating apparatus is the arm-and-rod, rack-and-pinion, or scissors type, each of which is operated by

Push-out side ventilators provide extra
air circulation when temperatures soar.

use of gears. One gear at the base of the column support is operated
by a wheel handle. A chain running from the lower gear to one attached to the horizontal rod at the top of the greenhouse (beneath
the sash) sets the rod in motion. Attached to the rod are "elbows"
which are fastened to the sash. Control with this type of ventilating
equipment can be precise. However, you should bear in mind that
you are the one who must operate the ventilators where they are
manual and you must be alert to weather changes.

Without a doubt, considerable pleasure and much more accurate
growing control will be yours if you can possibly install automatic
ventilating equipment from the start. In the long run it pays big

dividends in economy, too, by a more careful control of temperatures which might damage your plants and by preventing loss of heat from within the greenhouse when temperatures outside drop rapidly.

The Lord and Burnham Company manufactures a superb automatic ventilating system which uses a "brain" to do all the raising and lowering of the ventilators throughout the day. A semi-automatic ventilating device made by various greenhouse firms uses a simple exhaust fan operated by a thermostat. As the fan revolves, old air is expelled and light aluminum louvers open to admit fresh air through side vents and/or foundation louvers. Many home greenhouses use this type of equipment.

Still another type of automatic ventilation is one which was developed at Washington State College several years ago. Cupolas astride the greenhouse ridge contain exhaust fans. When cooler air is called for, the fans are activated thermostatically and draw the warm air from the greenhouse, discharging it outdoors. The same thermostat activates louvers in the foundation through which fresh air arrives. This type of ventilation has real advantages in an area where wind is a problem.

Whatever your ventilator, cover the ventilators with Saran cloth (plastic screen) to keep out birds which can damage plants and also to keep out the larger insects.

There are three primary reasons for ventilating a greenhouse: (1) To control temperatures. (2) To permit an intake of fresh air to provide the plants with needed gases, especially carbon dioxide. (3) To aid in controlling humidity.

Just as fertilizer and water form a partnership when it comes to producing good greenhouse plants, so do temperature, ventilation, and humidity, especially where the matter of disease incidence is concerned.

A good, relatively high humidity is considered essential for optimum growth of most greenhouse plants, other than those which like arid conditions. To provide this humidity, keep the walks and areas beneath the benches moist.

Normally the greenhouse is not ventilated while the heat is on, although there are some exceptions. It may seem inconsistent to apply heat while at the same time allowing some of that heat to escape through the vents. But the idea is to drive out, late in the day, some of the moisture-laden air which would otherwise condense on the foliage of the plants. Such moisture is an open invitation to mildew and botrytis blight. This ventilation need only be of a few minutes' duration, just enough to get the warm air circulating about the plants and to move out the excess moisture in the air. But it is important.

Sudden drops in temperature are particularly harmful to botrytis-prone plants such as chrysanthemums, carnations, and cyclamen, and to roses, snapdragons, and all crops susceptible to mildew. So it is evident that you cannot afford to neglect temperature control during the night or during the day. Frequently the fluctuations are greatest during the late afternoon when, after a sunny day, a sudden temperature drop from the 80's to the 50 or 60-degree mark may occur. If you have automatic controls, this temperature fluctuation can be handled much more easily.

During the winter months when ventilators may be closed or nearly so, the problem of poor air circulation can become a serious one. The dead air which exists in corners and pockets is conducive to disease. Also, when the air does not circulate properly, much of the heat lies above the plants and the temperature around the plants remains relatively cool. This can be offset by installing circulating fans. The warm air is thus brought down around the plants and dead air is moved out as part of the circulation pattern. You needn't be afraid that such fans will create a draft around your plants; actually, the movement of air is so smooth that you will barely be aware that the air is moving.

It is no secret that proper temperatures are important to the production of potted plants and flowers. If you do not know the optimum temperatures for particular plants, check the recommendations in this book. It is true, however, that many plants also have a fairly wide range of temperatures within which they can grow. The important thing is to maintain not only a reasonably correct but as uniform a temperature as possible without sudden variations.

A humidity recorder in a greenhouse may be misleading, for the humidity on the surface of the leaf is considerably higher than that which is recorded. If you use a recorder, try to keep the recorded humidity below 70 per cent for most crops. You can do so by turning on your heat, for the warmer the air is, the lower the relative humidity, even when the same quantity of moisture is present. When you turn on your heat, though, remember to be sure to leave your ventilators open to allow some of the warm moisture-laden air to escape.

CHAPTER VI
Light and Shade

Lighting Installations

In accordance with their individual needs, all plants must have light. The optimum light for one plant may be only a few foot-candles. (A foot-candle of light is the amount of light given off by a single candle at a 1-foot distance.) Another may require the full intensity of the sunlight. "Just any old light" will not do for a great many plants. This is one of the reasons why it is very important to consider the compatibility of the various plants you wish to grow in your greenhouse.

Lengthening the ordinary daylight period will increase the growth rate of plants. During any 24-hour period the maximum period for lighting plants is about 16 hours. If 600 foot-candles of artificial light are provided for 16 hours per day to supplement a deficiency in sunlight, you may expect good growth from your plants. If artificial light intensity equivalent to 1,000 foot-candles is provided, you will not need to provide the artificial light for as many hours each day.

First of all, you must provide for regular lighting in your greenhouse. Place drop cords at important spots, such as over work benches so that on short winter evenings you can indulge in your favorite hobby. Then, if you intend growing plants of different light responses, install 60-watt incandescent lamps using reflectors every 4 feet over 4-foot benches or beds. (The reflectors may be ordinary "pie tins.") Use 100-watt lamps at 5-foot intervals over 5-foot beds. Suspend the lamps 5 feet above the beds or benches.

Automatic timing devices are available to turn the lights on and off as needed. Latest USDA research with intermittent lighting has shown that many plants do not require long periods of artificial light; a short flashing of light at the prescribed time will suffice. The timing devices are still rather costly to install, but they do, of course, reduce the electricity cost drastically.

Those plants directly beneath the light will receive the maximum intensity, while those which are further away will not be receiving as much light. This means that without proper reflectors on your lights beneath the bench the growth of your plants will be uneven. Use 40-watt fluorescent lamps in channel-type fixtures. Four such lamps will properly illuminate about 24 square feet. The reflector should be made of moisture-proof material which will not rust. This will insure permanent equal light over the area illuminated. Since fluorescent lamps give off practically no heat, the lights can be placed close to the growing plants.

There are some fine fluorescent lamps developed particularly for plant growth. Among them are the Gro-Lux lamps manufactured by Sylvania Electric Products Company. Among the plants which have been known to do exceptionally well under Gro-Lux lamps are seedlings of sapphire lobelia, petunia, salvia, alyssum, and lettuce.

Westinghouse has an excellent fluorescent lamp used for light gardening or supplemental greenhouse lighting called Agro-Lite. Another good lamp for plant growing is Vita-Lite, manufactured by Duro-Lite Lamps, Inc.

The Sylvania Company has devised the following helpful hints for better growing results with Gro-Lux fluorescent lamps:

LIGHT INTENSITIES:

A. *For germinating seeds and rooting cuttings:* 10-lamp watts per square foot of growing area. The light source should be 6 to 8 inches above the soil or planting media.

B. *For low-energy growing plants:* 15-lamp watts per square foot of growing area. The light source should be 12 to 15 inches above plant tops. Many of the household plants fall into this classification.

C. *For high-energy growing plants:* 20-lamp watts per square foot of growing area. The light source should be 12 to 15 inches above plant tops. Plants such as chrysanthemums, carnations, roses, tomatoes, beans, and most vegetable crops fall into this classification.

LENGTH OF LIGHT PERIOD (PHOTO PERIOD):

> *For the germination of seeds and rooting cuttings:* A light period of 16 hours produces satisfactory results. With newly germinated seedlings and rooted cuttings, prior to transplanting, a longer light period of up to 20 hours may be used with good results.

According to research done at the A and M College of Texas, the manner of blending the color of fluorescent lamps is important. It recommends that both the white fluorescent lamps, which produce a blue light, and the warm-white fluorescent lamps, which produce light with more red rays, be used. Standard white fluorescent lamps produce low, stocky plants. The warm-white fluorescent lamps tend to make plants grow taller.

Fluorescent lamps make it possible for the shut-in to have his own greenhouse right within the home. One indoor greenhouse makes it possible to grow up to 864 plants in any vacant corner of the home. It takes only 8 square feet of floor space. Almost any number of shelves can be used or removed as needed. Four 40-watt fluorescent tubes are used on each shelf, which measures 2-by-4 feet.

Shading

Shading can be provided simply and inexpensively. The greenhouse could even be shaded with mud—but don't! Always keep in mind that the shading on your greenhouse can add to—or detract from—its attractiveness. There are two principal reasons for shading a greenhouse: (1) to keep temperatures down within the greenhouse, and (2) to reduce light intensity for those plants which need less light at certain times of the year.

During the winter months, of course, except where plants are being grown in areas where the winter light is quite bright, shading is of no concern. In fact, in most places during the winter months, it is highly important to have the glass as clean and clear as possible. It is amazing how large a percentage of light is blotted out by dirty glass.

The density of shade applied depends upon the plant or plants in question. Some require more shade than others. If you are growing a variety of plants, some compromise will likely have to be made. When you apply a shading compound to the outside of the glass it is important to spread it evenly over the entire greenhouse, except where heavier applications are needed for a group of plants. Uneven application will provide uneven light transmission which can affect some plants a great deal.

In order to keep from applying shading and taking it down alternately it is best to "divide" your shading, putting part of it on your glass and part of it on the inside of the greenhouse. For the outside there are some fine shading compounds which you can use. These compounds provide an easy-to-apply material that sticks well, need no additives, and will not be difficult to remove when the time comes.

The shading material which you use on your greenhouse should not be harmful to the paint on the bars. Your aluminum bars or bar caps can be corroded by shading compounds which contain alkali. Neither clay nor lime should ever be used on aluminum.

Here is a good formula for a homemade shading compound: mix together 8 pounds of white lead to 1 gallon of kerosene. Then add ¼ pint of linseed oil to the mixture to keep it from flaking off.

Shading which has been on the glass during the summer months can be removed by wetting the glass, brushing, and washing it off with water. If an extra heavy coat of shading material is not removable in this manner, use trisodium phosphate at the rate of 20 pounds in 100 gallons of water. Brush or spray this on the roof and let it set for 10 minutes, then brush it well. Next, flush it off with clear water. Trisodium phosphate will burn leaves and flowers of plants, so be sure that none falls on plants on the outside; cover your plants inside and close the ventilators to make sure it does not get on the plants in your greenhouse. The sprayer will need washing out, too, after the job is done.

There are other methods which you can use for shading the outside of your home greenhouse. Slat frames, made of ordinary laths properly spaced, can be fastened to the greenhouse when needed and removed quite easily. Various companies manufacture roller-type slat shades which are made of redwood or aluminum. They are attractive and long-lasting. Ordinary Japanese bamboo roller shades can be used for shading the outside of the greenhouse. They are less expensive, but they do not last long. Shrimp netting is often used to shade the greenhouse, and if you can find it, army camouflage netting material is excellent.

Saran cloth (plastic screen) is ideal for shading the greenhouse.

It can be purchased in different gauges, so that you may have the amount of shade that you require for various plants.

For the inside of your greenhouse you have a number of materials to choose from, depending upon the degree of shading sought. There is Saran cloth, opaque polyethylene, shrimp netting, and common cheesecloth. If you suspend such material from the inside of your greenhouse, and shade the outside, you will have protection for your plants even when the weather is changeable. A sudden rainstorm, for instance, can remove most or all of the outside shading, but the inside shading will protect your plants until the outside can be replaced. Incidentally, it is a good idea during the spring to delay application of the outside shading until heavy spring rains have passed.

CHAPTER VII

The Indispensable and the Luxurious

It is nice to own a "Cadillac" greenhouse, with all the frills and ideas which can make operation as simple as possible, but you can do quite well with a "Model T" greenhouse. The latter merely takes more of your personal attention—which you may prefer.

But let's name a few of the essential things that you will need for your greenhouse. First of all, you will need a work room, work bench, or potting area. If you have the space for a special room, so much the better. The work room can contain closets in which to store your work clothes, implements, and other paraphernalia. There should be a special closet, under lock and key, in which to keep all insecticides, fungicides, and any other poisonous materials. A sink is an important item for a work room. If there is room for the installation of a laundry tray, this makes an ideal place in which to wash pots or to provide subsurface watering of seed flats when needed.

Of course the single most important item for your work room, or for a spot within your greenhouse if you do not plan a regular work room, is the work bench. The bottom of a good work bench should be constructed of heavy planks. Use pipe legs, cement legs, or 4-by-4 posts to support the bench. Be sure to construct your work bench at a height which is most suitable for you.

A "special" which you may want to consider when you build your greenhouse benches is to use corrugated asbestos cement board such as Transite in the bottom of the benches. The cement boards will last the life of the greenhouse and the corrugation aids drainage.

You can conserve space by using bins beneath the bench to hold potting soil, sand, compost or leafmold, and peatmoss. The back of your work bench should be edged with a foot-high board and the sides with boards of around 8 or 9 inches high to contain the soil. A sturdy work bench itself holds a considerable quantity of soil. A work bench within the greenhouse, of course, must be more or less stationary. But a work bench constructed in a work room can be equipped with rollers which make it possible to move it from spot to spot. The bins beneath the work bench may also be equipped with rollers so that you can move them into an outdoor potting area during the summer months.

There are some tools and implements used in the greenhouse which are absolutely essential. Among them: a trowel; a spotting or dibble board; flats; scissors; spraying and dusting equipment; dibble sticks; clay or plastic pots; plant bands; peat pots; cultivators; soil scope; a watering can equipped with a fine sprinkler; sprinkler bulb; a tamping block to firm sand in the propagating bed or soil in seed flats; a tamping stick for certain kinds of potting; plant markers; gloves; wooden tweezers with which to handle tiny seedlings; a stiff brush for pot washing; and all of the ordinary handyman tools such as pliers, hammer, screwdriver, and chisel.

Then there must be sieves or soil-preparing machinery of some sort. If you are going to be preparing large quantities of soil, you will want a soil shredder. They come in various sizes and there are several good makes. But the average home greenhouse does not require equipment of this latter sort. Most amateurs find that simple sifting screens are sufficient. It is always wise to have a small sifting screen beside your work bench for small quantities of soil. And in a shed or lean-to near the greenhouse it is wise to have a "V"-type sieve for larger quantities of soil. A sifting screen may be suspended by wires above the potting bench to sift soil in cradle fashion down onto the bench. Actually, it is wise to have two different meshes of screen for sieves. One should be made of window screen for fine-soil sifting to prepare soil for seed flats, etc. The other should be of larger size and made of hardware cloth of $\frac{1}{4}$ to $\frac{3}{8}$-inch mesh.

Among the items which are nice to have, but not altogether necessary, are a fogging nozzle; a Vibra seeder with which to sow fine seeds evenly; soil-sterilizing equipment; electric propagating-bed cable; a soil-testing kit; and any number of other items which are nice, if you have a use for them and wish to indulge that much more in your hobby.

Flat size varies in many parts of the country. Unless you plan to make your own flats, investigate the commercial greenhouses of your area to learn the dimensions of flats used there. The flats you choose may govern the width of the greenhouse benches you construct. The regular flat depth is 3 inches. For bulbs, deeper flats are used, usually 4 inches.

There are almost as many different kinds of containers which you can use for potting as there are different sorts of greenhouse structures. Popular since greenhouses began have been clay pots and there is much to be said for their use. They allow greater aeration of the potted soil and make watering simple. But plastic pots are used more and more by amateurs and commercial growers alike. With any nonporous container, since the pot walls will not absorb moisture, care must be taken not to water too much. There are sev-

Ordinary juice cans with perforated bottoms can be used to start seedlings.

eral kinds of plant bands on the market today, including those made of veneer, tarpaper, plastic, and organic matter.

Highly popular nowadays are peat pots. They are especially good if you are starting seedlings which do not transplant well—the peat pot, soil, plant, and all can be transplanted into other pots or outside at the proper time.

Peat pots are used mostly in the smaller sizes. But for clay pots or plastic pots you will want various sizes from the small to the larger. If you are growing certain types of specimen plants, especially those to be used in a conservatory or on a patio, you will probably also want some wooden tubs.

Don't stint on the quality of the equipment you buy. Probably in no place is this of greater importance than in the matter of the sprayer or duster which you use. The very best sprayers are those which use high pressure because they atomize the moisture better, thereby making it possible to cover smaller surfaces more thoroughly. This insures better insect and disease control. Be sure that you have separate sprayers to use for plant spraying, weed control, and for application of shading material to the outside of the greenhouse. The smallest greenhouses need only quart-size sprayers.

The newest type of fan is the turbulator. It is designed to prevent a high relative humidity and maintain a more even temperature at plant level. It assures a better circulation of air, which, in turn, assures a healthier and more vigorous growth of plants.

An electric humidifier is mighty nice to have for those plants which require ample humidity, although it is not absolutely necessary. The better types of humidifier use a water reservoir made of heavy-gauge copper. You can use a humidifier which needs to be filled manually or one which can be connected to the water line for automatic filling, containing a built-in float valve.

There are lots of things for the do-it-yourselfer to make for use in the greenhouse. Cultivators, for one. Make a simple, blade-type cultivator by taking a piece of wire clothes hanger and flattening out a 2-to-3-inch portion of the hanger with a hammer and iron. Fashion this into a closed "Y," with the closed portion of the "Y" in front. Braid two pieces of the "tail" and insert the braid into a bamboo handle. Such an implement is ideal for slicing tiny weeds and for cultivating the soil in a bench of cut flowers or in flats. The hook of a coat hanger can be used to make a single-pointed cultivator. Simply insert the other end into a wooden or bamboo handle. Multi-

Handy homemade go-cart for hauling bedding plants, etc.

ples of this type of cultivator can be made by combining two, three, or more of the hooks, twisting the other ends together and inserting them into a bamboo handle.

If you use a standard-size flat, you can probably find a dibble or spotting board to fit it. But if not, you can make one yourself with pieces of tapered dowels: fasten them to one side of a board which fits the inside of your flats; place a handle on the opposite side for easy application and removal of the spotting board.

Depending upon where you live and the threat to your greenhouse by attitudes of nature, you will want to provide whatever protection is necessary. If you live in an area where winters are cold, beware of ice or snow sliding from the roof of the building to which your greenhouse is attached. Place a buffer of hardware cloth beneath the eaves of the building so that the brunt of the force will be caught by the baffle, rather than by the greenhouse glass. The baffle should be well supported and far enough above the greenhouse so that the sudden weight will not cause it to sag into the glass. Place fine-mesh wire over the rest of the greenhouse to shunt the ice and snow beyond the greenhouse roof as it leaves the baffle. You may use a board instead of hardware cloth as a baffle, but if you do, remove it as soon as the danger from falling ice or snow has disappeared, for a solid object throws shade on your plants below.

As noted, double-strength greenhouse glass will prevent all but very heavy hailstones from penetrating. To prevent hail damage, stretch rabbit-wire fencing over rails fastened to the greenhouse. The wire should be supported far enough above the glass level to insure proper opening of the vents in the roof. Remove the hail guards during summer months.

Supplying Carbon Dioxide

Research has shown that a deficiency of carbon dioxide (CO_2) curtails plant growth, stopping it altogether if the deficiency is too great. Naturally, if there is plenty of CO_2 in the atmosphere for a plant's requirements, the addition of more CO_2 is of little consequence. In other words, when dark winter conditions have reduced a certain plant's growth, the demand for CO_2, which amounts to aerial fertilization, is less, just as the demand for fertilizer from the soil is reduced. But even though growth has been slowed on certain plants during dark weather, there may still be a need for supplemental CO_2, because of reduced ventilation.

Introducing CO_2 into the greenhouse is a far easier matter than it used to be. Now it is possible to get a CO_2 greenhouse generator which is engineered exclusively for greenhouse use, and produces the gas at a fairly low cost. Automatic controls introduce the carbon dioxide at the time it is wanted and determine the correct amount. This system distributes the mixture uniformly throughout the greenhouse, burning gas outside the greenhouse to produce the CO_2.

The use of an open-flame gas burner *inside* the greenhouse has been questioned because of the danger to humans from carbon monoxide given off along with the carbon dioxide. Information from gas companies, however, has been to the effect that "scrubbed" natural gas does not present this problem. The tiny amount of carbon monoxide which may be given off is absorbed along with the carbon dioxide by the plants.

But there is a potential danger for the plants themselves which should be considered—the trace gases which may be given off when an open-flame burner is used within the greenhouse. Some of these trace gases need only be present in the amounts of 30 to 40 parts per million to damage crops. Ethylene gas is one of the worst. The danger increases when a house is frozen over during the winter and little ventilation exists. Perhaps at least some of this danger might be reduced by allowing some ventilation at all times. At any rate, you should take a second look at the matter of how to provide CO_2 in the greenhouse.

Some amateur growers have been burning alcohol in ordinary coffee cans to produce CO_2, but this presents a certain hazard to those walking up and down the aisles where the cans are placed, inasmuch as alcohol burns with an almost invisible flame and so it is easy for someone to be burned by it. If the alcohol is put in a kerosene lantern, the hazard is somewhat reduced.

Another method is to create a "system" overhead where there is no danger to those in the greenhouse. A reservoir cut from a 5-gallon tin is suspended from one of the greenhouse frame pipes. From the reservoir runs a 1-inch pipe. Placed at intervals in the house are 1½-inch standpipes into which methyl alcohol from the reservoir is fed—a measured amount each morning. The alcohol is usually burned only on dark days. In experiments, better growth, finer foliage, and a better grade of roses have resulted from the CO_2 being converted by the burning of the alcohol.

Melting of dry ice is probably the simplest manner of inducing CO_2 into a greenhouse. Regardless of the method used, do not be afraid of getting too much carbon dioxide into your greenhouse. Plants are not hurt by heavy amounts.

CHAPTER VIII

"Framing" Your Plants

You can stretch the usefulness of your greenhouse a great deal by having auxiliary growing areas such as coldframes, hotbeds, lath houses, cloth houses, pits, etc. You will also stretch the dollars of your investment, for it is much cheaper to construct a coldframe or other auxiliary growing area than it is to build another greenhouse.

Coldframes and Hotbeds

Coldframes have several uses. If you use your greenhouse to start plants which you intend to put in the garden later on, the cold-frame is the ideal place to harden the plants before they go outdoors. Plants need this intermediate stage between the warmth of a greenhouse and the outdoors. The coldframe is also the ideal place to start any seedlings and cuttings in the spring. From there they can go directly outside. At the end of the summer, the coldframe can supply protection for tender or semi-hardy plants which will not take the rigors of winter's cold. The coldframe is also an excellent place to store potted or flatted bulbs in the fall until they have made proper roots and before being taken into the greenhouse for forcing. Coldframes can be used as a temporary storage place for many different potted or flatted plants, especially if some heat can be provided.

A simple coldframe is little more than an open box, fit snugly to the ground and covered with sash. One of the most important things to remember as you prepare to build one is to locate it properly. First, pick a site with excellent drainage. (If you can't, remove about 2 feet of the soil and replace it with good drainage material.) Also, place the frame where it will get full sunshine—you can always provide shade.

The summer is a good time to construct a coldframe. Most home gardeners prefer to build theirs of semi-portable wooden materials, although some have found that more permanent construction pays off in the long run. However, wooden coldframes, made of a durable wood, will last for a long time. I suggest rough bench-lumber redwood: it will last 8 or 10 years without treatment. Good tight coldframes will give protection even in the coldest of temperatures without supplementary heat, provided the frame is extended into the soil far enough to get below the frost line.

Although you can make coldframes of any size, it is best to construct the box so that standard coldframe sash can be used. Standard sash is 3 feet by 6 feet.

Be sure that the floor of the coldframe is absolutely level; otherwise, uneven watering and drainage will result. The headboard of the frames should be 18 inches above the inner soil surface and the footboard 12 inches (both taller if larger plants are to be housed in the frame). The side boards which run between the top and the bottom boards should be cut to fit the slope.

As noted before, in milder areas the coldframe can fit into the ground, the outside edges banked with sand or soil to make sure that it is reasonably tight. In colder areas, a foundation should be extended from 18 to 24 inches into the ground. The foundation may merely be an extension of the wooden material used in the box (it must be treated to prevent rotting) or it can be of poured concrete, cinder blocks, bricks, etc.

It is best to use regular drip-free greenhouse sash rails. It is important that the coldframe be so constructed that there is no dripping of moisture on the plants inside. And the rails add strength to the coldframe.

Put slat racks on the floor. Make them in easy-to-move units and treat them well with a wood preservative. The racks will make it possible to move flats easily and to keep them clean. Or you can place a layer of sand in the bottom of the coldframe and cover it with hardware cloth to facilitate movement of flats and pots and to keep them cleaner.

Provide your frames with "arms" which can be used to hold the sash open at various degrees to give you the ventilation you will want each day. And be sure that you have a way to secure the sash tightly to prevent it from being blown off in heavy windstorms.

If you have more than one coldframe, allow enough room between them and between your frames and buildings for easy handling and stacking of the sash. Make the aisles wide enough so wheelbarrows or other carting equipment can be used to move the flats and pots. By placing handles on the ends of your sash, you make the job of moving or replacing them much easier.

Coldframes are turned into hotbeds very simply by being provided with heat. Most home gardeners find it simplest and best to heat the hotbed with small electric heating units or electric cables. An electric cable should be placed within a layer of sand in the bottom of the frame. Wooden slats should be used to protect the cable. The slats will allow the heat from the cable to filter around the plants in the hotbed.

If the weather becomes severely cold and additional heat is needed in a hurry, string 100-watt bulbs inside the frame. Further protection can be added by covering the sash with protective material such as straw or hay. When the weather is mild the cables should be turned off. As the days become warmer in the spring, pay particular attention to ventilation of coldframes and hotbeds. It only takes a short period of direct sunlight to heat up a frame, even when it is cool outside.

Shade for coldframes and hotbeds is usually provided by slatted frames placed directly on top of the sash. However, I recommend the use of frames containing plastic screen (Saran cloth), inasmuch as they are much lighter to use.

After each season's use the sash should be inspected and repaired. Replace any broken glass, clean the sash, and paint them. If sash are not stored indoors, be sure that they are properly fastened to prevent wind damage.

Sash Houses

Closely akin to the coldframe and hotbed is the sash house. It is far superior to a coldframe for various reasons. First of all, you can work inside without lifting the sash. In addition, you can control temperatures better and provide more air for the plants when the house has to be closed because of cold weather. A simple way to construct a sash house is to cover the walls of the frame with canvas. The canvas can be rolled on long rollers and raised or lowered to provide ventilation. Ordinary coldframe sash form the roof of the sash house, lending it its name. In effect, it is a greenhouse. This is especially true when you use a unit heater or some other means of heating it. The fine new plastics, of course, are ideal to use for either the coldframes or sash houses.

Cloth Houses

Growing cut flowers or potted plants in cloth houses during the summer substantially improves their quality. The cloth excludes bees and other insects active in pollination and curtails other pest and disease destruction. Damage which might be inflicted by heavy rains and strong winds is offset too, provided, of course, the cloth house is strong. The frame used for a cloth house should be sturdy and properly braced. Ordinary cheesecloth is used to cover it.

Light intensity is reduced for those plants growing under cloth, while temperatures are from 8 to 10 degrees cooler than outside during the warmest part of the day. The relative humidity is also higher during the day. A combination of all these factors plus slower air movement and greater uniformity of soil moisture result in longer stems and larger flower heads. Adequate drainage beneath the cloth house is of utmost importance, especially if the flowers are being grown in ground beds.

Among the plants which do very well under cloth are: asters, snapdragons, chrysanthemums, zinnias, dahlias, calendulas, and roses. Such potted plants as azaleas, hydrangeas, gardenias, kalanchoës, fuchsias, and tuberous begonias also do well.

Shade Houses

Traditionally, the shade house is constructed of lath or slats. If properly made, the building can be very attractive as well as useful.

Many gardeners like the lath or shade house for hardening off various plants in the spring. The shade house protects the plants

Garden shade house is ideal for tuberous begonias and fuchsias.

from sun, wind, and from heavy rains and hailstorms. Many home gardeners like to do their potting during the hotter months of the year in the lath house.

You need not go to a great deal of expense to build a lath house; it requires only the sort of construction work that the average handyman can do. The sections of a lath house can be built on the ground and assembled on a previously erected framework. Or the framework can be built first and the laths or slats nailed to the posts and supporting boards afterwards. One of the simplest ways in which to erect a shade house, and very attractive, too, is to cover your framework with plastic screen. No matter what material you use for providing the shade on the roof and walls, be sure that the framework is well constructed and properly anchored.

There is on the market at least one aluminum lath house which features an adjustable, movable, secondary roof for complete shade-rain-sun control. It has certain features which are highly desirable, one of which is that of eliminating most of the drip which occurs from the old-style lath houses. Because of the adjustable roof there is complete weather control. A simple manual chain and sprocket control enables the gardener to adjust the panels of the roof structure to any degree of sun, rain, or shade. The structure is exceptionally sturdy and will stand heavy winds without damage.

Pits

An old-fashioned and inexpensive way to have an additional growing area or, in fact, almost a greenhouse in itself, is by constructing a pit. I am not too enthusiastic about this sort of growing area, since it does not provide a greenhouse atmosphere—and does give off a musty, damp smell.

To start a pit house, dig an ordinary deep pit—where drainage is exceptionally good. You need have the aisle area of the pit only dug deep enough for you to stand erect and the areas where growing is to take place only deep enough to hold the benches—and any necessary storage space underneath—and to allow for sufficient head room above. Construct the benches so that air can circulate around them.

As a rule, hotbed sash is used to cover the pit. You can heat the pit in the various ways outlined in Chapter IV and provide ventilation with a simple push-up system which allows for the raising of roof sash, which should be hinged to the ridge. Best results are obtained when the foundation goes below the frost line.

CHAPTER IX

Compatibility Is Important

One of the main causes of failure in a home greenhouse is lack of compatibility of plants. The home greenhouse gardener, especially when his greenhouse is new, is tremendously thrilled by the thoughts of being able to grow any and all of the various cut flowers and potted plants which he has always enjoyed. But his enthusiasm will fade with each failure, and only by being very careful about which plants he grows together will he be able to point with pride to successes.

Compatability involves more than just consideration of temperature, light, moisture, and humidity. There are mechanical factors to be considered also. For instance, it takes considerable head room to produce sweet peas. If your greenhouse is high enough for sweet peas, then you can also grow other plants that like that extra head room, provided, of course, the plants are otherwise compatible. There is also the matter of benches versus beds: if your greenhouse has only benches and no ground beds, this will restrict the variety of plants and cut flowers you can grow. Space and timing also enter into the matter of compatibility. You must plan ahead so that you will have space available for those seasonable plants which you wish to grow. And you must consider the compatibility of those plants which will lap over, so to speak, the growing period of others which will follow.

The following charts should be very handy for the home greenhouse gardener. Through correct application of the information

The overhead shelves can be shifted so that too much
shade does not hit any bed below for too long a time.

given here, it should be possible to plan, time, and grow plants so
that they can best be converted into contented hours and ultimate
pleasure.

COMPATABILITY CHART

Key: PLANT NAME: Refers to name most commonly used.
METHOD: Usual propagation method; B, bulb. C, cutting. D, division. S, seed.
BEST STARTING TIME: 1, January. 2, February. 3, March. 4, April. 5, May.
6, June. 7, July. 8, August. 9, September. 10, October. 11, November.
12, December. (Each number denotes entire month, unless otherwise
noted.)
POTTING OR BENCHING TIME: Numerals indicate various months as with "Best
starting time." Cl, clumps. Fl, flat. Pr, progressively, as needed.
FLOWERING OR MATURITY PERIOD: Numerals indicate months.
ADDITIONAL INFORMATION: Specific information at a glance.

COOL GREENHOUSE (45 to 50 degrees F.)

PLANT NAME	METHOD	BEST STARTING TIME	POTTING OR BENCHING TIME	FLOWERING OR MATURITY PERIOD	ADDITIONAL INFORMATION
Agathaea	S	1	7	12–5	
Ageratum	S	8/15	9	2–5	
Alyssum	S	8/15	8/15	12–4	
Anemones	B	9	9	1–3	
Aster	S	12–4	2–6	4–7	Winter, artificial light
Boston yellow daisy	C	7–8	11	2/15–5	
Bouvardia	C	2	5	12–1	Pinch 9/1
Browallia	S	7–8	9–10	1–5	
Buddleia asiatica	C	2–3	9	11–1	
Calceolaria	S	7–8	10	5–6	
Calendula	S	7–12	9–2	11–5	40 deg. best
Campanula	—	—	—	5	Cl, 12–1
Candytuft	S	12	Fl, 1	5–6	Keep on dry side
Carnation	C	12–3	5–6	11/25	
Centaurea cyanus	S	12	2	4–6	Artificial light
Chrysanthemum,					
Early	C	3	5	9–10	Short days
Mid-season	C	4	6	10–1	Short days
Late	C	4–5	7/15	12–2	Short days
Annual	S	10–1	12–2	4–7	Short days
Cineraria	S	5–8	7–10	12/25–3	
Clarkia	S	12	Fl, 1/25	5	Keep on dry side
Cyclamen	S	7–8	—	12–3 11–4	16–18 months needed
Daphne	—	—	2/1	4–5	Use coldframe plants
Didiscus	S	8	10	2–4	
Eupatorium	S	3–4	6	10	
Feverfew	S	12	2	5–6	
Forget-me-not	S	3	9	12–4	
Freesia	B	8–9	8–9	12–2	
Genista	C	3–6	9–10	3–4	45 deg. best
Gladiolus	B	12–1	12–1	5–6	
Godetia	S	12	Fl, 1/25	6	Keep on dry side
Gypsophila, annual	S	9	—	Spring	
Iris	B	10/25	10/25	1–2	Refrain from moving rooted plants
Larkspur	S	11	1	3–6	
Marguerite	C	3	8–11	12–1	

PLANT NAME	METHOD	BEST STARTING TIME	POTTING OR BENCHING TIME	FLOWERING OR MATURITY PERIOD	ADDITIONAL INFORMATION
Marigold	S	8/1	9/15	11–1	Winter flowering
Nasturtium	S	9	9	12–6	
Nemesia	S	12	Fl, 1/25	5–6	Keep on dry side
Pansy	S	7–8	11	12–3	Additional light
Primula					
sinensis	S	3–4	5	4–6	
malacoides	S	8	10	3–5	
obconica	S	5	7	1–3	
Ranunculus	B	10	10	2–4	
Salpiglossis	S	12	2	5–6	
Schizanthus	S	8	10	3–4	Pinch 9, 10/15
Snapdragon	S	11	1	3–6	
		1	3	4–6	
		8–11	10–1	12–5	
Stevia	C	3–4	9	12–2	
Stock	S	11–2	1–4	4–6	
		7–9	8–10	12/25–2	
Sweet pea	S	1–2	1–2	4–6	
		6	6	9–12	
		8–11	8–11	11–5	
Zinnia	S	3–5	4–6	6	

MODERATE TO WARM GREENHOUSE
(55 to 70 degrees F.)

PLANT NAME	METHOD	BEST STARTING TIME	POTTING OR BENCHING TIME	FLOWERING OR MATURITY PERIOD	OPTIMUM TEMPERATURE
Amaryllis	B	9	10	1–2	60 deg.
Asparagus plumosus				Following	
or sprengeri	S	5	6	May	60 deg.
Astilbe	—	—	Cl, 11	2–3	55–60 deg.
Azalea	C	3–5	1	2/15	Forcing, 60 deg.
Begonia,			year		
Christmas	C	11	later–11	12–1	55–60 deg.
Begonia					
semperflorens	S	1–2	4	8–2	50 deg.

PLANT NAME	METHOD	BEST STARTING TIME	POTTING OR BENCHING TIME	FLOWERING OR MATURITY PERIOD	OPTIMUM TEMPERATURE
Bougainvillea	C	3–4	6	4–5	50 deg. Oct.–Mar. then 60 deg.
Calla, white	B	9–12	9–12	2	55 deg.
Calla, yellow	B	11	11	3–4	60 deg.
Christmas cactus	C	3–6	10	12–2	60 deg.
Coleus	C	9	10	3–6	55 deg.
Daffodil	B	10	1–2	4 weeks	45–50 deg., storage until rooted. Force 55–60 deg.
Euphorbia fulgens	C	—	7–8	1	50–60 deg.
Fern, Boston	Runners	7	—	Year	60 deg.
Gardenia	C	11–12	9	12/25–6	60–65 deg.
Geranium	C	7–8	8–10	5	55 deg.
Gerbera	S	2–3		12—	55–60 deg.
	D	6	8–9		
Gloxinia	B	1–2	1–3	6–8	
	S	3	1–3	8–9	60 deg.
Hyacinth	B	10	1–2	3–5 weeks	35 deg. until Jan.; then force 55–60 deg.
Hydrangea	C	2–7	Pr.	4–5, year	50–70 deg.
Kalanchoë	S	1	8–9	12	60 deg.
Lantana	C	8–9	9	5—	60 deg.
Lilium					
auratum	B	8–9	5	1	55–60 deg.
candidum	B	8–9	3/15–3/30	5	45–60 deg.
Erabu	B	11–12	11–12	2–4	60–70 deg.
formosum	B	11–12	9	1	55–60 deg.
giganteum	B	11–12	11–12	2–4	60–70 deg.
regal	B	1	3	3–4	55–60 deg.
speciosum album	B	8	8	1	55 deg.
speciosum rubrum	B	4–5	4–5	9–10	55 deg.
	B	7–8	7–8	12–1	55 deg.
	B	11–12	11–12	5–6	55 deg.
pumilum (*tenuifolium*)	B	10	10	5	Coldframe until Mar. 1, then 55 deg.
tigrinum	B	6–7	6–7	10–11	55 deg.

PLANT NAME	METHOD	BEST STARTING TIME	POTTING OR BENCHING TIME	FLOWERING OR MATURITY PERIOD	OPTIMUM TEMPERATURE
Philodendron	C	10	11	—	55–60 deg.
Poinsettia	C	6–8	9–10	12/15—	60–65 deg.
Roses in pots	—	Pot on arrival	1	4	Cool until started, then 55–60 deg.
Saintpaulia	C	12–4	3–5	11–2	60 deg.
Tulips					
Breeder	B	10	2	2–4	55–70 deg.
Darwin	B	10	1–2	2–4	35 deg. until rooted, then 55–60 deg.
Double early	B	10	1–2	2–3	35 deg. until rooted, then 55–60 deg.
Single early	B	10	1–2	2–3	35 deg. until rooted, then 55–60 deg.

CHAPTER X

The Growing Medium— Soils and Soil-Free Mixes

The ideal soil for greenhouse use is not something which just happens. Unless you are fortunate enough to own land which has been properly cropped over a period of years, it is wise to start a program of soil-building in order to provide good greenhouse soil for your plants. First-class soil for your greenhouse plants is one of those variables which has much to do with creating high quality plants and flowers. If you must buy your soil instead of getting it from your garden, you are at the "mercy" of circumstances, for you will continually be dealing with untried soil. At best, this is risky business, for no two soils are alike, either in their physical or chemical makeup, and only with careful analysis can you hope to provide the right kind of soil for your plants, when it is derived from different sources. Because of this difficulty many home greenhouse growers have found it simpler to turn to the inert mixes described later in this chapter.

Building a Good Greenhouse Soil

It is not difficult to build good greenhouse soil, if you start with topsoil, not subsoil. You should have the soil analyzed so you will know what you have to start with and what must be done to put the soil into the best condition. Your county agent or state college experiment station can provide you with such information as needed for making soil samples and having the soil properly tested.

Here are some good seeding mixtures for building organic matter into various types of soil. The proportions are based on plots of 100 by 100 feet.

Low land which is moist and heavy should be planted with the following cover crop: 1½ pounds of Kentucky bluegrass, 1 pound of timothy, ½ pound of red top, ½ pound of red clover, ½ pound of alsike clover, and ¼ pound of ladino clover.

On dry land where growing conditions are not too good use: 1 pound of Kentucky bluegrass, 1 pound of timothy, 1 pound of orchard grass, ½ pound of red top, 1 pound of red clover, and ¼ pound of ladino clover.

Where moisture is ample but not overabundant: 2 pounds of Kentucky bluegrass, 1 pound of timothy, 1 pound of red clover, and ¼ pound of ladino clover.

Domestic ryegrass (not perennial ryegrass) is also good in these mixtures. It makes a heavy root growth and will add much humus.

Any of these mixtures will do a good job of improving the soil structure and fertility. The clovers, in particular, will add nitrogen to the soil, thereby encouraging the growth of the grasses besides leaving additional nitrogen for the green plants themselves.

In some areas lime may be needed on the soil before the plot is seeded. Add the lime when the land is prepared for the cover crop. At the same time add 75 pounds of 5–10–10 fertilizer to the plot or, instead, 1½ to 2 tons of phosphated manure. The cover crop should be started as early in the spring as possible or in mid-August and wintered through in mild regions where growth continues, more or less, through the winter.

In the fall (or spring) mow the cover crop and allow it to lie on the ground. At the same time, if clover was omitted from the seed mixture or if the clover stand wasn't heavy enough, add 100 pounds of 10–10–10 to the suggested plot. Otherwise, add 100 pounds of 0–10–10. The mown crop and fertilizer should then be thoroughly tilled or spaded into the soil at least three times about four to six weeks before you plan to use it in the greenhouse. If the soil you start with is in pretty good condition, one year of this program may do the trick. In other cases two years are enough but, if the land is typical of most I've seen, the process described above should be repeated three times before the soil is used. By determining the approximate amount of soil to be used each year, once the program is under way you can always have in process the amount of soil you will need for the coming year and the two years following. Of course, if your greenhouse program is new, you can "manufacture" the soil you need for your immediate program in a matter of hours by combining components such as humus, sand, leafmold, peatmoss, manure, etc. with soil in the proportions needed.

The soil to be used in the spring can be worked up in the fall. Even though you have done a good job of building your soil through the cover-crop method, it is still a good idea to check the amount of organic matter in your soil before you use it. Add leafmold, peatmoss, or rotted manure, if it seems to be insufficient.

Soil Structure

The addition of organic matter—well-rotted manure, peatmoss, leafmold, etc.—to the soil will improve the soil structure and provide the food for the soil bacteria which enable the plants to get the necessary nutrients from the soil. But such humus, alone, is not the answer to what constitutes the best soil structure. In fact, too much humus can be detrimental, because it can interfere with the "breathing" of the soil. Structure refers to the manner in which soil particles (sand, silt, or clay) are bound together into granules. Just how heavy a soil you have depends upon the structure plus the amount of organic matter in the soil. Structure often becomes confused with texture in the minds of gardeners. Texture refers to the proportionate amount of sand, silt, or clay particles present, not the way the particles are arranged.

When particles of clay or clay-loam soil function independently of one another, the soil cannot be used successfully, because it is too compact. The particles must be grouped together in stable granules which are not easily broken down by water in order for the soil to be a useful one.

The formation of stable granules in soil is brought about by the repeated wetting and drying of a soil. Humus (finely divided and partially decayed organic matter) acts as a cementing material to bind together particles of clay. As the soil dries out, the film of water around the masses of soil contracts and presses the particles together. Organic matter in the soil holds the particles together when the drying is completed. The importance of organic matter in the soil, therefore, becomes very apparent. The reason why sod soil is repeatedly referred to by writers and growers as the ideal soil is because the grass adds much organic matter to the soil and, thus, provides the proper structure.

Basically, there are three types of soil structure: grain, crumb, and puddled. A grainy soil structure is loose and open with large individual pore spaces. These spaces allow ample air circulation and water movement. The cultivation of such a (sandy) soil is easy. It warms quickly and permits early crops outdoors because the warm soil provides "bottom" warmth, much as does the cable in a greenhouse bed. But there is also an important fault in a sandy, loose soil. Looseness can make the soil incapable of retaining sufficient moisture and nutrient materials. This sort of soil is apt to be infertile and droughty. To remedy this, ample organic matter is needed.

A puddle structure usually results in a clay soil where the majority of the particles are extremely fine. This type can be amended by the addition of sand and humus. Correctly managed, aggregates of proper size and nature can be developed from such fine particles, and a soil which is loose, open, and friable results. On the other hand, if this type of soil is mishandled, the aggregates may break down and form a puddled soil which will not produce good plants.

The ideal type for greenhouse plants and for most outdoor plants, for that matter, is the crumb soil, for it contains some particles which are large and function separately and others which are small to medium sized and cluster together to form granules and aggregates. Usually this type of structure occurs in loam, which has large pore spaces like a sandy soil to facilitate drainage and air movement, and numberless small pore spaces like a clay soil to retain water and nutrients.

Soil Sterilization

Soil "sterilization" is somewhat of a misnomer inasmuch as the soil is actually pasteurized,—steamed at 180 degrees F. for 30 minutes. The gains to be made through soil sterilization by steam are several. A good program of soil sterilization saves plants and work in these ways: (1) Such pests as symphyllids, nematodes, and grubs are killed. (2) Disease organisms which cause root rot, wilt, etc., are destroyed. (3) Weed seeds are killed, eliminating hours of work. (4) Soil structure is improved; in many instances, the improvement is considerable. (5) Old soil can be reused without the time and work needed to replace it with fresh soil.

Whether the soil is old or new, it should be sterilized. Soil should be completely prepared, with the peatmoss and manure added *before* sterilization.

In hot weather, use a chemical such as Vapam—instead of steam —for sterilizing the soil, and allow at least two to three weeks of good aeration after the chemical treatment. You should not steam-sterilize during the summer or you will interfere with the decomposition process of the soil—which is accelerated in hot weather.

As we said, steam sterilization is actually steam pasteurization, and during the process of pasteurization harmful bacteria are killed along with most of the beneficial ones. However, the bacteria which create ammonia survive better than others. Hence, after the soil is steamed, the build-up of ammonifying bacteria is more rapid. In the summer months, the build-up is so rapid that even heavy leaching or drying of the steamed soil fails to reduce the excessive rate of the ammonifying build-up. And while the ammonifying bacteria are necessary for plant nutrition, too much ammonia in the soil can cause root damage. At other times of the year, the build-up of ammonifying bacteria subsides after the soil has had an opportunity to "rest" a bit before it is used for crops.

For a long time it was thought that soil should stand several days before planting was done. The build-up of salts in the soil from the dead bodies of organisms was what prompted this belief. But you can avoid delay by following this method. First of all, the soil must thoroughly cool before the plants can be placed in it. After steaming but before planting, apply 1 to 1½ pounds of gypsum (calcium phosphate) to a cubic yard of soil. Should you use superphosphate, remember that it is about half gypsum. This will prevent an excessive accumulation of ammonia. By planting at once, after cooling, a toxic build-up of manganese will not be possible before the young plants are established. Then water the new plants well, keeping the soil moist. This will keep the soil concentration diluted. Following this procedure makes soil leaching unnecessary.

For soils that are heavy and tight use peatmoss before steam pasteurizing. This will allow enough oxygen to enable the bacteria to do their work. Don't use too much peat, however, for it soaks up much oxygen as it decomposes. Keep the soil well cultivated afterward to encourage air to enter the lower parts of the soil sterilized. Also avoid overwetness or the ammonia build-up will be too rapid.

Remember to use great care to prevent recontamination of the soil after you have pasteurized it.

Fumigants containing chloropicrin or methyl bromide are best for greenhouses, coldframes, or outdoor seed beds. Follow the directions of the manufacturer very carefully, both as to precautions concerning your plants and yourself, and to get the desired results.

pH Adjustment

There is considerable misunderstanding concerning the pH requirements of plants. Simply, pH refers to the acidity or alkalinity of the soil. The condition of the soil is designated by a scale which uses 7.0 at the middle point. All figures below 7.0 denote an acid condition and all above 7.0 denote an alkaline condition of the soil.

Because a preferred pH requirement of a certain plant may be 6.5 (this is the best pH for the majority of greenhouse plants), it does not mean you should attempt to keep the pH exactly 6.5—this is practically impossible to do. With a soil that is well fertilized and contains a high amount of organic matter, the pH should be kept between 6 and 7 when the ideal requirement is 6.5. Soil testing kits and tools are simple to handle, and the job of giving an acidity test is easy, if you follow the directions of the manufacturer.

In most areas there is a need to raise the pH rather than lower it. Dolomitic lime is considered the best means of raising it, although calcite, sodium nitrate, calcium nitrate, and potassium nitrate are also alkalizing materials. To lower the pH, sulfur has the greatest reaction; other acidifying materials are ammonium nitrate, ammonium sulfate, monoammonium phosphate, diammonium phosphate, urea, ferrous sulfate, and aluminum sulfate. It is well to keep in mind that almost all liquid fertilizers are acid-forming. When you use them frequently, a drop in the pH may occur, unless lime is used occasionally.

Artificial Soils

As noted, the scarcity of good soil has brought about the adoption of various mixes for greenhouse plants. There are two basic sorts of mixes: (1) The University of California mix. (2) The peat-lite mixes developed at Cornell University. These artificial soils are only satisfactory when the components are carefully and thoroughly mixed. The gardener using them must learn to adapt the feeding of his plants to the mix at hand, for these inert materials call for more fertilizer than normal soil does.

For one cubic yard of the California mix use 11 bushels of shredded German or Canadian sphagnum peatmoss; 11 bushels of fine sand (0.5 to 0.05 millimeters); 4 ounces of potassium nitrate; 4 ounces of potassium sulfate; 7½ pounds of dolomitic limestone; 2½ pounds of calcium limestone; and 2½ pounds of 20 per cent superphosphate. This mix contains a moderate amount of available nitrogen and potassium fertilizer but requires supplemental feeding starting 10 days after planting.

For one cubic yard of the Cornell peat-lite mix use 11 bushels of shredded German or Canadian sphagnum peatmoss; 11 bushels of number 2 vermiculite, horticultural grade; 10 pounds of ground limestone, preferably dolomitic; 2½ pounds of 20 per cent superphosphate, powdered; 3 to 4 pounds of ammonium nitrate, fertilizer grade (or 12 pounds of 5–10–5 fertilizer instead of the ammonium nitrate). If the peatmoss is very dry, a small amount of water may be added to reduce the dust problem during mixing.

An alternate peat-lite mix substitutes horticultural perlite for the vermiculite. If ammonium nitrate is used, additional potassium must be added before planting, because this mixture contains no potash. Use potassium chloride (muriate of potash) at ½ pound per cubic yard of mix, or use 5–10–5 at the rate of 16 pounds per cubic yard instead of ammonium nitrate and potassium chloride.

A third formula for one cubic yard of peat-lite mix calls for 11 bushels of shredded German or Canadian sphagnum peatmoss; 11 bushels of vermiculite or perlite; 10 pounds of ground limestone, preferably dolomitic; and 2½ pounds of 20 per cent superphosphate, powdered. This mixture will need nitrogen and potassium as soon as the seedlings are transplanted.

CHAPTER XI

Fertilizer and Water Are Partners

Almost from the time that crops were first cultivated by our ancestors there has been a realization that some sort of feeding of plants was necessary. Yet, strangely enough, there is no part of the growing of plants which is so misunderstood as is the fertilizing of them.

Exercise every care when feeding your plants. Never apply a strong concentration of fertilizers when the soil is dry, or the roots will suffer damage. Fertilizer and water work as a team. Nutrients from the soil can move into the roots only when the fertilizer elements are in solution. Water carries out its bargain in the partnership by moving fertilizer elements and manufactured food from one place to another within the plant.

Apply fertilizer in larger amounts when the plants are making a rapid growth. Diminish the amount as plant growth slows down. Refrain from feeding plants when they are resting. Remember, it is better to make weak applications and feed the plants more often than to feed the plants too heavily at any one time. Use either a liquid or water-soluble, high-analysis plant food.

Soil testing should never be a "one-shot" operation. Soil should be tested before it is used and at various times thereafter. It is best to make soil tests when a plant's growing period is in its ascendency, so that you will know what your feeding requirements are in time for the heavy growing period.

Always keep in mind that young plants cannot absorb fertilizer as rapidly as older plants. Remember, too, that large plants need to be fed more often.

Here are soil nutrient ranges for most florist crops under normal conditions: nitrates 15 to 25 parts per million; phosphorus 8 to 12 ppm; potash 20 to 30 ppm; and calcium 150 ppm. The total of all nutrients in the soil should run from 40 to 50 ppm. When it gets as high as 75 ppm, you had better leach the soil to reduce the amounts.

Prepare a chart on your plants, listing the various nutrient requirements, the amount of fertilizer required for each feeding, and the dates when feeding is made. It is very important to feed greenhouse plants on a regular basis. Whenever feeding is done in a hit-or-miss fashion, the plants are bound to suffer. Plants, unfortunately, have no way to call out when they need food, other than through deficiency symptoms, which are described later in this chapter. As a matter of fact, some plants, such as chrysanthemums and carnations, are so slow about letting you know that a deficiency of some sort exists that before it becomes apparent, the damage is done. This again emphasizes the importance of soil testing.

On the average, most of the plants grown in a greenhouse should be fed every ten days to two weeks, provided, of course, you use a dilute solution. You may stretch your feedings to three week intervals but you need to feed a little more at each application.

Light soils do not hold fertilizers as long as heavier soils. With a sandy soil feed more often than with a heavier one.

The yearly amount of both phosphorus and trace elements can be added to the soil at the time it is prepared for your plants. But you must add nitrogen and potassium more regularly to compensate for that taken up by the plants and that leached out in watering.

If nitrogen is all that is needed, there certainly is no sense in applying phosphorus or potassium as well. On the other hand, the sort of nitrogenous fertilizer given should be considered. Ammonium sulfate is quickly available but it causes the soil to become more acid. If this is not a problem and nitrogen is needed in a hurry, fine! But if the acidity is already too great, calcium nitrate can be used to alkalize the soil.

Where a greater amount of phosporus is needed, superphosphate is the answer. It can be obtained in 16, 20, and 45-per-cent strengths. Use a level 5-inch potful of superphosphate to a wheelbarrow of soil. It is not easily leached from the soil.

The principal sources of potassium are muriate of potash (potassium chloride) and potassium sulfate. These two fertilizers leach out readily inasmuch as they are immediately soluble.

Nitrogen and potassium can be given your plants at the rate of 1 ounce of calcium nitrate or ammonium sulfate and ½ ounce of muriate of potash in 2 gallons of water. Remember to be sure that the soil is moist at the time of feeding.

The term "balanced" fertilizer, and the reference to fertilizers as 20–20–20, 6–10–4, 5–3–2, and the like, can sound very confusing to anyone who does not know what is meant by such terms. Actually, a balanced fertilizer is one which has about the right proportions of the main elements needed for the area in which the fertilizer is to be used. But inasmuch as soils vary considerably, even in relatively limited areas, you may find that some of the plants which you grow in your greenhouse will do better with a fertilizer which is balanced differently from some offered for general sale.

When you read the analysis of a mixture on the bag and see 6–10–4, this is what is meant: there are 6 pounds of nitrogen, 10 pounds of phosphorus, and 4 pounds of potash to 100 pounds of the mixture. The balance of the 100 pounds is filler which has no plant value. The analysis on the bag as indicated by the figures is always in the same order—nitrogen first, phosphorus next, and potash last. You can have a fertilizer manufacturer mix any proportion which you find is best suited for your particular use.

We hear a great deal today about the slow-release types of fertilizers, such as Uramite and Nitroform. After considerable research with both, Cornell University recommended the following: ½ teaspoon of either material per 4-inch pot of soil; 2 teaspoons per 7-inch pot of soil; $\frac{2}{10}$ of a pound per bushel of soil; and 4½ pounds per cubic yard of soil. Ohio State University, reporting on similar research, recommended 1½ teaspoon per 6-inch pot of soil; 2½-inch potful per bushel of soil; and a heaping 3-inch potful to a wheelbarrow full of soil (2½ bushels).

The slow-release fertilizers are recommended mainly for those plants which last a long time, inasmuch as they give fertilization for up to two years or more. There are two grades in the material, medium granules and coarse granules. The coarser granules break down over a longer period. These new-type fertilizers have a small percentage of nutrients which are immediately available to get new plants started. From then on, the nutrients are doled out slowly and plant roots are not endangered by excessive fertilizer being released at one time. Because of the fact that the fertilizer is pretty much used as it is released, there is little lost by dissipation through leaching.

MagAmp is another slow-release fertilizer. It is used principally on plants grown in containers, such as potted shrubs or trees for patio or outdoor use. When used in the original potting soil, this material will produce good-looking plants over a long period without the need for continuous feeding. Other good controlled release fertilizers are Osmocote (various formulations); Gro-Tabs (14-4-6) and The Pill (20-10-5). The last two are agriform planting tablets.

Many greenhouse gardeners still use dry fertilizers, but most of them have found that soluble fertilizers are easier to use and are better in several ways. With soluble fertilizers the plant food is available to plants almost at once and distribution of nutrients is more even.

Means of Application

You can apply liquid fertilizers in many ways. There are automatic plant-feeding systems which run from the simple Hozon proportioner to the more complicated injector systems such as Fert-o-ject. Such devices take liquid fertilizer from the container and properly proportion it with water, so that as you water, the plant is also fed. The Fert-o-ject system can provide food to plants every time they are watered. The low-cost water-powered Hydrocare Injector is used for applying fertilizers, insecticides, fungicides, soil sterilants, growth regulants or herbicides. Water rate or pressure does not affect its accuracy.

A homemade feeding system can be constructed in this manner: use a large stoneware container in which to mix and hold the fertilizer. Use a non-corroding, rubber impeller pump for pumping the fertilizer into the greenhouse. A separate pipeline should be used, for if the regular water line is used, corrosion can cause trouble at an inopportune time. Outlets, with hose connections, can be placed on the fertilizer line throughout the greenhouse. Thirty-pound pressure is adequate on the line and the fertilizer hose should be equipped with a valve for a quick and easy shutoff of fertilizer.

The simplest fertilizer proportioner for the small home greenhouse is the Hozon nozzle. It is calibrated at 1–15 which means that 1 gallon of solution is sucked into 15 gallons of water, making a total of 16 gallons coming out the end of the hose. The Hozon proportioner is available in garden centers and greenhouse supply firms.

An even simpler method of applying liquid fertilizer in a home greenhouse is a pressure insect sprayer can with an open hose (with nozzle removed).

Organic vs. Inorganic Fertilizers

There is no surer way for a horticultural writer to stick out his neck than to become a proponent of organic fertilizer as opposed to inorganic, or vice versa. Among amateur growers, this can almost lead to bloodshed, especially by those who advocate organic fertilizers and are strong in their belief that theirs is the only way to feed plants. But this is far from the truth, for a plant couldn't care less where its food comes from, organic or inorganic sources.

Ask yourself, do the plants need additional organic matter? If so, can you purchase animal manure or other organic fertilizer cheaply enough to make it practical to supply both that organic material and the fertilizer needed by means of the organic manure alone? Or would it be cheaper to use peatmoss, leafmold, etc., to give your soil needed organic matter and provide the nutrients by way of a chemical fertilizer? One more question which needs asking: are some of your plants in need of a mulch? If so, perhaps you can use animal manure to provide both the mulching material and most of the nutrients.

Watering and Humidity

When you water your plants, do so thoroughly. Then allow the soil to approach the dry side before watering again. Don't, however, allow your plants to wilt before watering them. When salts become excessive, leaching is required. (See section of this chapter on Salts Concentration and Plant Deficiencies.)

Damage to plants in ground beds can be prevented by using simple inverted **V**-shaped wires to fend off the hose.

Whenever you water potted plants or feed them with a liquid fertilizer, fill the pots brimful with solution at each feeding. The plants will then be fed equally (or watered equally) and thus insure even growth of the plants. In the case of benched plants be sure that you water or feed from both sides of the bench. Or if necessary to feed or water from one side all the time, use a nozzle extension so that you can place the water or liquid fertilizer on the far side of the bench without washing the soil or any mulch which may be on the bench. If water is applied from one side of a bench continuously, without the use of an extension nozzle, the soil will become humped on the far side, and, eventually, one side of the bench will be receiving more water and fertilizer than the other.

There are several forms of automatic watering, including the misting system. (See Chapter XIII on Propagation.) One sort of automatic watering device uses a tensiometer which turns on the water supply as the soil becomes dry and turns it off when enough water has been applied. A time clock can also be used to turn off the water. Another sort of automatic watering device especially adapted to bench watering uses a float valve system to turn the water off and on.

Among the most modern of automatic watering systems is the Chapin Watermatic system for watering pot plants. Many commercial growers are using this system today and it is adaptable to amateur greenhouses where a uniformity of pot sizes is possible. This system uses a plastic tube from which tiny plastic lines run to each pot. Lead weights hold the tubes in the pots. There is a moisture scale and a pilot plant which sets upon the scale. As the moisture in the pilot or indicator plant evaporates, its weight lightens and water is provided all of the plants watered with the system. Weekly adjustment must be made in the scale to compensate for the increased weight of the plant on the scale. This system also needs a check valve every few feet where there is a "fall" in the greenhouse. Before installing such a system, it is important to check the water pressure to make sure whether or not changes are necessary. By growing plants which are adaptable to the use of this system, and using automatic heat and ventilation, etc., it is possible to leave the greenhouse for days and to have all of the essential things done to keep your plants happy and alive.

Water faucets should always be placed in convenient spots. The best places are along the aisles just beneath the bench. Be sure the faucets are set back far enough to prevent stumbling over them. A single-aisle greenhouse, up to 100 feet in length, needs only one faucet, in the middle of the house. Place a faucet in each aisle. A snap-on hose connection on each faucet will make changing the hose easy if one hose is to be used on all aisles.

Simplest and cheapest way to provide humidity in the greenhouse is simply by applying moisture to the aisles and beneath the benches as humidity is needed. The simplest automatic or semi-automatic way to increase humidity is with an atomized spray. Plants requiring more exact humidity control call for a humidistat to activate the spray of water when necessary.

Salts Concentration and Plant Deficiencies

Far more damage to greenhouse plants results from a concentration of salts in the soil than many growers realize. Highly soluble salts can be part of the fertilizers or be residues of these fertilizers. Or they can result when you reuse soil which was used for other plants. This very often happens when a highly fed crop, such as chrysanthemums, is followed by another crop.

There are various things which you can do to offset a high-salt condition. Leaching the soil heavily is one of the best methods, if you have raised benches. To do this, water the bench heavily, until the water runs out the bottom. Allow the bench to drain well. Then, after an hour, water again until the water drains out of the bottom of the bench once more. Repeat this process once more after another hour. It takes the first heavy watering to bring the material into solution. Successive waterings push the dissolved material on through.

You can use an application of sawdust or similar material, such as corncobs, to "take up" excess nitrates, but this is a temporary solution and may lead to even greater trouble. The danger lies in the fact that as soon as the sawdust or corncobs start to decompose, they will release nitrates, and unless your plants are growing quite rapidly, you have to water quite heavily for a while.

If you can raise or lower your pH to a point at which the element in question is tied up or made insoluble in the soil, changing the pH is a good way to correct a high-salt concentration. This means, of course, adding another material which will take part of the excessive nitrate or other offensive element out of solution.

The best idea of all is to avoid such a situation in the first place. Make regular soil tests and test new soil or soil which is to be reused before a new crop goes into it. Then you can make any necessary adjustments beforehand.

Nitrogen deficiency: The foliage appears light green, growth is stunted, the stalks are slender and there are few new shoot breaks. Also, the leaves are small and the lower ones are of lighter yellow than the upper leaves. The yellowing is followed by a drying to a light brown color but there is little actual leaf dropping. The effect on the plant may be general, or localized on the older, lower leaves.

Phosphorus deficiency: Growth is retarded and the foliage is dark green. Sometimes the area between the veins on the lower leaves is yellow. More often it is purplish, especially on the petiole or leaf stems. Leaves drop prematurely. Again the effect may be general or localized on the older, lower leaves.

Potassium deficiency: The effects are usually local and on the older, lower leaves. The lower leaves appear mottled and the areas near the top ends and margins are usually necrotic. Yellowing starts at the margin of the leaves and continues toward the center. Afterward the margins become brown and curve under, with older leaves dropping.

Deficiencies of some minor elements, too, may have a very detrimental effect on crops.

Insufficient magnesium may cause older, lower leaves to become chlorotic (yellowed) and later necrotic. The chlorosis exists between the veins and the margins of the leaves curl upward or downward, or may develop a puckering effect.

Iron deficiency is localized in the new leaves. Veins remain green but the leaves become chlorotic between the veins. Necrosis of leaf margins and tip will be noted when the problem is acute.

A manganese deficiency causes the plants to have blooms poor in size and color. A checkered or finely netted appearance hits the foliage and it becomes necrotic, mainly on the new leaves.

If sulfur is deficient, new leaves are light green with the veins lighter than the adjoining interveinal areas. Necrotic spots likely will occur.

The terminal bud usually dies when a *calcium deficiency* is present. Young leaves show a necrotic condition beginning at the tips and margins. Often the young leaves have a hook on the tip.

Boron deficiency also affects the young leaves. There is a breakdown of the young leaves at the base, and the stems and petioles become brittle. With both boron and calcium deficiencies, the roots die, especially the tips.

CHAPTER XII

Growth Regulators

Just as we think that the ultimate has been reached in growing techniques, along comes someone who says "it ain't so." And so it will always be. That is one of the chief reasons why the growing of plants in greenhouses or outside is so intriguing. There will always be new growing techniques, new fertilizers, and new growth regulators to stir gardeners, making it possible for them to produce bigger (or smaller), better-flowered, better-fruited, healthier plants in less time than ever before.

The most exciting thing at hand is the matter of regulating the growth of plants with chemicals. It all began in 1926 when a Japanese plant pathologist, while investigating a rice seedling disease, observed a fungus, *Gibberella fujikuroi,* which gave off a substance that caused rice seedlings to grow themselves to death. The actual chemical, later named gibberellic acid, was isolated in 1935 by other Japanese scientists. It first came to the attention of western scientists in 1949 when the U.S.D.A. reported success in dwarfing a test plant without harm to the plant. Early experiments with gibberellic acid caused bush beans to produce twining vines and grow as tall as pole types. It did almost the same thing for dwarf peas, stimulated flowering stocks so that the linear growth was better and faster, reduced the flowering time for biennials, and other wondrous things. In short, it set scientific minds racing as it became apparent that here was a whole new concept for plant-growing awaiting refinement.

Great strides were made during the next fifteen to sixteen years.

Introduced were the chemicals B-9, Amo-1618, Cycocel or CCC, and Phosfon. Refinements of these chemicals have continued since their introduction.

There are now chemicals that improve the form and attractiveness of many kinds of excessively tall-growing ornamentals; shorten the stem height of various flowers and plants which hitherto were considered too tall for greenhouse subjects; restrict the excessive vegetative growth which occurs on some plants around the flowers such as azaleas; extend the production period of others; reduce the necessity of pruning for some woody plants; improve the flowering of various annuals and other plants, etc. The shorter internodes and more compact plants among poinsettias and chrysanthemums when growth retardants are used eliminate the necessity for staking the plants. Also, the plants require less water and are less apt to be injured by heat, drought, or a build-up of salts in the soil. But it requires good judgment and close adherence to instructions to use such chemicals properly.

For some as yet unknown reason the retardants do not work on all plants. And they work on various plants with different degrees of success. Even varieties within a certain species make a difference. Results may be outstanding on one variety, mediocre on another, and negligible on a third.

It is wise as you use a growth retardant (or growth stretcher) to follow directions of the manufacturer very carefully. Even then, use the material on an experimental basis at first, to get the "feel" of the material under your own growing conditions. It is not as dangerous to most plants to receive an overdose of growth retardant (provided it is not too great) as it would be to overfeed a plant to the same degree.

Growth regulators, too, are tempermental. They do not all respond in the same manner in accordance with the seasons. Some do a better job when used in the winter, others are best in the summer.

Much of the scientific research which has been done on a national scale in regard to growth regulators on herbaceous plants and other ornamentals has been under the direction of Dr. Neil Stuart (now retired) physiologist, and Dr. Henry Marc Cathey, Head, Ornamentals Research Division of the U.S.D.A. at Beltsville, Maryland. Most of the following recommendations are a direct result of their work in this field.

Generally, growth regulators are applied by spraying the plants or by drenching the soil. When plants are sprayed, they must be in good turgid (firm) condition. Foliage must be dry, and no water should be applied to the plants for 24 hours after treatment. Also, you should use only a fiberglass or plastic sprayer, for some of these chemicals react on metal containers. Spraying should also be done with a fine mist, applying enough of the material to cover thoroughly the top third of the plant.

Growth regulators have a wonderful effect on garden annuals. Most annuals respond to the use of B-9 as a spray. The material should be applied at the time of transplanting the seedlings. No wetting agent need be added to B-9, inasmuch as it has the necessary wetting agent within it. However, be sure to start with a fresh solution of B-9 each time. Overdoing the application by applying the retardant to the dripping point destroys much of its effectiveness—it need be only misted on the plants.

The benefits of B-9 carry over into the garden, providing the plants with a certain resistance to their garden environment. A side benefit which has been noted is the reduction of damage which occurs in cities from air pollution or smog.

When a growth retardant is used as a soil treatment, it is usually necessary to stick with the single treatment. But with spray retardants it is possible to apply the material two, three, or more times. Following the first application, there should not be another until the plant starts to elongate again.

Cycocel is best used as a drench. Many commercial growers who produce red poinsettias have found that Cycocel-treated plants have much less height, deeper green foliage, stronger stems, and red bracts. If small plants are being potted or panned, treatment with Cycocel should not occur until active root development is observed. Cycocel works well as a growth retardant on azaleas and rhododendrons as well as on many other woody plants. A wetting agent such as Dreft or some other detergent should be used with Cycocel.

Research in regard to using growth regulators on foliage plants is still in its infancy. But the prospects are that it will exert a vast influence on the choice of plant material used as foliage plants in the future. For instance, spraying normally tall aphelandras with B-9 keeps them to a desirable height.

Phosfon used as a soil drench likewise holds down the height of many plants, making some very useful as indoor plants and others acceptable for outdoor use where too much height would otherwise restrict their use.

Potted hollies, when grown with the aid of growth regulators, are now possible. Early research has shown that when a growth regulator is used, such plants, complete with bright red berries, will be possible for any period of the year.

There is another fascinating new idea offered by the U.S.D.A. research. It consists of using gibberellic acid to induce the flowering of a single bud by breaking its dormancy. Research has shown that a single drop of 1 per-cent solution gibberellic acid when placed at the base of a bud of a rhododendron, after the top scale has been peeled off, will cause the bud to flower quickly at a 65-degree temperature. This has great possibilities as a "home idea" whereby the lady of the house can bring into flower one bud at a time or all at once.

CHAPTER XIII

Propagation

Propagation by Seeds

If all the miracles that have taken place were listed in order of importance, the miracle of the seed would have to be placed high on that list. Tucked within the shell of a seed is the embryo plant ready for a trip to maturity, once the right combination of moisture, light, and temperature are provided to trigger its growth.

There never has been a quality plant produced from poor or worn-out seed. The reliable seed firms deal only in fresh seed which has been produced and handled according to rigid specifications to ensure that it goes to you in A-1 condition. So if you experience poor germination, check your own system of storing, sowing, and starting the seed, before you blame the seedsman. The grower is to blame far more often for failures than is the seedsman.

When you purchase seed, buy only enough to supply your present needs comfortably; do not have so much left over that you will be tempted to save it for use next year. Remember, the viability of seed depends, first of all, upon its freshness.

Second most important is the manner in which the seed is stored. There are four main enemies of seeds in storage: (1) excessive humidity; (2) excessive temperature; (3) air; (4) rodents. Always store seeds in airtight, rodent-proof jars at a temperature of around 50 degrees and in a place where the humidity is not excessive.

Should you find it necessary to store seeds for any length of time, test the seed to be sure that the viability is still good enough to insure you sufficient plants. Count out a given number of seeds—50 or 100—and place them between two pieces of moist blotting paper or soft muslin. Keep it evenly moist and at a temperature between 65 and 75 degrees. Then count the good sprouts to see what the percentage of germination is.

The section of the greenhouse in which you start your seeds should be in apple-pie order. Germinating seeds and seedlings are very touchy about their surroundings. A drafty, leaky greenhouse in which the temperature variance is considerable is the surest place around to kill off seedlings—or the seeds, themselves, may never germinate. At best, the germination will be poor.

The benches should be sound and sterilized between crops of seedlings. To get longer life out of the propagating bench, treat it periodically with a wood preservative. The same thing can be done with your seed flats. If you use pots or similar containers, be sure that they are sterilized before each new use.

Guard against all sorts of pests from slugs to birds. Slugs can quickly mow down a flat of seedlings; birds will fly through open ventilators for a meal of tender seedlings. Get rid of the slugs with poison bait and keep the birds out by screening the ventilator openings from beneath.

Heat is extremely important when you propagate. You should be able to control your heat accurately 24 hours a day. Bottom heat, particularly desirable for propagating cuttings, is also desirable for starting many seeds.

Most gardeners prefer a light soil for their seeding medium, for it enables the seedlings to push through easily—and to be removed without damage to their root system. A good light soil mixture for the majority of seeds consists of one part loam, one part leafmold, and two parts sand. The mixture should be sterilized. Top the mixture with $\frac{1}{2}$ to $\frac{3}{4}$ inch of vermiculite, after you have firmed the soil and leveled it. Do not firm the vermiculite.

Other good media in which to start seeds are vermiculite, sand, sphagnum and peatmoss, used alone or in various combinations. These materials, however, have no plant foods in them, and without nutrients the young seedlings will become spindling unless fed. For feeding these young plants, give them potassium nitrate or other soluble fertilizer at the rate of 1 teaspoonful to 1 gallon of water.

Without moisture, nothing happens. With too much, damp-off and other problems occur. The germinating medium should be soaked before the seeds are planted. A good system is to place each flat in a deep pan or sink of water which will allow the flat to be soaked from beneath. Use a fine rose sprinkler to moisten the vermiculite, if it does not become wet enough. Be extremely careful to avoid contaminating the flats again. This initial wetting should be enough for good germination.

If you use waterproof inserts for your seed flats, place the insert on the bottom of the flat. Cover the insert with a layer of pea-size gravel. Then add a thin layer of screened peatmoss to prevent the soil from sifting into the gravel. Use the germinating medium recommended above. In the center of each seed flat place a small pot, directly on the bottom of the insert. Add water through the pot, if needed, to keep the medium moist. The moss between the gravel and the soil will act as a wick to pull the moisture into the soil.

There are other methods to keep the flats moist. One is to use a shallow container into which the flats may be placed to keep them moist. It takes some practice to learn how to provide the right amount of water from beneath to keep the flats moist but not wet. Either is a far better method than watering the flats from above before all the seeds have emerged. If you water from above, there is bound to be some packing and crusting of the soil. You should water from above, of course, when fine seeds are not covered and must be watered into the soil.

A few growers prefer a constant-water-level seedbed for starting seeds. This requires a watertight bench.

Time-clock controlled misting nozzles are the surest way to insure uniform moisture at all times. The danger of neglecting to water on time is eliminated by the fine, misty spray which comes for a few seconds periodically. The cost is reasonable and the germination results are remarkable.

One of the age-old methods of preventing your seed flats from drying out is by covering the flats, after sowing, with panes of glass and topping the glass with newspapers until the seeds germinate. Better yet, try the new Plasticovers which are light-gauge, flexible plastic tubes that fit completely around each seed flat. Moisture evaporation cannot take place. It is important, however, to remove the covers at once when the seeds are up, or growth will become soft and straggly.

A good extra precaution to take with seeds is treating them with a fungicide. For the average packet of small seeds use an amount equal in size to half a match head. To obtain even distribution of the fungicide on all seeds in the packet, close the packet and shake it vigorously. Avoid using too much fungicide or more harm than good may be done. Good materials for this purpose are Semesan, Arasan, Ferbam, and Tersan.

Hard seed coats are a real problem with some seeds. Some can be soaked in water for 24 hours, or until the seeds swell up. But white varieties should not be soaked, for they rot easily. An English treatment for hard-coated seeds is to soak the seed in boiling water, leaving the seed there until it shows signs of softening. Strong sulfuric acid is also used for soaking hard-coated seeds. The length of time for the soaking depends upon the kind of seed.

One of the simplest methods to "soften up" hard-coated seeds is to bury them in moist peatmoss or soil in a warm place. Bacteria and fungi will decompose the seed coats in time. Palms, cotoneasters, and such nutlike seeds as hazelnuts are treated in this way for best results. Common frost can be used to split the seed coats of apricots, almonds, plums, and peaches, enabling the embryos to get started when properly planted thereafter.

Stratification is used to help many seeds of trees and shrubs, such as cotoneasters, hawthorns, snowberries, walnuts, and stone fruits. Stratification is accomplished by mixing the seed with peatmoss and sand and keeping it moist and cold (40 to 41 degrees) for a period of two to four months, depending upon the kind of seed. Sand and peatmoss can also be placed in layers with the seed between. Stratification can also be accomplished by mixing the seed with moist peat and sand and placing it outdoors for the winter but, should you try this method, be sure the mixture is screened or placed where rodents will not get at it. One trouble with this method is that there may not be enough days at the strategic temperature and two winters may sometimes be necessary.

SOWING SEED

When seed is sown in the greenhouse it can either be broadcast or sown in rows. The latter is better because it allows for better aeration and prevents crowding which is an open invitation to damp-off and other fungus diseases. Whenever the weather is warm, the danger from overcrowding of seedlings is greater.

To make rows, take a ½-inch piece of wood, cut it to fit from one side of the flat to the other, and make slight depressions from ⅛ to ¼-inch deep in the moist vermiculite or soil. Be sure the depressions are of uniform depth, according to the seed being planted, and about 2 inches apart, in most instances.

Sow the seeds uniformly and thinly along the depressions and then cover lightly with dry vermiculite, peatmoss, or sand. Only a scattering of particles should be placed among fine seeds. Note, though: the *extremely* fine seeds, such as begonias and petunias, should not be covered at all. The best way to treat such seeds is to place finely shredded sphagnum moss in the depressions, moisten it and then sow the seed in the rows. Water it in gently. Most gardeners, following the sowing of a seed flat, prefer to sprinkle it lightly.

Seed flats should be placed in a draft-free place and covered. Most of the seeds for greenhouse plants prefer a germinating temperature of 65 to 70 degrees nights (68 degrees is ideal) and daytime temperature of 84 degrees. This includes most of the popular spring annuals. But there are some seeds, such as delphinium, larkspur, and snapdragons, which should have a germinating temperature of 60 degrees. Bottom heat may be supplied by placing the flats on electric cables. This aids germination considerably. You can germinate seeds with air temperature of around 50 degrees, but this will reduce the percentage of germination unless you can provide for extra heat to get directly at the seed flats.

Whether or not the flats are covered with glass or plastic sleeves, if the sun is bright, they should be shaded with newspapers or burlap as well until germination starts, unless they are placed in semi-shaded locations. As the seeds start to germinate, remove the newspapers or burlap and gradually allow the seeds full exposure to the sunlight and air.

By the time the seed has germinated, the panes of glass or plastic sleeves should be removed from the seed flats or conditions will be ripe for spindling growth and disease attack. Do the removing in stages. Begin with a crack the thickness of a toothpick and gradually lift the glass on the flats to expose the seedlings to the air and sun as they emerge, until they are given full exposure.

Get the germinated seedlings out of the germination environment as soon as possible to prevent poor growth. The seedlings will respond to the "tougher" atmosphere of a cooler temperature, more air, and more light. They will quickly become stronger. It takes extra vigilance at this point. The flats must not dry out. Neither must they be overwatered. The fine seeds, especially, must be watched in this regard. If the tiny plants dry out, they quickly die. As the seedlings begin to grow, water them first with a watering can, using water which contains a good fungicide, such as Morton Soil Drench or Terraclor. Follow the directions carefully.

Once germination has taken place, the soil is kept a little drier to cause the plants to send down deeper roots in search of moisture. If the surface is quite moist, the seedlings will be content to keep the root system shallow. Gradually decreased watering will also tend to harden the plants. After the early waterings, switch to an adjustable nozzle on the hose. A light spraying four or five times a day is good during warm weather, but be sure the plants are dry before night.

The time for sowing certain seeds depends, of course, upon when you want the plants to mature. Be sure to check reliable sources concerning the length of time needed to produce each plant according to the best methods of growing used today. Also allow ample time for the seed to arrive.

Be certain that seed flats always set level. Otherwise, watering becomes uneven, one part of the flat getting too much and the other too little. If the days become overly bright or warm, shade your young seedlings. If you can provide this shade with cloth inside the greenhouse which can be quickly drawn overhead, this is best, for it can also be just as quickly removed. Many growers use newspapers for quick shading and this is certainly better than letting the plants suffer from excess light and heat while still young. However, newspapers have a tendency to draw moisture out of the plants, so the use of cloth above the flats is better.

Be sure to label your seed flats correctly and plainly so that there is no danger of mixups which might prove embarrassing. Label both the seed flats and the transplant flats. If the labels are to stay with the plants for a considerable period of time, use long-lasting ones. There are many kinds of good labels on the market today, including wooden, plastic, and aluminum.

The days listed as required for germination are minimum. It often takes longer for the seedlings to emerge. So do not be in too big a hurry to decide the sowing has been a failure. Sowing should be generous in accordance with the number of plants you wish to grow. Even with those seeds which germinate best, the number of strong seedlings which you will finally get will run only 50 per cent of the number of seeds originally planted. If you get from 65 to 75-per-cent germination of seeds, on the average, you are doing very well. Some will run considerably lower than that. Because the percentage of germination becomes poorer as the seeds age, even in good storage, pay close attention to the longevity recommendations. As noted before, to be on the safe side, test held-over seeds before you start the rest of them to be sure that they are viable enough to germinate properly. On the average, daytime temperatures should run 10 degrees F. higher than the night ones noted in the list for growing the seedlings.

SEED SOWING CHART

PLANT NAME	SEED LONGEVITY (Years)	GERMINATING PERIOD (Days)	OPTIMUM NIGHT TEMP. (degrees F.)
Aster	1	14–21	45–50
Begonia			
fibrous-			
rooted	2–3	14–21	60
tuberous	2–3	14–21	55–60
Calceolaria	2–3	14–21	45–55
Calendula	3–4	14–21	45–50
			40–45
Christmas			
cherry	1–2	21–28	50
Christmas			
pepper	1–2	21–28	50
Cineraria	2–3	14–21	45–55
Coleus	2–3	14–21	45–50
Cyclamen	3–5	42–50	55
Lupine,			
Russell	2	14–28	45–50
Mignonette	2–3	14–21	45–50
Nemesia	2–3	14–21	48–50
Pansies	1–2	14–21	45–50
Primula			
malacoides	2–3	14–21	45–50
obconica	1–2	21–28	50–55
Schizanthus	3–4	21–28	45–50
Shamrock	2–3	7–14	50–60
Snapdragon,			
single-stem	3–4	7–14	50
Statice			
annual	2–3	14–28	50
Limonium			
suworowi	2–3	14–21	50

PLANT NAME	SEED LONGEVITY (Years)	GERMINATING PERIOD (Days)	OPTIMUM NIGHT TEMP. (degrees F.)
Stock, direct-sown, raised beds	3–4	14	40–55
Sweet pea winter-flowering	2–3	14	45–50
spring-flowering	2–3	14	45–50
late	2–3	14	45–50
Vinca rosea	1	14–21	50
Violas	1–2	14–21	45–50

Propagating by Cuttings

Just a little short of the miracle of the seed is the miracle which makes it possible for a severed portion of a plant to push forward new roots and become a plant on its own. The characteristic of the variety is better preserved by a cutting than by a seed, as a rule. It also takes less time, in most cases, to prepare a fully mature plant from a cutting than with a seed. There are instances, however, when plants grown from cuttings do not possess the vigor of those grown from seeds.

The same physical conditions apply to the propagating surroundings for cuttings as those noted for propagation by seeds. A little more needs to be said about the heating controls, however. Attention must be paid to the temperature of both the air and the medium in which the cuttings are rooted. Consistent good results are only possible in the rooting of cuttings when automatic controls govern both the air and medium temperatures. The optimum air temperature for most cuttings is from 55 to 65 degrees, with an increase of 10 degrees (65 to 75) for the bottom heat. Note that bottom heat during the summer months is frequently not necessary.

The most reliable means of providing good, steady bottom heat with a minimum of variance in temperature is by an electric heating cable. Heating pipes beneath benches are unreliable because they become too warm at times and too cool at others. (The evenness of bottom heat is an important factor in the successful rooting of cuttings.) The old-style brick-bottomed propagating benches came as close to approximating the evenness of cable heat as anything.

When the heat is too great, there is danger of the cuttings becoming too dry. Electric cables, thermostatically controlled, provide exact temperatures at all times.

Sand was once the only rooting medium other than light soil. It still is the principal medium used, but there are many other fine rooting materials, such as vermiculite, perlite, peatmoss, sphagnum, Sponge-Rok, and others. These are good used alone, in various combinations, or with sand. If sand is used, it must be good clean sand which is obtained from deposits that have not been contaminated. (River sand is frequently contaminated by industrial waste matter and sewage.) When you put the sand in the propagating bench, water it thoroughly and use a wooden block to tamp it. Then with a dull butcher knife crevice the sand, and place and firm the cuttings into position, properly spaced according to kind. Sand should be sterilized both at the start and between batches of cuttings.

If vermiculite is used, cuttings may be poked in and no firming is necessary. Vermiculite need not be sterilized before its first use; the same is true of the other sterile media. Thereafter, though, between batches of cuttings it will require sterilization and careful removal of cutting debris.

Whenever you sterilize, include the bench as well as the medium. The best system of sterilization is by steam. Should you use a chemical of some sort for sterilizing, be sure that it is one which will not harm the cuttings.

A good combination idea for a rooting medium is one using sand beneath and vermiculite on the surface. Fill about half of the propagating bench with sand and bury the heating cable about an inch beneath the top of the sand. Over the top of the sand place panes of glass, edge to edge. Then fill the rest of the bench with vermiculite. This gives you the chief advantages of both media: the heat-conducting ability of the sand and the water-retention and easy-placement qualities of the vermiculite.

The medium should be neither too shallow nor too deep. Usually, if there is a problem, it is caused by having a medium too deep, for aeration is important in the rooting of cuttings, and if the cuttings are placed too deeply aeration is hindered. The medium should be only 3 to 4 inches deep so that the base of the cutting is not more than 1 to $1\frac{1}{4}$ inches from the top or bottom of the medium. This is even more important when a fine medium is used, for a coarse one is well aerated. The use of a combination of sand and vermiculite does call for a greater overall depth, but the upper layer is considered as the principal rooting area.

Aeration to the base of the cuttings can be increased by using ½ to 1 inch of pea gravel beneath the medium. The bottom of the bench should permit good drainage and passage of air. Cracks left between the boards can be covered with Saran cloth to prevent the medium from sifting through. Never use a coarse gravel beneath the medium or the medium will sift downward into the gravel.

Propagating cubes are relatively new to amateur greenhouse gardeners, but excellent for rooting cuttings. (They are used too for starting seeds.) Made of cellular phenolic foam, the cubes come in easily divided loaves. These cubes are non-splitting and water-absorbent. A cutting is stuck into the hole of a cube and the size of the hole adjusts to the cutting's diameter. Trace elements encourage rooting. Dibbling and firming are eliminated. The cubes are pathogen free. One good brand I know is The Good Earth (0-902 propagation medium), manufactured by Smithers Oasis.

MISTING

When misting is used for propagation, the medium depth is different: at least 6 inches deep. The sand should be fine, but if coarse sand is used, there should be more frequent misting. No matter which medium is used, the main thing to remember with mist propagation is that the bases of the cuttings should receive a constant supply of well-aerated water.

The sand for mist propagation should not be packed, just leveled. Steam-sterilize the bench and the sand before placing each batch of cuttings. As with regular propagation, make slits in the sand in which to place the cuttings. Do not water-in the cuttings afterwards; the misting will take care of this for you. Misting normally varies from 30 seconds to a full minute, depending upon the type of nozzles used and the time of year. The object is to have the mist regulated so that wilting is prevented. The interval between can be lengthened once the cuttings become callused and are able to absorb water, but never allow the cuttings to wilt.

Also use a weekly application of fertilizer when misting. Five ounces of 25–10–10 in 10 gallons of water is about right. To protect the cuttings from fungus diseases while the mist propagation is going on, use Ferbam in the same solution. The weekly application of fertilizer is necessary because of the leaching which takes place with misting and because the cuttings remain active all the time. Do not feed cuttings which are not under mist. Cuttings under mist must be removed promptly, lest they become too soft. No shading is necessary with misting.

Cuttings can be rooted directly in soil in small pots under mist, thereby saving a great deal of time and labor.

Some gardeners have found that a combination of equal parts of sphagnum peatmoss and soil makes a satisfactory rooting medium for plants in pots. The sphagnum-soil combination should be shredded first. (And be sure the mixture, pots, etc., are sterilized.) To raise the pH for certain plants add ground limestone. Never firm the soil in pots where the cuttings are being rooted under mist. Merely fill them loosely with the soil mixture and place them on the bench beneath the mist lines. To place cuttings, just push them into the loose soil without dibbling them. Again, no watering is needed, for the mist takes care of this. Apply weekly feedings of fertilizer.

Sphagnum in itself, either in regular propagation or under mist, is excellent for rooting cuttings. It is especially desirable where cuttings are rooted in flats or pots. The sphagnum should be finely ground; it works well in a 50–50 combination with sand. Leaf cuttings of begonias and African violets seem to work particularly well in sphagnum.

CARE OF CUTTINGS

What makes a good cutting? First of all, the stock plant it comes from must be strong and healthy, free of disease and pests. The plant part used for a cutting should have a good food supply in reserve to keep it alive and enable it to callus and form roots. Research has shown that those shoots which are well supplied with carbohydrates (sugar and starch) are the ones which do best during the rooting period. The food supply in stock plants should be built up in advance by good feeding, watering, and other favorable cultural practices.

If you have some particularly valuable plants from which you are most anxious to get the best cuttings possible, try notching or ringing the stems below the wood which you intend to use for cuttings. The movement of carbohydrates downward from the tips is then restricted by this action and the carbohydrates are concentrated in the stems above the wounds. Stock plants which are grown with their roots restricted will also have branches which are richer in carbo-hydrates. Young plants generally provide better cuttings than do older plants. If you are dealing with older plants, cut them back in advance to force them to produce young shoots for rooting.

The matter of preventing injury to cuttings as they are being taken and placed in the rooting medium cannot be overemphasized, for many young plants are lost at this point, either by the injury itself or by disease resulting from the injury. The utmost of cleanliness is needed, too, from the gardener's hands to the knife which he uses and the flat into which the cuttings may be laid. All must be steri-lized.

Softwood cuttings are the kind which concern more greenhouse gardeners than hardwood cuttings, although those growers who pro-duce azaleas, rhododendrons, and the like are concerned with the latter. Softwood cuttings should never be taken back into the hard-wood or the cuttings will root slowly and the stock plants will be longer in producing new cutting material.

Cuttings taken from the tip of the stem usually run from 3 to 5 inches long. Some prefer cuttings 2 to 4 inches long. There are also leaf-bud cuttings used on plants such as hydrangeas.

When taking an ordinary tip cutting, leave at least two or three mature leaves on the branch from which the cutting is taken. This will enable the branch to produce additional cuttings. Remove only those leaves from the cuttings that will interfere with their placement in the rooting medium. If you remove additional leaves or trim the remaining ones, you are robbing the cutting of some of its ability to manufacture food and will thereby delay root formation.

Take only a few cuttings at a time so that they do not wilt before placement. Cuttings quickly dehydrate and are injured. Be sure that the knife which you use for taking the cuttings is razor sharp and clean. Ragged edges too invite disease.

Most gardeners today use hormone-dust root stimulants on their cuttings. If used properly, these promote faster root growth. Con-stant use of a hormone powder eventually causes a build-up of the material in the propagating medium. So cut down on the amount you use as you add new batches of cuttings to the propagating medium. Otherwise you will experience trouble with cuttings which resent an overdose of the material.

If you started to use one of the rooting compounds, had good luck at first but later on ran into trouble, it was probably because of this concentration in the rooting medium. If you haven't yet used a rooting compound, do so, because it makes the job easier and shorter. These materials are available in powder or liquid form. The principal root acids are indolbutyric acid, naphthaleneacetic acid, and indoleacetic acid. Always check the directions carefully. Because a little of one of these materials is good does not mean that more is better.

Place your cuttings only deep enough for support and give them ample space for their foliage spread. Cuttings should always have as much light as they will take without wilting. When minor shading is necessary, provide it in a temporary fashion with cheesecloth above the propagating bench. Additional shading may be placed on the glass during such times of the year as it is necessary. Again— don't overdo it.

Increased humidity, where misting is not used, offsets the effects of greater light in the propagating areas; ample humidity is an aid in the rooting of cuttings. The rooting medium should be kept moist but not soggy and the amount of water applied will depend upon the kind of medium used. For instance, sand requires more water than does vermiculite, which holds the water better.

Most growers use overhead watering in the propagating bench. Some gardeners have had good results with subirrigation, in particular with the constant-water-level system. But since it is not easy to handle, amateurs prefer not to use it in the cutting bench.

The relative humidity for soft cuttings should be from 75 to 80 per cent during the winter and from 90 to 95 per cent during summer. It takes more than normal humidity to root cuttings properly. Nevertheless, humidity should not be overdone or the plants will soften and give you a problem when the plants go into a house where the humidity is less. There are good humidifiers available for greenhouse use. Some operate from water pressure and others by steam or compressed air.

Small amounts of cuttings requiring more humidity or heat can be started in flats covered with polyethylene tents. Homemade supports for the polyethylene can be made from wire coat hangers. If you have small amounts of cuttings to root you can use this system: Take a square of plastic film and place upon it a small amount of moistened sphagnum. Place regularly prepared cuttings so that the ends are stuck into the pile of moss. Then draw the edges of the film around the lower part of the cuttings and secure the film with a rubber band. Supply a constant temperature of 70 degrees and relatively high humidity. Remove the cuttings when rooted.

If you have a variety of cuttings to root which demand various conditions of temperature or bottom heat, you can use one of the above ideas for small amounts of cuttings, or you can partition your greenhouse, using additional heating pipe or finned pipe in the sections where more heat is needed.

Take the cuttings out of the bench when the roots are about ¼ inch long; if you let the roots grow longer, they will be easily damaged when the plants are removed—and also more difficult to pot.

Leaf cuttings are easy to root from African violets, echeveria, gloxinia, kalanchoë, peperomia, rex begonia, sansevieria, or streptocarpus. A leaf cutting can be made in conventional manner, sticking the petiole into the rooting medium or by laying a large leaf flat on the rooting medium, making a few cuts along the main veins, and "pinning" the leaf to the medium with toothpicks or hairpins. New plants start at points of injury. Some may also be rooted in water.

To remove the rooted cuttings, pry them loose gently with a putty knife or flattened stick by placing the blade beneath the roots. Be just as careful as possible to prevent root damage. Place the potted plants into as large pots as practicable. Small pots dry out too rapidly and it only takes a little wilting at this stage to check the plants and permanently damage them. The finest results are obtained from plants which are never given a setback at any time.

If you have cuttings shipped to you from another source (most growers now buy cuttings from specialists), be sure that you unpack them promptly upon arrival. Inspect them to be sure they are all right and then place them in the propagating bench or pots just as rapidly as possible. Keep the cuttings cool until you are ready to handle them.

HARDWOOD CUTTINGS

You can take some cuttings from perennials, shrubs, and trees almost any time of the year. But from November until spring is the best time for making hardwood cuttings of many deciduous plants and also from the new growth of conifers.

It is not difficult to make hardwood cuttings. A hardwood cutting is part of the stem of a deciduous tree or shrub taken when the plant is dormant and placed in the propagating bench so that roots will form around its base. For best results, take hardwood cuttings which are about the diameter of a pencil and 7 to 10 inches long. Most gardeners prefer to make the bottom cut about ¼ inch below a node. The top cut, unless it is a tip cutting, should be made just above a bud or node.

As most growers know, not all trees can be started from hardwood cuttings. Fruit trees, maples, oaks, lindens, birches, beeches, and most nut trees are normally started from grafts, by budding, or from seed. Grafting and budding are covered further on in this chapter.

In places where the soil freezes during the winter, the best idea is to tie hardwood cuttings in bundles and bury them in boxes of sawdust, soil, or sand until early spring. This is not a bad idea, even in milder climates. In either case, the bundles of cuttings should be stored in a cool place until it is time to place them outdoors for normal growth. Cool storage stimulates natural winter dormancy and by spring the cuttings will have formed calluses upon which the new roots will start. Using a rooting compound on the cuttings induces calluses and, therefore, better rooting.

In the spring hardwood cuttings should be placed in an outdoor propagating bed consisting of moist, loose soil containing ample humus. Bury the cuttings up to their necks in a wide V-shaped trench, leaving one or two eyes above the soil surface. Allow 6 to 8 inches between cuttings. If your soil is too heavy, mix some sand with it, for a heavy soil is not conducive to good rooting. Firm the soil about the cuttings and completely fill the trench, except for enough depression to assist in watering.

Be sure that your cuttings do not go into the rooting bed upside down. Only the lowest end of the cutting will produce roots, while the upper end will send out new shoots and leaves. A good way to avoid an error of this sort is to cut the upper end of the cuttings straight across and the lower end on a slant. Cuttings taken during the winter should be well rooted no later than next fall.

A good many semi-hardwood cuttings, such as lilacs, spiraeas, cotoneasters, hydrangeas, brooms, pyracanthas, and jasminums can be rooted in a cool greenhouse.

Conifer Cuttings

It is not as easy to root the cuttings of conifers by the usual methods of propagation as it is to root hardwood cuttings. (With the use of rooting compounds containing the right proportion of indolbutyric acid, however, the success in rooting conifers has been notable.) Among the best ones to try are the cedar, yew, juniper, chamaecyparis, arborvitae, and cryptomeria. Cuttings of these should be about 4 to 6 inches long. They should be rooted in pots, flats, or a propagating bench. Use a medium of good, clean sand, vermiculite, perlite, or other material or a combination of some of these materials. A good mixture is one of perlite, vermiculite, and peatmoss in about equal proportions.

The medium should be moist and the cuttings should be watered-in after placement. They root best in a 50-degree house with gentle bottom heat. Keep the cuttings constantly moist. Sufficient humidity is as important as bottom heat in assuring successful results.

Root Cuttings

Adventitious buds appear on the roots of some plants. Such roots may be used as cuttings. Rather thick portions of such roots should be used. Make sure that each section used for a cutting has at least one adventitious bud on it. The root cuttings can be started in any of the propagating mediums used for stem cuttings, or they will do quite well if started in soil. In most instances bottom heat is not necessary, although it helps with some species.

Plants to Start from Cuttings

Achimenes. Stem cutting made in late summer or fall. Bench or pot when rooted. Optimum night temperature 60–70 degrees. Matures winter and spring or late spring to fall.

African violet. Leaf cutting made any time of year. Pot when rooted. Optimum night temperature 60–70 degrees. Matures throughout the year.

Ageratum. Stem cutting made in August. Bench or pot in September. Optimum night temperature 55–60 degrees. Matures early spring.

Azalea. Stem cutting made in spring. Pot when rooted. Optimum night temperature 55–60 degrees. Matures mid-winter and spring.

Begonia, Christmas. Leaf or stem cuttings made in November. Pot when rooted. Optimum night temperature 55–60 degrees. Mature plant a year later.

Begonia, tuberous. Stem cutting made any time, bulb planted in February. Pot when rooted. Optimum night temperature 55–60 degrees. Matures spring and summer.

Begonia, wax. Stem cutting made any time. Pot when rooted. Optimum night temperature 55–60 degrees. Matures year around.

Boston yellow daisy. Stem cutting made in July to August. Pot or bench when rooted. Optimum night temperature 45–50 degrees. Matures from mid-February on.

Bougainvillea. Stem cutting made in March and April. Bench or pot when rooted. Optimum night temperature 60–70 degrees. Matures in April and May.

Bouvardia. Stem or root cuttings made in February. Bench or pot when rooted. Optimum night temperature 60–65 degrees. Matures in mid-winter.

Cacti and succulents. Leaf or stem cuttings made according to variety. Pot when rooted. Optimum night temperature 65–70 degrees. Matures at various times.

Calceolaria. Stem cutting made in August. Pot when rooted. Optimum night temperature 45–50 degrees. Matures in spring.

Carnation. Stem cutting made in May to August. Bench when rooted. Optimum night temperature 45–50 degrees. Matures in fall, winter, and spring.

Centaurea, foliage types. Stem cutting made in late September. Pot when rooted. Optimum night temperature 45–50 degrees. Matures from spring on.

Centropogon. Stem cutting made in fall. Pot when rooted. Optimum night temperature 60–70 degrees. Matures in spring.

Christmas cactus. Leaf or stem cuttings made in September. Pot in October. Optimum night temperature 55–60 degrees. Matures December to February.

Chrysanthemum, annual. Stem cutting made almost any time (April best). Bench when rooted. Optimum night temperature 45–50 degrees. Matures spring and summer.

Chrysanthemum, early. Stem cutting made in April and May. Bench or pot in late May or June. Optimum night temperature 45–50 degrees. Matures in September and October.

Chrysanthemum, mid-season. Stem cutting made in May. Bench or pot in June. Optimum night temperature 45–50 degrees. Matures in October through January.

Chrysanthemum, late. Stem cutting made in May. Pot in June or July. Optimum night temperature 45–50 degrees. Matures in December through February.

Clematis. Stem or leaf cuttings made in summer and early fall.

Bench or pot when rooted. Optimum night temperature 45–50 degrees. Matures in early spring.

Clerodendron. Stem cutting made in summer. Bench or pot when rooted. Optimum night temperature 60–70 degrees. Matures early spring or summer.

Coleus. Stem cutting made from September on. Pot when rooted. Optimum night temperature 55 degrees. Matures in spring.

Crossandra. Stem cutting made in May and June. Bench or pot when rooted. Optimum night temperature 70 degrees. Matures in 6 to 9 months.

Cytisus, genista. Stem cutting made in August. Pot in September and October. Optimum night temperature 45–50 degrees. Matures in March and April.

Episcia. Stem cuttings made in spring; divisions in fall. Pot when rooted. Optimum night temperature 60–70 degrees. Matures spring and summer the following year.

Feverfew. Stem cutting made in spring. Bench or pot when rooted. Optimum night temperature 50–55 degrees. Matures in fall and winter.

Forget-me-not. Stem cutting made in March. Bench or pot when rooted. Optimum night temperature 45–50 degrees. Matures in fall and winter.

Fuchsia. Stem cutting made in fall and winter. Pot when rooted. Optimum night temperature 50–60 degrees. Matures in spring through summer.

Gardenia. Stem cutting made in November and December. Bench or pot in September. Optimum night temperature 60–65 degrees. Matures from following Christmas on.

Gazinia. Stem cutting made in fall. Pot when rooted. Optimum night temperature 45–50 degrees. Matures in late spring and summer.

Geranium. Stem cutting made in August to October. Pot when rooted. Optimum night temperature 45–50 degrees. Matures from March on.

Gloxinias. Leaf cutting made from May to August. Pot when rooted. Optimum night temperature 60–65 degrees. Matures from June to August of following year.

Hoya carnosa. Stem cutting made in spring to fall. Bench or pot in fall. Optimum night temperature 65 degrees. Matures in late spring and summer.

Hydrangea. Stem, leaf-bud cutting made from mid-February to

July. Pot when rooted. Optimum night temperature 50–70 degrees. Matures in April and May.

Kalanchoë. Leaf cutting made in February and March. Pot when rooted. Optimum night temperature 50–60 degrees. Matures in December.

Lantana. Stem cutting made from August to December. Pot when rooted. Optimum night temperature 60 degrees. Matures in late spring and summer.

Marguerite. Stem cutting made in March. Bench or pot when rooted. Optimum night temperature 50–55 degrees. Matures from December on.

Orange. Stem cutting made any time. Pot when rooted. Optimum night temperature 45–50 degrees. Matures year-round.

Philodendron. Stem cutting made any time. Pot when rooted. Optimum night temperature 55–60 degrees. Matures year-round.

Poinsettia. Stem cutting made in June to August. Pot when rooted. Optimum night temperature 60–65 degrees. Matures at Christmas.

Rhododendron. Stem cutting made in spring. Pot when rooted. Optimum night temperature 55–60 degrees. Matures from mid-winter to spring.

Rondeletia. Stem cutting made in spring. Pot when rooted. Optimum night temperature 60–70 degrees. Matures in summer.

Sparmannia. Stem cutting in April. Pot when rooted. Optimum night temperature 45–60 degrees. Matures from spring on.

Stephanotis. Stem cutting made in fall or spring. Bench or pot when rooted. Optimum night temperature 65 degrees. Matures in spring to fall.

Stevia. Stem cutting made in late February or early April. Bench or pot when rooted. Optimum night temperature 40–50 degrees. Matures during winter months.

Swainsona. Stem cutting made in January. Bench when rooted. Optimum night temperature 50 degrees. Matures in late spring and summer.

Layering, Grafting, and Budding

LAYERING

Simple layering consists of fastening the branch of a shrub to the ground by means of a wire "pin" and heaping soil over the point where the branch touches the soil. When the covered part of the tree or shrub has rooted properly, it is merely severed from the parent plant and a new plant exists.

Air layering is the method of layering which you are most likely to use, especially if you have in the greenhouse a rubber tree, croton, or schefflera that has grown too tall. By airlayering, the plant is brought down to a more desirable size, while a new plant is created.

The stem of the plant to be air-layered must be wounded at the point where the roots are to form. Cut the plant from one-half to two-thirds through the stem. Hold the notch open by using a swatch of moss or a matchstick. Support the plant to keep it from cracking apart at the notch.

Sometimes a plant will have a tendency to knit back together at the point where it was notched. If so, use the girdle method to prevent the bark from growing together again. Remove a ring of bark ¼ to 1 inch wide on the stem, scraping the cambium layer from the exposed portion of the stem. Wounding the stem causes a damming up of carbohydrates and root-forming substances moving down the stem at the point of the wound. The combination of these two materials is needed to produce root growth.

Moist sphagnum moss should then be applied in a ball to the wounded area and for a few inches above and below it. Next, take a piece of polyethylene film and wrap it about the moss to retain the moisture. You can use ordinary polyethylene or you can get treated polyethylene made especially for the purpose. The special sort has fertilizer and root-inducing substances on one side. If you use it, rub the upper portion of the wound with the colored stripes of root-inducing materials to hasten the rooting.

Tie the polyethylene securely to the stem above and below the wound. When the roots are well formed (you can see them) completely sever the new plant from the old and pot it. You probably will not have to add moisture to the moss.

Never endeavor to air-layer too large a portion of an old plant. In the first place, attempting to root too old wood reduces the assurance of successful rooting. Also, enough roots must be grown to support a much larger plant without danger of losing it.

GRAFTING AND BUDDING

Most grafting is done on woody plants outdoors. However, greenhouse gardeners are finding more and more use for the grafting process. This is especially true with azaleas and rhododendrons grown for forcing in the greenhouse, where grafting has cut greatly the time required to produce a finished plant.

The whip or tongue grafting process is the one most desirable for this use, since the scion (the part being grafted on) used is of practically the same diameter as the understock (the plant upon which it is grafted); the quickest and best results are obtained with this method.

A long slanting cut is made across the bottom of the scion. Then a vertical tongue cut is made midway between the center and upper edge of this exposed surface. The plant upon which the scion is to be fastened is prepared in the same way, and the two pieces of wood are joined together with the cambium layers in contact.

The pieces are tied together with rubber budding strips, and a piece of polyethylene is wrapped around the area and fastened with a Twist-em or other quick fastener. No waxed string or wax from a hot grafting pot is necessary. The knitting process can be watched through the polyethylene and the rubber strip removed as soon as the union is completed and before any danger from girdling exists.

Budding is another method of grafting, though not many greenhouse growers use it. It is generally used in the production of fruit trees, rosebushes, etc., because it is simpler than grafting and requires less greenhouse space and equipment.

The plant which some greenhouse growers might wish to bud is the rose. It is usually budded in July or early August, but it can be done at any time when the bark slips readily from the wood when a knife is placed under the bark.

To bud a favorite rose to the understock, make a T-shaped slit in the bark of the understock at or close to the ground level. Then cut a well-developed bud with the petiole of the leaf attached from the variety of rose which you wish to graft on. Remove any wood which is still attached to the inside of the bark of the bud. Carefully peel back the slit in the understock just enough so that the bud may be inserted (sliding it down behind the back), fitting and holding it close to the wood of the understock. Wrap the bud firmly but carefully to avoid damage, with a soft twine or raffia. In 3 or 4 weeks' time remove the binding; the bud should have taken hold.

CHAPTER XIV

Do's and Don't's of Transplanting

Think of tiny seedlings and young rooted cuttings as babies and you won't go wrong when you handle them. You wouldn't treat a baby roughly for fear of harming it. Neither should you treat tiny plants roughly.

Transplanting is not a difficult job, but even a seemingly small error can cause trouble. First of all, you need the right tool. For transplanting seedlings (or rooted cuttings) you need transplant flats, plant bands, peat pots, plastic pots, or clay pots. Or you may transplant directly into a bench from the seed flat or pot. You will also need a dibble stick (smooth, splinter-free stick about 8 to 9 inches long with one end tapered and the other end rounded); a putty knife or paddle-shaped stick; a dibble or spotting board (a board with attached pegs to make holes in the soil of the transplant flat); labels; wooden tweezers; and a sprinkling can.

The transplant flats should be filled brimful with soil, using a well-drained, friable soil. Heavy, poorly drained soils need the addition of peatmoss and sand. Sterilized soil is best. Otherwise, you run the risk of damp-off or other plant diseases. The soil used should be put through a ¼-inch mesh screen. Remove air pockets in the soil by firming it. Then again fill the flats to overflowing. This time, do not firm the soil.

If only a few plants are to be transplanted into a flat or if the plants are going into pots or bands, you can use your forefinger to make holes for seedlings or cuttings. But if you are working with a number of seedlings, use a dibble board to form the holes. In general, a 15-x-20-inch flat should have 10 rows of plants running lengthwise and 10 rows across the flat.

Good timing, proper preparation of soil, careful handling of plants followed by prompt and thorough watering are necessary for successful transplanting. Seedlings should be transplanted when the first true leaves appear. Cuttings are ready for potting or transplanting when they have roots that are about ½ inch in length. Handle them with care.

A few hours before removing plants from the seed flats or beds, water them well so that more soil will cling to the roots when they are lifted. Use a putty knife or wooden paddle to pry beneath the seedlings or cuttings. You can cut down through the soil between plants, making little blocks around each. Some of the roots will be cut, but this is better than having an insufficient amount of soil clinging to the roots. Use wooden tweezers to remove the very tiny seedlings such as begonias. (This process is called "pricking off" seedlings.) Discard all but perfect plants.

The soil in your transplant flat should be reasonably moist but not wet. Press the dibble board firmly into the soil so that good holes are made. Remove only a few plants at a time from the cutting box or seed flat. Gently grasp one seedling, holding it by its leaves and carefully guide the roots with the tapered end of the dibble stick into the hole in which it is to be planted. With the rounded end of the stick, firm the soil about each plant, being careful not to squeeze the soil about the plant roughly enough to damage the plant.

Do your transplanting in a shaded spot, completing a flat as rapidly as possible. Immediately upon finishing the flat, sprinkle it gently with the watering can and remove it to a shaded spot for 2 or 3 days until the seedlings have started to take hold. Then give the plants all the light they need. Most bedding and vegetable plants, once recovered from the shock of transplanting, will take full sun. Of course, there are many other seedlings which will need regular protection from the full effect of the sun's rays.

The water you use should contain some good fungicide such as Semesan, Morsodren, or Shield to aid in controlling damp-off. Watering newly transplanted flats from the bottom is an ideal method. If the tiny hair roots of seedlings or cuttings get dry the plants will be crippled or die. So if the seedlings you have removed are not being planted quickly enough, dip their roots in a can of room-warm water and shade them until you can place them in the transplant flat.

This need for transplanting the seedlings as rapidly as possible cannot be overemphasized. If they are going into flats, fill a flat as quickly as possible and then follow the procedures above. If the cuttings or seedlings are going into individual pots or plant bands, do only the number which you can handle promptly and then remove them to a shaded area. Those plants going into a bench should be handled in the same manner. Plant only a few at a time before watering them.

Large-mouthed snifters and rose bowls provide room enough for the hand. Smaller bowls require use of tongs and dibble stick.

Be sure to set the transplant flats in a level place free of severe drafts or windy spots. Watering of young seedlings is especially delicate. Don't allow them to become too dry, but do not keep them sopping wet. Moist but leaning toward the dry side is the ideal situation. From time to time, "cultivate" the transplant flats by dragging the pointed end of the dibble stick between the rows of plants, applying only a slight pressure. This will break up the crust on top of the soil and make it possible for the water to penetrate better. A non-ionic wetting agent, such as Aqua-Gro, is a good idea. Such a material wets the soil deeper after application than plain water does. Also, stir the soil surface of plants in plant bands, peat pots, plastic pots, or clay pots frequently but take care not to disturb the roots. This cultivating can stop when the plants begin to fill in the flats enough to stifle weed growth and shade the soil about them. If you used sterilized soil, as you should have in your transplant flats, you should have no weed problems and probably no disease problems.

Give the young plants a booster feeding just as soon as they start to take hold and grow—not before—using 1 tablespoonful of nitrate of soda or ammonium sulfate to 2 gallons of water. Just a word of caution: Be sure to remove all sickly plants at once, if any should appear in the flat. Then treat the soil about the area with a good fungicide such as those noted above.

Shortly after transplanting, start hardening the young plants: reduce the water, giving them just enough to keep them from wilting, and give the plants less heat than they received while being propagated.

CHAPTER XV

Potting Like An Expert

Potting plants is not a difficult job. On the contrary, it is quite simple if you pay attention to a few basic rules.

Most of the information you need in regard to correct soil for pot plants is contained in Chapter X. The important things to keep in mind are that good aeration and drainage are absolute necessities. The restricted root area of a potted plant, compared to that of a plant in a bench, makes this imperative. Soil for potted plants should be light, airy, and, of course, sterilized. Smaller pots call for finer soil which has been run through a $\frac{1}{4}$-inch sieve. Coarser soil can be used in large pots.

One of the most important factors is moisture content. The soil should be neither too dry nor too wet. Here is a good test: Take a firmed ball of soil, hold it in the air, and let it drop. If it shatters as it hits the potting bench, it is just right. If it still clings together in a wet mass, it is too wet. If the soil fails to form a ball in the first place, it is too dry. The tender, hair roots of a young plant need the best of soil conditions in order to start growth as early as possible after transplanting.

The commercial grower of greenhouse plants becomes very familiar with pot sizes and terminology. Often this is an area of mystification for the amateur greenhouse grower. What is a 2, 3, 4, 5, or 6-inch pot? What is meant by a three-quarter pot or by a pan? What is a standard pot?

Generally speaking, the maximum inside diameter of a standard pot measures the same as the pot's height top-to-bottom. In other words, a 3-inch pot measures 3 inches in diameter on the inside at the top of the pot and 3 inches from the top of the pot to the bottom. Pans are of the same diameter measurements as standard pots but only half as deep. A three-quarter pot measures the same in diameter as a standard pot but it is only three-quarters as tall.

These measurements refer to clay pots. Plastic, aluminum, and square pots are measured from top to bottom and side to side.

Over the years, preferences have evolved in regard to sizes or types of pots with various plants. For instance, pans are nearly always used for seed germination and are excellent for shallow-rooted plants, such as poinsettias. Three-quarter pots are excellent for lilies, azaleas, etc. Primroses and calceolarias seem to balance out better in three-quarter pots. The shorter the pot the wider the base; hence during watering or other handling there is less likelihood that it will topple over.

All clay pots, new or old, should be soaked before they are used. This will prevent them from drawing excessive moisture from the soil, causing the plants to dehydrate. Old pots should be thoroughly scrubbed and sterilized before they are used.

Always an irritation are the algae which grow on pots, discoloring them and making them slimy and disagreeable to handle. But there is an easy way to do away with this problem. Immerse the pots in a copper naphthenate solution (in mineral spirits) containing 3 per cent copper for about 10 seconds. Allow the pots to dry for 3 days before using. That will provide protection against algae for about 9 months, long enough in most cases. Number 10 Cuprinol and other wood preservatives with the same constituents are suitable for this purpose.

But do not shift plants from one pot into a treated pot of the same size, for when the roots touch the treated pot severe root injury may result. But you may transfer a plant into a larger treated pot without hurting its growth. Commercial growers have successfully used pots treated as above for cyclamen, African violets, chrysanthemums, geraniums, hydrangeas, poinsettias, and many other plants. The cost for treating pots in this manner is insignificant compared to the amount of good it does.

Kinds of Pots

For some time now there has been a kind of battle going on between the manufacturers of clay pots and those who manufacture other types such as aluminum and plastic. I have no intention of getting into this battle except to point out the good points of each kind.

Plastic and aluminum containers, when used in place of clay pots, call for an entirely different method of watering. This, in turn, influences the amount of fertilizer which may be used. The grower, therefore, who is considering a switch from clay pots to something else should look into watering, feeding, and pot porosity.

A flat filled with plants in plastic or aluminum pots is much lighter to handle than one filled with clay-potted plants. On the other hand, some gardeners feel that it takes a clay pot to make a nice plant look complete.

It is quite easy to overwater when you use a plastic or aluminum pot because of the lack of porosity. If you are using conventional feeding (instead of applying soluble fertilizer with each watering), you will need to decrease the frequency of feeding or the plants will become overfed. Clay pots provide more humidity because of the moisture which escapes through the sides of the pots. On the other hand, when plastic pots are used, less nutrients are required, because there is less leaching from them.

If you use glazed pottery this, too, calls for special attention: There must be an abundance of drainage material in the bottom, especially in those with no drainage holes. The addition of charcoal in the lower soil is also advisable to keep the soil sweet. Not only watering but also feeding should be restricted.

Peat pots are very good for preparing plants for the bench to follow others which have already flowered. The young plants can be brought along in the peat pots and timed for just the right moment to go into the bench.

Most any of the seedlings or cuttings which you grow will do better at the start in peat pots, rather than in clay pots or flats. Then, when the time comes to put the plants into the bench, there is no disturbance of the root system and the plants go right on growing without interruption, for they are planted pots and all. This also saves time. Peat pots are available in various sizes ranging from 1½-inch to 4-inch round and square.

Plant bands are used much as peat pots are, for starting plants to go into benches or for annuals to be planted outdoors later on.

Aluminum pots in smaller sizes are used for some pot plants, principally foliage plants. In the larger sizes the question which you must decide upon is largely between clay and plastic.

How To Pot

Small pots usually do not require drainage material. If you use a piece of crockery, place it over the hole of the pot with the curved side up. If you use gravel or other drainage material, place a layer of it in the bottom in such a manner as to allow the water to move through the hole in the bottom of the pot. Five or 6-inch pots should have about an inch of drainage in the bottom and larger pots as much as 2 inches. The sifting of soil into the drainage area can be prevented by placing a layer of sphagnum moss over the drainage.

All cuttings and seedlings which you are about to pot should have been watered beforehand.

Place enough soil into the pot so that the plant's roots will rest on the soil, leaving the plant at its proper height in the pot. Be sure that the plant is placed in the center and at the same depth it was in the seed flat or propagating bed. Then add additional soil to bring the level to within $\frac{1}{2}$ inch of the top of the pot. Firm the soil slightly and rap the pot against the bench to settle the soil about the roots.

Whenever you are potting more than one of a given kind of plant, be sure that the space left at the top of the pots is equal. This will insure equal watering and feeding of the plants thereafter. When you firm the soil around the plant, do so with the thumb and forefinger of each hand. Do not press against the stem or stock of the plant, for this may injure it. The amount of watering space left at the top will depend upon the size of the pot. Larger pots need considerably more space than small ones. It is surprising what difference in growth will be noted when like plants are potted unevenly and receive uneven amounts of food and water.

Particular attention must be paid to shade and moisture for seedlings and cuttings potted for the first time. Don't allow them to dry out or their growth will be checked, and it is always difficult to get a plant growing again once this has happened. But don't overwater.

Repotting Plants

As a rule, the best time to repot an old plant is following the flowering period or just as new growth is beginning. Those plants which are to be repotted should also be watered beforehand. There is no strict rule as to when a plant should be repotted. Generally, though there are exceptions, it is when the root mass in the bottom of the pot has become rather heavy. In fact, repotting should occur before this becomes severe. If the root ball is tight, it will be some time after repotting before moisture will penetrate it properly. That is another good reason for having the soil moist before it goes into the new pot.

You will become experienced in determining when a plant is ready to be repotted. But until you have reached that stage, the surest indication of a need for repotting is the root-ball condition. To examine the root ball of a plant, place the tips of the fingers of one hand on the surface of the soil in the pot just inside the lip; then invert the plant and rap it sharply against the potting bench. This will jar the plant and its soil loose from the pot. The soil should be moist whenever you do this. After determining whether or not the plant is ready for repotting, gently replace it into the pot. Avoid shattering the soil about the root ball.

For most plants, it is a good idea to gradually step up the size of pot being used. Gradual periodic repotting has an invigorating effect upon the plant. But there are some plants which do equally well when shifted directly from a 2 or 3½-inch pot to a 6-inch pot. As you go along and experiment in your own greenhouse, you will determine which plant prefers which system.

There is no question but that direct-shift—transference of a small plant into its final-sized pot in one jump—saves much work. But such a method has certain dangers. You must be particularly careful about watering and feeding. The small plant in a large soil area does not use up a great deal of water. So water sparingly. Then, too, fertilizer increases in the soil as microorganisms convert it, and the resulting build-up of salts can be lethal to small plants. Consequently, do not fertilize with nitrogen until the plant has used up the available fertilizer already in the soil and shows a need for additional.

As with seedlings and cuttings, the repotted plant should be placed at the same depth as it was before. (There are a few exceptions, such as with cyclamens, which must be placed a little higher each time they are repotted.) Rap the pot sharply after repotting to be sure that soil is settled about the roots and air pockets are eliminated.

Potted plants should always set upon some bench-covering medium which will allow for good drainage beneath them. Sand,

If potted plants are to follow a bench
crop, place polyethylene plastic over the soil.

perlite, cinders, or other good materials are available for this purpose. The pots must also be set level and the medium covering the
bench will help to insure level placement. The medium also provides needed humidity about the plants. When plant roots find their
way into the medium covering the bench it is usually a sign that
they are ready for repotting. If not, sever these wandering roots.

There comes a point when it is not practical to increase the size
of the pot into which a plant will go. When this is true, it calls for
this procedure: Remove the plant from the old pot and loosen some
of the old root ball. Remove as much of the old soil as you can

with a dibble stick. Tuck new, fresh soil wherever you can into the bottom of the pot, around the sides, and on top. Use good soil that contains the nutrients needed by the plant. Use your dibble to work the fresh soil in around the root ball. By having the root ball well moistened before it is replaced, less damage is apt to occur.

Never skimp on the room between plants. It always results in inferior plants, spindling and lopsided. It is better to produce fewer plants of high quality rather than a large number of poor to mediocre ones.

CHAPTER XVI

How to Beat the Pests and Diseases

How to Spray and Fumigate

"Plants may come and plants may go, but the bugs go on forever." Breathes there a gardener who has not thought something like that many, many times? To some gardeners, controlling pest and disease is a difficult chore, but it need not be. The secret is merely a matter of being properly equipped to do the job and doing the job on a regular schedule!

Here are seven rules to follow:

(1) Choose the material which seems to be more specifically designed for your needs than the others and which also, if possible, offers you the most for the money.

(2) Follow directions carefully. Be sure you read the label correctly and use only the amount of dust or spray recommended for the specific insect or disease you are after. Too little is often worse than none at all and using too much can injure the plants.

(3) Have special measuring utensils. Keep on hand a tablespoon, teaspoon, graduated cup, pint, quart, and gallon measuring containers. Use them for nothing else.

(4) Spray thoroughly. Insecticides and fungicides often kill by contact. Consequently, thorough coverage is necessary. To be certain of getting spray material on all pests and diseased areas, spray the trunk, branches, tops and bottoms of leaves, and the soil around the plant.

(5) Never spray during the heat of the day. It is always best to

spray in the morning or early evening. If the plants are moist, however, the spray material may be diluted somewhat and not be as effective. Slight moisture on the plants, though, causes dusts to stick better.

(6) Do not syringe or water plants until material has had time to be effective.

(7) Put your spray or dusting equipment away clean. This goes for the measuring utensils, too. Keep your equipment in top working condition.

Contact sprays do the job on sucking insects. Some contact sprays also have a fumigant action, making them doubly effective. Among the contact sprays you will find Lindane, nicotine, Malathion, rotenone, pyrethrum, etc. With them you can kill aphis, leaf hoppers, thrips, scale insects in the crawler stage, lacebugs and other sucking insects.

One of the safest insecticides to use on edible plants, as far as humans are concerned, is rotenone. It can be used to control both sucking and chewing insects but it must be used frequently, as its residual life is short.

Many soil insects must also be controlled to prevent later damage to the upper portions of the plants. Soil insecticides, such as Lindane, are used like a liquid fertilizer. Follow directions carefully. Soil sterilization is the best means of controlling soil-borne pests and diseases. Many viruses can also be controlled through sterilization.

To kill chewing insects, however, you must use a stomach poison, which kills by paralysis, or a fumigant.

Most insecticides are also available in dust form. Use Captan, Fermate, Zineb, Maneb, and other chemicals to control the various diseases which attack plants. Tie in with the control program a real effort at sanitation.

Sometimes a home gardener will switch from one insecticide to another because he has found plants infected again after a few days. This does not mean that the first material was not right. Pests move around rapidly and plants may be reinfested shortly after they have been rid of their pests. You can pretty much rely upon the claims made for pesticides or fungicides, provided that you use the materials according to the directions and repeat the applications as recommended.

Check the pressure of your equipment. It takes about 250 pounds or more to atomize a spray properly so that it will get into all of the places where insects and diseases hide. Nozzles wear out, too, and often the hole in the disk becomes enlarged after use. This makes the droplets larger than they should be and coverage not good enough to get a good kill of insects. A multi-headed sprayer is more apt to produce good results.

It takes the addition of a good spreader (unless the material you are using already contains a spreader) to produce the best coverage. Among the good spreader materials now on the market are Triton B 1956 and DuPont Spreader–Sticker. For some purposes, common household detergents such as Tide and Dreft will work. The hardness or softness of the water also makes a difference. By testing, work out your own formulations regarding the amount of spreader to use.

You must be aware of the potential danger of the powerful materials used for pest control. At no time is the danger greater than during the summer months. The risk is considerably greater when the temperature is 85 degrees F. or above. For this reason, when day temperatures are high, use aerosols and some spray materials at night. If you fumigate at night the greenhouse can be aired in early morning. Still, look out for a possible residue which might be dangerous to you.

During the summer it is easy to become careless. When it is hot, one becomes less willing to don a mask and heavy clothing to protect lungs and body from deadly fumes or mists. One of the hardest things chemical manufacturers and horticultural writers have to put across is the fact that some materials can readily be absorbed through the skin, and the final outcome can be just as serious as if the material were inhaled or swallowed. Heed the manufacturer's warnings.

Also, if daytime application is necessary in summer, have someone standing by. A lone individual could be overcome by heat and not be discovered until too late.

Remember, too, that gas-mask canisters have expiration dates. Replace them before the time has lapsed.

Further, advise everyone to have on hand a $\frac{1}{100}$-grain atropine sulfate prescription and be familiar with how to use it. This will then be available for immediate use in case of accident while spraying with organic phosphates. Also get one of the charts available nowadays which give the antidotes for the chemicals you handle.

Just by way of review, the symptoms of organic phosphate poisoning are a tightness of the chest, headache, nausea, or difficult breathing. If any of these symptoms occur, get out of the greenhouse and into the fresh air at once.

Even with the best precautions, accidents can happen. Should an applicator or hose break and shower you with material, wash yourself off immediately and thoroughly with soap and water. Often such an accident will occur when a nozzle or hose is being cleaned. Wearing goggles and rubber gloves can be the means of saving your eyesight or preventing other injuries, if an accident occurs. Also, avoid contact with the foliage of plants immediately after spraying or dusting.

Insect and Weed Control

It is all too easy, when accepting the gift of a plant or cutting, to place it among our other plants or cuttings without being sure that the newcomer is clean and free of insects or diseases. Whenever you buy plants, too, be sure you buy from a reliable dealer. But whether you buy them or receive them as gifts, set the new purchases apart at first from your other plants until you are sure that insects and diseases are not being brought into your greenhouse.

Spray, dust, or fumigate the new plants or cuttings before mixing them in with the plants you already have. Anything which is badly diseased should be discarded.

Keep debris from accumulating in your greenhouse. It is beneath old boards, flats, dirty pots, etc., that sow bugs, symphylids, slugs, snails, cutworms, and other destructive insects hide.

Improper ventilation is an open invitation to diseases, and it encourages some insects, too.

In the greenhouse and garden, keep the weeds down, for weeds are the natural hiding place for insects. Insects breed rapidly in the weeds and then march in on your plants. They quite often bring diseases with them, too, for many insects are vectors or carriers.

An excellent, non-volatile, long-lasting chemical for weeds is CMU (Karmex W. Monuron Herbicide). It will do a first-rate job of controlling weeds under raised benches or between V-bottom beds. One application will control weeds for up to two years or more when not much leaching takes place. Use it at the rate of 2 level tablespoonfuls in 1 gallon of water to 100 square feet.

Sodium arsenite is another good control for weeds in the greenhouse. It is also non-volatile and long-lasting. It does have one drawback, however. It is poisonous in concentrated form and must be kept away from children and pets. For greenhouse weed control, use it at the rate of 1 ounce of 40-per-cent material per quart of water. From 2 to 4 quarts of the mixture are required for 100 linear feet of walk.

The problem becomes different when it comes to controlling weeds between ground beds, for some of the chemicals could be picked up by the roots of the crops, too. But relatively safe to use between ground beds is sodium isopropyl xanthate. It is a temporary control, not long-lasting like the materials you can use beneath raised benches. And you must make this material fresh each time you use it. Use 1 pound to 10 gallons of water and add a wetting agent to produce a more effective kill. Be sure that you keep the material from contact with desirable plants. Spray the weeds when they are not more than ½-inch high.

Diagnose Problems Correctly

A great many greenhouse gardeners fail to diagnose their plants' ailments correctly and do the wrong thing for diseased plants, only to discover, too late, that their plants have been severely damaged or ruined. I know of an instance where a grower had some beautiful standard chrysanthemums which should have been a fine crop except that they showed spotting of the foliage. He sprayed his plants vigorously with Fermate. But his problem actually was caused by foliar nematodes, which he should have been battling with parathion spray or dust applied to the lower foliage. He discovered his error but not in time to save his plants.

A common mistake I have witnessed is one where the grower, knowing that a prescribed doseage of an insecticide is good, decides that two or three times more would be better. Damage almost inevitably results from an overdose.

Be absolutely certain what your trouble is. If you cannot determine that, do not apply insecticides or fungicides indiscriminately. If necessary, contact your county agent, your experiment station, your state college, or another grower who knows what the trouble is. Then do what is necessary.

Storage of Pesticides and Fungicides

Many fungicides and pesticides will last for several years if properly stored, but emulsions break down rapidly and should be replaced yearly. Signs of breaking down are these: salting-out or settling of emulsions, balling and lumping of wettable powders and dusts.

To be safe, whenever you purchase pesticides, mark the exact date of purchase on the package. Never store pesticides or fungicides with weed killers, for they absorb some of the fumes of herbicides and cause injury to your plants when used.

Always keep pesticides and fungicides in their original containers and under lock and key. The original containers supply valuable information on the labels concerning the safe use of the material as well as properly identifying it. Be sure to store chemicals in a cool, dry place.

Pest and Disease Charts

The charts which follow provide quick-reference information concerning the pests and diseases which attack greenhouse plants, including symptoms and methods of control. There is no overall cure for all problems, but much freedom from pest and disease troubles will result when you follow good cultural procedures. Try always to use a preventive rather than a corrective system of controlling pests and diseases. For the more common pests and diseases, spray before you notice any symptoms and follow a system of regular application.

In general, first try those sprays and dusts that are relatively harmless to humans when used properly. For example, materials based on pyrethrum and/or rotenone will often bring proper control of the more easily killed pests, such as aphids.

Information included in the following charts is based upon research done at Ohio State, Cornell, Michigan State, and Pennsylvania State Universities, the United States Department of Agriculture at Beltsville, Maryland, and numerous other research institutions, both public and private.

NOTE: Some states prohibit the use of certain pesticides by amateur growers, restricting usage to commercial operators experienced in the application of pesticides highly toxic to man. Such chemicals are not included in the chart.

INSECT CONTROL CHART
(For foliage plants, see Chapter XVIII)

PEST	USUAL PLANTS AFFECTED	SYMPTOMS	CONTROL (REPEAT AS NEEDED)
Ants, grasshoppers	Any	Chewing evidence	Vapona or Diazinon sprays
Aphids	Any	Plant covered with sticky substance; tender leaves, stems attacked	Diazinon, Lindane, Malathion or Sevin sprays; Dibrom 8 or Lindane vaporized from steam pipes; Dithio bomb
Corn earworm	Any, especially chrysanthemums	Flowers eaten	Sevin spray
Cutworms	Any	Chewing evidence	Dylox spray or dust
Earthworms	Any	Visual (castings, holes)	Sterilization of soil
Foliar nematodes	Christmas begonias, chrysanthemums	Wedge-shaped brown areas on leaves, leaf shrivelling	Diazinon or Zectran sprays
Leaf miner	Aster, azalea, chrysanthemum	Winding white trails or broad whitish spots on green leaf surface	Diazinon or Zectran sprays
Leaf roller, leaf hopper, sow bugs, mum midge, tarnished plant bug	Any	Leaves spotted, dwarfed, or rolled up	Malathion, Sevin, or Zectran sprays
Mealybug	Any	White, cottony-appearing insects	Diazinon, Malathion, or Zectran sprays; Malathion, or Vapona bomb; Malathion dust

PEST	USUAL PLANTS AFFECTED	SYMPTOMS	CONTROL (REPEAT AS NEEDED)
Mite	Begonia, ivy, African violet, cyclamen, snapdragon, gloxinia, foliage plants	Stunted, distorted growth; poor flowering; discolored, brown, or dry leaves	Diazinon, Kelthane, or Tedion sprays
Nematodes	Bare soil	Various	Steam sterilize soil and clay pots; use chemicals on plastic pots; fumigate with chloropicrin, EDB, Fumazone, Mylone, Nemadrench, Nemagon, Vapam or VC-13
Red spider mite (normal)	Any	Same as for mite	Chlorobenzilate, Diazinon, Kelthane, Malathion, Morestan, or Tedion sprays; Chlorobenzilate, or Malathion bombs
Red spider mite (resistant)	Any	Same as above for normal red spider	Pentac or Morestan sprays
Root aphids	Fern, palm, poinsettia, foliage plants	Poor growth and foliage color	Lindane—1 oz. 25 per-cent Wettable Powder per 30 gal. (apply like a fertilizer to potted plants)
Rose midge, strawberry root worm, Fuller's rose weevil	Rose, etc	Leaves covered with cone-like galls; loss of vitality; later, chewed leaves with weevils	Diazinon spray; three applications on plants, soil, walks 14 days apart, for larvae; Metaldehyde slug bait for adult weevils

PEST	USUAL PLANTS AFFECTED	SYMPTOMS	CONTROL (REPEAT AS NEEDED)
Scale, soft brown, armored	Any	Scale-like insects on foliage or stems	Diazinon, Malathion, or Zectran sprays; Vapona bomb
Slugs, snails	Any	Chewing evidence	Metaldehyde bait; Slugit or Zectran sprays
Spittle bug	Any	Stunted growth	Lindane spray
Symphylids	Any	Stunted growth	Lindane—see root aphids; for bench crops use 1 oz. 25 percent WP per 100 sq. ft. in any convenient amount of water
Thrips	Any	Deformed, silvery foliage; shriveled buds, flowers	Malathion bomb or dust; Lindane or Malathion sprays
Thrips	Gladiolus corms	Corms shrivel, discolor	Malathion or Lindane sprays
White fly	Any	Foliage spotted, chlorotic; growth stunted	Malathion or Zectran sprays; Vapona bomb

DISEASE CONTROL CHART
(For foliage plants, see Chapter XVIII)

DISEASE OR DISORDER	USUAL PLANTS AFFECTED	SYMPTOMS	CONTROL
Aternaria blight	Chrysanthemum	Flower tissues rot	Captan or Zineb mist sprays or dusts twice weekly as flowers open
Ascochyta blight	Chrysanthemum	Flower tissues rot; petals fall away	Captan or Zineb mist sprays or dusts twice weekly as flowers open
Blackleg (Pythium)	Geranium	Blackened areas on stems	Dexon soil drench may help prevent infection—will not prevent death of infected plants; discard diseased plants
Black mold	Rose	Black mold evident on dormant plants	Soak plants in one pt. formaldehyde to 40 gal. water or 1 lb. potassium permangnate to 25 gal. water for 2 hours
Black spot	Rose, English ivy, chrysanthemum	Black spots on foliage	Captan or Ferbam sprays, for roses; Phaltan, Captan, Ferbam, Zineb, or Ziram sprays or dusts, for chrysanthemums—avoid overhead syringing
Botrytis or petal blight	Chrysanthemum, snapdragons, others	Brownish-gray mold, petal spotting	Captan, Zineb, or Maneb mist sprays or dusts twice weekly as flowers open; Botran spray—may injure plants; Terraclor spray or dust; remove infected flowers; keep flowers dry

DISEASE OR DISORDER	USUAL PLANTS AFFECTED	SYMPTOMS	CONTROL
Branch rot	Geranium, carnation	Rot on plants	Captan or Zineb sprays regularly; Agrimycin 17 sprays regularly for geranium (don't injure stems tearing off flower stalks—break off just underneath flower head); Captan or Zineb sprays for carnation; keep foliage and stems dry
Canker	Camellias, rose, gardenia	Lesion or wounded area	Remove and destroy infected shoots; sterilize shears after each cut by dipping in rubbing alcohol; avoid leaving stubs
Chlorosis	Azalea, rose, chrysanthemum, gardenia, snapdragon, hydrangea	Paling or yellowing of foliage	Check drainage and pH; check for soil insects; avoid over fertilization; check pest chart
Crinkles	Geranium	Water-soaked areas on foliage	Destroy plants that have this virus
Damping-off	Any (seedlings)	Rotting of plant at soil line	Terraclor or Semesan; Morsodren; Shield; steam-sterilize soil and containers (not plastic pots); avoid recontamination
Foliar dieback	Snapdragon	Leaf tip wilts, then stem dies	Destroy plant
Gall	Azalea	Pinkish-white puffy growths on leaves	Pick off leaves or use Bordeaux spray
Leaf scorch	Lily	Tips of leaves die; entire lower leaves may die	Apply lime to soil; try to keep pH at 6.5 to 7.5

DISEASE OR DISORDER	USUAL PLANTS AFFECTED	SYMPTOMS	CONTROL
Leaf spots, foliage blights caused by fungi	Aster, azalea, begonia, carnation, chrysanthemum, cyclamen, gardenia, geranium, hydrangea	Discolored area on leaves with rather definite outline	Phaltan, Captan, Ferbam, Zineb, or Ziram sprays applied thoroughly to cover all leaves, stems; pick off and destroy badly infected leaves, keep foliage dry, give more space and air
Leaf spots and bacterial blight	Foliage plants, geranium	Leaf and flower spotting; badly infected plants may die	Agrimycin 17 sprays; weekly spraying necessary; keep foliage dry
Leaf spot, physiological	(See Chapter XVIII, Foliage Plants)		
Mildew, powdery	Calendula, rose, chrysanthemum, hydrangea, African violet, snapdragon	White powdery appearance on foliage and stems	Actidone, Karathane, Mildew, Morestan, or Phaltan sprays; avoid drafts, but ensure good air circulation; sulfur dust or spray; sulfur vaporized from steam pipes or electric vaporizers—sulfur often bleaches flowers
Mosaic	Any	Irregular yellow spots; dwarfed ruffled leaves; virus—spread by aphids	Destroy badly infected plants
Ringspot virus	Peperomia	Brown or yellow rings on leaves; sometimes necrotic; leaves inclined to curl	No known control except destroying diseased plant portion

DISEASE OR DISORDER	USUAL PLANTS AFFECTED	SYMPTOMS	CONTROL
Root rot (Pythium) (Phytophthora)	Any	Rotting of roots	Dexon soil drench for Pythium or Phytophthora rot on any plant; use Phaltan, Kaptan, Ferbam, Zineb or Ziram sprays on stem and leaves
	Lily	Rotting of roots	Dexon or Shield soil drench
(Erwinia -bacterial)	Calla	Rotting of root and rhizome	2 oz. Spergon in 1 gal. water for 3-hr. soak or 1 part formaldehyde in 50 parts water for 1-hr. soak; use non-metal containers and plant while wet; remove rotted portion of calla rhizome prior to treatment; steam soil and pots
Rust	Aster, snapdragon, carnation	Rust spots on foliage	Captan, Maneb, sulfur, or Zineb sprays or dusts; keep foliage dry and new growth covered lightly with fungicide
Sooty mold	Most foliage plants	Sooty deposit on foliage	Controlling scale controls this fungus
Spotted wilt	Calla	White or yellow spots or rings on leaves; distorted flowers	Keep thrips under control; destroy infected plants
Stem rot (Rhizoctonia)	Any		Terraclor, Semesan, Morsodren, or Shield; don't plant deep; avoid overwatering
(Pythium)	Any		Dexon soil drench

DISEASE OR DISORDER	USUAL PLANTS AFFECTED	SYMPTOMS	CONTROL
(Xantho-monas —bacterial)	Geranium		Agrimycin 17 sprays; don't root cuttings under mist; buy cultured stock
(Sclerotinia)	Snapdragon		Steam-sterilize soil to kill black sclerotia which form in lower stem area and drop on soil
Stunt	Chrysanthe-mum, cyclamen	Stunted, poor growth	Destroy infected plants; buy stunt-free plants
Wilt			
(Fusarium)	Aster		Steam-sterilize soil and pots (not plastic or peat); treat seed with Cuprocide to kill spores on surface
(Verticil-lium)	Begonia, cineraria		Steam-sterilize soil and pots; propagate from disease-free begonia plants
(Fusarium and bacterial)	Carnation		Steam-sterilize soil and flats; propagate from disease-free plants (cultured stock)
(Verticil-lium	Chrysanthe-mum		Steam-sterilize soil and pots; buy cultured cuttings
Yellows	Asters, chrys-anthemums, many others	Yellowing, sickly appear-ance of plant; if not fatal, flowers are poor	Grow under cloth or plastic if outside; Malathion sprays re-peatedly; spread by leafhoppers

CHAPTER XVII

Flowering Plants

Most of the plants which are grown in the greenhouse sport flowers of some sort or other, even the many plants listed as foliage plants. But many of the latter have blooms which are only of secondary interest. This chapter deals with the plants which are normally thought of as flowering potted plants, plus a few of the foliage plants which produce reasonably spectacular blooms.

Achimene. Achimenes are less well known than many other flowering potted plants but newer varieties developed recently have made them more popular. Foliage is elm-like with variations as to species. Petunia-like flowers of white, pink, rose, red, violet, purple, and blue. Colors may be solid or variegated. Stem cuttings made in late summer and fall. Height: 1 to 2 ft.

African violet (*Saintpaulia*). This cheery little plant will bloom almost perpetually, provided conditions are right.

African violets are started from leaf cuttings, divisions, or from seed. Select the best, large mature leaves from disease-free plants for propagation.

One of the most critical factors in the culture of African violets is light. With either too much or too little light the *Saintpaulia* will not bloom properly. Actually, it prefers about 1,100 foot-candles of light. In simpler terms, it should have fairly good light, but not the direct rays of the sun. Provide indoor shading and, as needed, shading on the glass to protect the plants. If the petioles or leaf stems are long, this indicates the plant is not getting enough light. If the petioles are too short, it is getting too much light.

Never water the *Saintpaulia* with cold water. Use room-temperature water and apply it carefully over the lip of the pot. Or water by placing the pot in a saucer of water. Keep the soil moderately moist, watering only as the plant requires it.

Provide good air circulation. African violets prefer a reversal of usual temperature pattern, doing best with night temperatures of 70 to 75 degrees F. and 60 degrees F. daytime temperature.

Saintpaulias are not heavy feeders. In fact, overfeeding damages these plants. Use a completely soluble fertilizer, preferably one which is lower in nitrogen than a balanced fertilizer. Lower nitrogen encourages flowering. Apply weak solutions fairly often. Mite is the worst insect attacking African violets. Grows 4 to 6 inches high.

Amaryllis. The amaryllis is grown from a bulb. Start it in a tray, covering the roots with dry soil. Keep it at 60 degrees and pot as soon as the roots have begun to show good growth activity. Thereafter, a good growing temperature is 55. Water sparingly until after the flower bud is above the neck of the bulb, then keep it on the moist side. After the flowers are gone and the stem turns yellowish, remove it with a sharp razor. At this point feed the plant with a teaspoon of complete plant food. Supply plenty of water when the foliage is growing. It has strap-like stemless leaves and umbels of large, fragrant showy flowers in a wide range of colors including pink and red. 2 to 4 feet tall.

Anthurium. The "blooms" of anthuriums are spectacular. Actually, the very tiny yellow flowers are crowded into a dense spadix, beneath which is a leathery spathe of bright red of one sort or another, or white. The cut blooms of anthuriums hold up exceptionally well, making them ideal for corsage wear or for arrangements. The species which do best are *A. andraeanum, scherzerianum* and the Shaffer Hybrids.

Start anthuriums from divisions or cuttings which are made of the rhizomes or suckers. They root easily in a 75-degree temperature. They can also be grown from seeds. However, it is really best to buy started plants from a specialist, because they are very slow growing. You will need to repot the plants about once every three or four years, depending upon how rapidly they grow.

Use a rough, fiberous loam for anthuriums. Be sure that drainage is excellent. Instead of soil, you can use a mixture of peat, sand, sphagnum, and decayed osmunda fiber.

Keep the plants well watered and provide high humidity. The

best growing temperature for anthuriums is 60 to 65 degrees. Give the plants plenty of shade in the spring, summer, and fall and some shade is necessary during bright winter days.

Aphelandra. This is a glamorous plant with attractive twisted, dark green foliage with a silvery sheen between main veins and spectacular flowers of orange-scarlet. Keep it warm, preferably 65 degrees at night and 72 during the day. Never let it dry out. Provide diffused light and fresh air but no drafts. Feed it every 10 to 14 days with a complete fertilizer. Start from stem cuttings any time. 1 to 2 feet in height.

Ardisia. The ardisia's bright red berries qualify it for this chapter on flowering pot plants. Its leathery, shiny, serrated leaves are extremely attractive. It likes a night temperature of 65 degree F. and a day temperature of 75. Keep it reasonably moist and provide good ventilation free of drafts. Full light, except during the summer months, is fine. Feed once a month with a balanced fertilizer. Start from stem cuttings as shoots appear. 1 to 2 feet tall.

Aster. Dwarf asters make good potted plants. Give them plenty of moisture, full light (except where light intensity is considerable), plenty of fresh air, freedom from drafts, and temperatures of 65 degrees at nights and 75 by day. Colors: white, blue, rose, crimson, and deep scarlet. Rich green, elliptic-shaped leaves. Start from seed. 8 to 14 inches tall.

Astilbe. Commonly called spiraea by florists, the astilbe is a lovely plant with feathery blooms in delicate shades of pink, lavender, and white. Airy branches. It is relatively easy to force provided it is given full light, good ventilation, and plenty of water. Never allow astilbe to dry out. Start by seed or divisions in fall. 19 inches to 2 feet tall.

Azalea and Rhododendron. Growing azaleas and rhododendrons from cuttings is a lengthy process. It is simpler to start with established plants and force them. Start them at 60 degrees and increase the temperatures to 70 to initiate bud formation. During the winter months the plants will stand the direct rays of the sun; at other times shade is necessary. Never allow azaleas or rhododendrons to dry out or they will rapidly defoliate and die. Both plants do well in a straight peatmoss medium, provided they are fed twice a month with a good fertilizer such as liquid fish emulsion. Give them an abundance of fresh air. Start from stem cuttings in spring. Wide variety of colors and heights.

Begonia, Christmas. Christmas begonias are usually started from leaf cuttings in fall. After they are in pots, keep them a little on the dry side, but water thoroughly when watering.

Christmas begonias like a humid atmosphere, plenty of ventilation minus drafts, and full light during the winter months. As brighter spring days approach, protect the plants to prevent foliage burning. A weak feeding of a balanced fertilizer should be applied every 3 to 4 weeks. Keep old blooms and other decayed plant material removed from around the plants to prevent disease. All begonias like good fibrous soil and good drainage. Various shades of pink. 12 to 18 inches high.

Begonia, fibrous-rooted. The fibrous-rooted or semperflorens begonia will always be one of the gardener's favorite plants. It is started from stem cuttings or from seed any time. The seed is extremely fine and must be watered in as described in Chapter XIII.

Promptly remove all old flowers and poor foliage to prevent rot. Fibrous begonias like humidity and should be fed about every 2 weeks with a dilute liquid fertilizer. They like good air circulation and a cool growing temperature is preferred.

One of the reasons for the popularity of the fibrous begonia is that it changes with the light. Given full sun, it will produce flowers of a darker color and foliage with a reddish tinge. Grown in the shade, the foliage will be a medium green and the pink-flowering variety will always have light pink flowers.

Begonia, tuberous. Tuberous begonias are among the loveliest of potted plants and some make beautiful hanging baskets, too. There are many different types: camellia-like flowers; basket or hanging type; fimbriatas; carnation-flowered; picotee and ruffled varieties. And there are many colors too: white, pink, orange, red, and variations.

Tuberous begonias are started from seed November thru February or tubers in early spring. Keep them moist at all times and never allow them to become dry. They prefer a cool temperature (60 degrees) and plenty of fresh air. The plants must be shaded. They are heavy feeders and should have a good liquid fish fertilizer every other week. 8 inches to 2 feet tall.

Bouvardia. This is a lovely, dainty flower for corsages. It can also be used in small arrangements. Plants produce clusters of small tubular pink or white flowers. Propagation is by stem cuttings made at a nodule or joint. The plants can be flowered either in pots or in benches. Allow about a foot of space each way when the plants are benched.

Avoid acid peatmoss in the soil mixture, inasmuch as bouvardias like a neutral to slightly alkaline soil. I would recommend as a soil mixture one containing 1 part of well-rotted manure, 2 parts of leafmold, and 2 parts of light loam. Add sand if the soil is heavy.

Bouvardias need ample water when the plants are growing well, especially during the summer. Cut down on the water and allow the plants to rest somewhat after they have finished blooming.

The best night temperature is 60 to 65 degrees. Do not try to grow them below 55 degrees. During late spring and summer the plants need some shade but during the winter give them full sun. Be sure air circulation is good, for the plants are susceptible to mildew.

Feeding bouvardias with manure water from time to time is a good idea. Otherwise use a balanced fertilizer. If you pinch the plants during June, July, and August, you will produce a heavier crop of flowers during the winter. Bouvardia is responsive to light, so it can be flowered throughout the season by shading and lighting to shorten or increase the length of the light period.

Bromeliad. Most of this group have formerly been thought of as foliage plants. However, growth regulators have made it possible to trigger the flowering of bromeliads almost at will. They produce brilliant, spectacular clusters of flowers in a wide variety of colors, and stiff pineapple-like leaves. They should be kept on the dry side and fed occasionally with a dilute fertilizer. Provide a light, well-drained soil. Start from offsets as they appear.

Browallia. This plant has lovely metallic-blue or violet-blue flowers. *B. speciosa major* is the most popular because of its larger flowers. All like a 60-degree night temperature but can be grown cooler. Some shade is needed during the summer, full sun the rest of the time. Water sparingly at the start and then keep them slightly on the moist side later. Feed rather dilute nutrients during early stages, increasing the fertilizer as the plants get larger. For good growth, pinch the plants frequently while small. Start from seeds sown from June to August. Low to medium height.

Calceolaria. The pouch-like flowers, wide range of riotous colors, and soft medium green foliage make calceolarias real favorites with nearly everyone. These South American plants like a temperature of 60 degrees days and 50 at night. Keep them a little on the dry side but do not allow them to wilt. Keep the humidity down and avoid drafts but provide good ventilation. Calceolarias will not stand direct sun but need some protection by shading. Too much shade, however, causes the plants to stretch too much, so shade with cloth inside and reduce the shade when the weather is dark. Guard constantly against aphids. Once entrenched in the flowers, they are practically impossible to dislodge. Calceolarias should be fed occasionally with a balanced fertilizer, although they are not heavy feeders. They like a fiberous, loamy soil and are started from seeds sown in July and August. 12 to 18 inches tall.

Camellia. The camellia does very well in the greenhouse, provided you can give it the space required horizontally and vertically. The flowers are beautiful for corsages. An evergreen shrub with waxy, long-lasting flowers of pink, red, white, or variegated, its leaves are shiny and leathery in texture.

Although you can start camellias from cuttings, it is slow. You are better off buying established plants from a commercial grower. Grow your plants in large tubs, pots, or in ground beds. Camellias should not be overpotted, nor should they be repotted too often. When repotting is done or when the soil is to be replaced in the pots or tubs, do this right after flowering.

Although camellias will tolerate a fairly wide range of soils, they must have a very acid one. The pH should be 4.5 to 5.0. You need plenty of organic matter and good drainage. I would recommend a soil using equal parts of acid peatmoss and good loam with some sand used where the soil is heavy. Do not use manure in the soil.

Supply camellias with ample humidity and plenty of water. In ground beds watering is comparatively easy. In pots or tubs the job can become more complicated if the root ball becomes too compacted. To be sure that the entire root ball is receiving sufficient water, it is a good idea to immerse the pots or tubs for a considerable time at each watering to make sure that the impacted roots do not dry out. Keep the humidity high during the foliage growing season by frequent syringing of the plants and aisles. When the blooms begin to form, however, reduce the humidity and be very careful about slopping the water on the plants. It may cause a spotting of the flowers.

During the blooming period camellias should be grown at 40 to 45 degrees. After the plants are through blooming, the temperature should be increased to 50 to 60 degrees in order to start new growth and build up the plants for the coming year.

Light shade should be supplied to plants in early spring and fall in the greenhouse. You can place the tubbed or potted plants in a lath or other protected area during the summer or provide them with considerable shade during that time. Give the plants good ventilation at all times.

Although camellias do not feed too heavily, they should have three or four feedings per year. A 6–10–8 formula is a good fertilizer. If you desire high quality flowers, disbud the plants, leaving only the terminal bud at the tip of each axil.

Chenille plant. The chenille plant, *Acalypha hispida* is an outstanding tropical plant with foxtail-like spikes in the axils of the leaves. They are pendant, showy, bright red and run from 8 to 18 inches long. Plants are started from cuttings taken at any time. Temperatures preferred are 65 degrees at night and 80 during daytime. Bright sun is preferred. This shrubby plant likes a rich, well-drained, loamy soil. Feed it with a balanced fertilizer, such as 10–10–10, at the rate of 1 ounce to 3 gallons of water every 4 weeks. 18 to 30 inches tall.

Christmas pepper. The colorful peppers (purplish-red color) of this shiny, smooth-leaved plant qualify it for inclusion in this chapter. It likes full sunlight, good ventilation without drafts, a 50-degree night temperature, and 60 to 65 by day. Its soil should consist of 2 parts fibrous loam, 1 part leafmold, and 1 part sand. Provide good drainage and keep the plant moist but not wet. Feed it with a light application of balanced fertilizer every three weeks. It is highly touchy about fumes. Start from seed sown February to June. 12 to 14 inches high.

Chrysanthemum. Chrysanthemums can be grown from cuttings started at any time of year. Be sure stock plants are strong and free from disease. Use tip cuttings 3 to 4 inches long. Practice utmost sanitation with chrysanthemums from beginning to end.

Potted chrysanthemums can be grown single-stemmed, one flower per stem, or they can be pinched to make a cluster of flowers on each. Keep humidity up and provide ample ventilation. They like a well-drained, porous soil for the copious amount of water which they take. They should be kept moist but never soaked. Water thoroughly when you do water and then allow the surface to get slightly dry before watering again. To each bushel of soil mixture add one 4 or 5-inch pot of 0–20–0 (superphosphate) fertilizer. Be sure the soil is sterilized. Give plants full sun.

By shade and light manipulation, they can be made to flower

Chrysanthemums and calceolarias, among
the loveliest of potted plants to grow.

any week of the year. The chrysanthemum is a short-day plant and so sets buds when it is exposed to a short day (12 hours or less). The short fall days provide the required conditions for normal flowering. To prevent bud setting so plants will flower at other times, lights are needed. A single, 4-foot bed should be equipped with 60-watt bulbs with separate reflectors, spaced every 4 feet. Two 4-foot beds can be lighted with one row of 100-watt bulbs with reflectors, spaced every 6 feet. Three 4-foot beds can be lighted with 1 row of 150-watt bulbs and reflectors every 9 feet. The bulbs should be placed 60 inches above the soil and the reflectors must be held up off the bulbs. It takes $1\frac{1}{4}$ watts per square foot of area covered including benches and walks.

Chrysanthemums for out-of-season flowering are listed by response groups. For instance, a 7-week response means that the particular variety will flower 7 weeks after the short-day treatment is started. A 13-week group of plants requires 13 weeks of short-day treatment, etc. Application of light, of course, prevents bud formation regardless of the response group into which any given variety may fall. It takes 7 foot-candles of light to prevent buds from forming. The maximum allowable period of uninterrupted darkness is 7 hours. The best idea is to apply 4 hours of light nightly from 10 P.M. to 2 A.M., thus breaking up the period of uninterrupted darkness.

At the end of the lighting period apply black cloth shading to induce flowering. This is not necessary during the normal fall flowering season. Shade should not be applied until late in the afternoon. Do not give the plants more than 12 hours of darkness. There are some excellent catalogues available today which list the exact timing for lighting and shading of various chrysanthemum varieties which you wish to grow out of season (Check Chapter VI for additional information on light and shade.)

Cineraria. Cinerarias are heavy heads of colorful daisy-like flowers in vivid colors of pink, lavender, purple, and blue, often combined with white, and large, hairy leaves of rich green. They are grown from seeds sown in mid-June until November. Although these plants should be kept on the dry side, they must never be allowed to become truly dry. Once wilted, they quickly deteriorate. Give them full sunlight and keep them out of drafty places. Plants will flower immediately when they become pot-bound. To get larger plants, repot them promptly. Feed occasionally with a balanced fertilizer.

Never allow aphids to become entrenched on cinerarias for they are almost impossible to dislodge. They prefer a 50–60-degree temperature range. 12 to 18 inches tall.

Citrus. Small-fruited citrus with their shiny, leathery foliage and fragrant white blooms are very enjoyable plants to grow. They are usually started from cuttings any time and prefer 55 to 60 degrees. Give them a well-drained soil with ample organic matter. Feed them regularly with a balanced fertilizer. Guard against scale and spider mites. Varying heights.

Combination pots. Combination pots, as such, are not grown. Instead, a variety of suitable plants which will stand the overcrowded condition of a combination pot are grown and are then assembled into a single large pot when wanted. Choose compatible plants for combination pots. Among plants which are good for combinations are geraniums, fuchsias, alyssums, ageratums, small cinerarias, dracaenas, various bulbous plants, and many others. When you construct a combination pot give it some thought and be sure to shape it properly, placing smaller and trailing plants toward the front, medium-sized ones in between, and taller plants in the center.

Crossandra. This lovely, dwarf, waxy-leaved plant with spikes of salmon-orange flowers is becoming more and more popular. It is grown from either seed sown in February and March or cuttings made in May and June. It likes a soil rich in humus. A good one consists of equal parts of leafmold, well-rotted manure, and sand plus a double portion of loam. Once the seedlings have passed through a period of growth in transplant flats, place two to four in a 6-inch pot. During the early stages the plants will need shade but thereafter can take full sun except when the sun is hot. Ventilate the plants well and grow them at 70 degrees. When the weather is bright, water the plants well; reduce watering during dark weather. Plant grows 10 to 14 inches high.

Cyclamen. Cyclamen—with its flowers of white and all shades of pink, and its heart-shaped, long-stemmed, dark green leaves—is usually grown from seeds sown from August to November. However, a leaf cutting with a small fragment of the corm attached to the petiole will produce a rooted cutting.

Cyclamen want plenty of sunshine during fall, winter, and spring, but need some shade during the summer months. They like lots of cool fresh air and prefer a temperature of 50 degrees at night and 60 during the day.

Cyclamen are long-term plants requiring about 15 months to produce a large, high-quality plant from seed. However, smaller plants can be produced in a period of 8 to 9 months.

Provide the plants with ample moisture at all times. Water over the edge of the pot and do not pour water onto the bulb of the plant. Be sure that drainage is excellent. Once potted, feeding a cyclamen with a moderate amount of fertilizer every 2 to 3 weeks is sufficient. The plants like good humidity.

When first potting, see that the corm barely shows above the soil line. Thereafter with each repotting, raise the corm until it is finally resting on top of the soil. Provide a soil mixture consisting of ½ garden loam, ¼ sand, and ¼ peatmoss or leafmold. Grows from 8 to 14 inches tall.

Dahlia. The little Unwin or Coltness dahlias make fine potted plants. They are bright and cheerful plants which can be used for short periods of time in the house or planted in the garden. There are both singles and doubles and they come in pink, white, and yellow. Give the plants full sunshine, ample water (once they are well established), and good ventilation. Humidity should be moderate and they prefer a fairly warm growing temperature. The plants are started from seeds sown in October to January or from tubers planted December thru February. 12 to 18 inches tall.

Daphne. Wear a sprig of daphne and everyone will know of your whereabouts. Its fragrance is delightful. Its flowers of white tinged with pink are borne in terminal clusters.

Daphnes should have a soil which is light, well-drained, and close to neutral. These small shrubs will not stand too much acidity. If your soil is on the acid side, use lime to amend it. The plants will need some shade during bright weather and should be grown at 45 to 50 degrees. Start from cuttings.

Flowering maple (*Abutilon*). *Abutilon* is liked for its bell-shaped flowers of yellow, white, and pink and attractive maple-like foliage, and can be used both indoors and out. It is handled similarly to geraniums (see Chapter XXI). To get a well-branched plant, pinch it occasionally. Grown from seeds or cuttings in May. Varying heights from 1 foot up.

Fuchsia. See Chapter XXI.

Gardenia. Once the queen of all corsage flowers, the gardenia is still high on the list. Admittedly, cut gardenias do not stand rough treatment: they bruise easily. But for my money, the lovely fragrance and beauty of the gardenia flower is hard to top. The evergreen shrub has large, shiny, thick leaves. Gardenias are propagated from cuttings and the utmost sanitation must be practiced when the cuttings are made and taken, since gardenias are highly susceptible to canker and other diseases. Gardenias must have an acid soil, preferably with a pH of 4.5 to 5.0 but never greater than 5.5. I recommend a soil which is ⅓ to ½ acid peatmoss, the rest good loam. Heavy soil should be lightened with sand as necessary. After the plants are established, provide them with a good peat mulch. Should chlorosis (yellowing) develop from a pH which has risen above 5.5, you can correct it by spraying the foliage with ferrous sulfate at the rate of 1 ounce to 2 gallons of water, applying this every two weeks until the chlorosis has disappeared. Or use one of the newer chelated irons.

Gardenias need plenty of water and humidity. However, overdoing the watering can produce chlorosis. But keep the plants on the moist side at all times. Sixty-four degrees is an ideal night temperature. The plants prefer a moist atmosphere with ample humidity, but some ventilation is necessary. Provide them with a light shade during the bright days of summer and when necessary in the spring and fall. During the winter months give the plants ample light. Avoid sudden changes in temperature or application of air or the plants will show their resentment by dropping their buds. Each spring and summer feed the plants with two or three applications of 6–8–6 or 5–10–5. Thereafter, feed the plants with ammonium sulfate at the rate of 1 ounce to 2 gallons of water every two weeks. When the plants are small, they can be built into bushier, better producing plants by pinching. If the plants are pinched after late August, the winter crop of flowers will be reduced.

If you give gardenias extra light from September 15 on, they will produce more flowers for Christmas, since they are light-responders. Giving them extra light from October 15 on results in heavier flowering in January.

Genista. This old-fashioned plant is no longer grown as much as it should be. It is a relative of the sweet pea and produces an abundance of yellow, pea-like flowers. It is grown from cuttings taken in February and does well outside during the summer months. Keep the genista on the dry side and provide it with full sunshine. It likes ample ventilation, moderate feeding, and a 60 to 65-degree temperature. Grows from 18 to 24 inches.

Geranium. See Chapter XXI.

Gloxinia. This lovely Brazilian is one of the most beautiful of potted plants. There are many fine hybrids available today, including Panzer's Red and Marbott's Pink. The plants are more or less flat with huge lush green leaves and large bell-shaped flowers.

Keep gloxinias moist but do not water over the leaves, for this may cause rotting of leaves or tuber. Water carefully over the edge of the pot and be sure that the drainage is good. Avoid direct sunlight; provide indoor and, as needed, on-the-glass shade. These plants like 65 to 70-degree temperature. Give them good ventilation but avoid drafts. Feed the plants every two weeks with a weak solution of liquid ammonium sulfate or fish emulsion. Use the latter at the rate of 1 tablespoon to a quart of water. Plants can be started from leaf cuttings from May to August, seeds late August to October, or tubers December thru February. Newly started seedlings and tubers should be watered sparingly. Space the plants well at all stages of growth. When a gloxinia has finished blooming, gradually withhold water until it is dried off. Store the tuber where the temperature is about 50 degrees, keeping it slightly moist to prevent shriveling. When it shows signs of active growth, knock off the old soil and repot in fresh soil.

Hydrangea. Growing hydrangeas from cuttings is a long-drawn-out process. Most commercial growers prefer to buy dormant plants for forcing. I advise you to do the same. If you do want to start them from cuttings, take your cuttings during the spring, using good live wood.

Hydrangeas like good light but must be protected from the direct rays of the sun which burn the foliage and flowers. Watering is important. Hydrangeas wilt rapidly when thirsty. Once wilted, the plant will be damaged. But waterlogging the plant also damages it. Give hydrangeas plenty of good fresh air.

Hydrangeas are heavy feeders and respond well to a feeding every two to three weeks with a fertilizer heavy in nitrogen (25–10–10).

Hydrangeas should be started at 55 degrees and the temperature gradually increased to 60. After the buds have reached dime size, the plants can be grown at 62 degrees or even as high as 65. Hydrangeas like a good rich, well-drained loam.

One of the most interesting matters in growing hydrangeas is that of color determination. If you have a soil on the heavily acid side (5.0 to 5.5), the flowers will be blue. If the pH runs from 6.0 to

6.2, the flowers will be pink. If you desire pink or red flowers, feed your hydrangeas with superphosphate on a regular basis throughout the growing of the plants. Lime can be used to change the pH of the soil instead of superphosphate, but the latter is the better way.

If blue flowers are desired, the phosphorus should be eliminated during the spring forcing period only. It will not harm the plants to have the phosphorus withheld during the spring if they have been properly fed during the previous summer and fall. I recommend aluminum nitrate (not aluminum sulfate) for bluing hydrangeas.

Jerusalem cherry. This is a bright cheery Christmas plant with shiny, red berries and dark green foliage. It is grown from seed sown in February, producing good plants in 5 or 6-inch pots for Christmas. Don't start the seeds too early or the fruit will look faded at Christmas. A Jerusalem cherry does well when grown at 50 degrees and it likes good fresh air, but no drafts. Avoid exposure to artifical gas fumes or other bad air conditions which will cause its leaves to drop. Except where the sun may be intolerably hot, the plant likes full light. Feed every 3 to 4 weeks with a light application of a balanced fertilizer to keep the foliage green and hold the fruit after maturity. Give it good drainage and ample water but allow it to approach the dry side between waterings. The Jerusalem cherry likes a good loamy soil. During the summer months the plant can be placed outdoors and brought in again in the fall. Grows 12 to 16 inches tall.

Kalanchoë. This is one of the more durable plants that should be grown more than it is. It has glossy, fleshy, light-green foliage, and terminal clusters of small yellow, purple, or scarlet flowers. It grows from seed or from cuttings and can be timed for various periods of the year in much the same manner as chrysanthemums. Kalanchoës like to be kept reasonably moist. Never let them dry out or be too wet. They do well in a 50 to 60-degree temperature. Give them plenty of fresh air but avoid drafts. They prefer full sunlight. Feed every 2 weeks with a balanced, liquid fertilizer. Robust, erect-growing plant up to 18 inches tall. See Chapter XIX.

Poinsettia. Poinsettia, the traditional Christmas plant, is a bit more tricky to grow than some plants. However, it is most rewarding. It is grown from cuttings taken during the summer and, once rooted, they are potted directly into sterilized soil. Poinsettias are extremely touchy about drafts and moisture. They should be kept moist and supplied with plenty of humidity. Allowing a poinsettia to dry off may cause it to drop its foliage quickly. Give poinsettias full light and follow these temperature recommendations: Plants grown at 60 degrees nights and 80 degrees days will require 65 days to mature. Grown at 60 degrees nights and 70 degrees daytime will require 75 days to mature. At 60 degrees nights and 60 degrees daytime, 85 days is required to mature poinsettias.

Of special importance, avoid any night light on your poinsettia plants. They are light responders and any light given them after darkness falls will delay their flowering. However, you can turn light to your advantage and insure good flowering at Christmas by applying lights (similar to lighting used for chrysanthemums) from September 20 to October 7 in most areas. This prevents bud initiation before you want it.

Primrose. Although obconica primroses are old-time favorites, I advise against growing them in the greenhouse. Some people are allergic to them—it might be you or someone in your family, or it might be a visitor to your greenhouse. So regardless of their beauty, it is hardly worth the risk to grow them.

However, malacoides primroses—light green, hairy foliage, and many-flowered umbels of rose and lilac blooms—do not have that effect on humans. They are grown from seed sown in August and September. Primroses should be grown cool, given plenty of ventilation, and kept moist at all times. Water may be reduced somewhat during the winter months. Avoid splashing water into the crowns to avoid rot. Provide fair humidity and feed primroses lightly until well established. After that, give them a dilute complete liquid feeding every other week. Grow 8 to 20 inches tall.

Rose. Potted rambler and tea roses are covered in Chapter XXIII.

CHAPTER XVIII

Fabulous Foliage Plants

With your home greenhouse you can grow a great many lovely foliage plants, but there are some special cultural factors to note.

Soil

The best soil for foliage plants is one that is low in clay, well-drained, capable of holding moisture well, high in organic matter, and sterilized. Here are some excellent soil combinations for potting and repotting: (1) ½ coarse, acid sphagnum peatmoss and ½ coarse sand or perlite; (2) 1 part peatmoss, 2 parts leafmold, and 1 part sharp sand; (3) 2 parts peat and 1 part sandy loam; (4) 3 parts peatmoss, 1 part well-rotted manure, and 1 part sandy loam or compost.

Except for dieffenbachias, the pH for foliage plants should run between 5.0 and 6.0. Dieffenbachias need a pH of 6.0 to 6.5 to do their best. For good pH control of foliage plants, add two 2½-inch potfuls of 20-per-cent superphosphate to 1 bushel of soil. When nitrogen and potash are low, add 2 tablespoonfuls of a well-balanced fertilizer such as 10–10–10 per bushel of soil, instead of the superphosphate. Test your soil from time to time with a home soil-testing kit.

When repotting from small pots to large pots, it is a good idea to use peatmoss instead of soil mixture. Peatmoss gives you a well-aerated area for root development. The original root ball will stay moist better, too. But for pothos or peperomias, use a ½ peat and ½ coarse sand or perlite mixture, instead of straight peatmoss.

Temperature, Humidity, Watering, and Feeding of Foliage Plants

The best temperatures for most foliage plants are between 80 and 85 degrees F. during the day and around 65 degrees F. at night. At these temperatures, maximum growth at a rapid pace can be expected.

Most foliage plants prefer a high humidity in the greenhouse. If you have a humidistat, establish a relative humidity of 75 to 80 per cent for the majority of foliage plants. If you are growing a wide range of foliage plants and include among them peperomias, dracaenas, cordylines, dieffenbachias, sansevierias, and pothos, which prefer a lower humidity, then you will have to strike some sort of compromise. You can provide a high humidity with fog nozzles, humidifiers, and with frequent hand syringing. Make the mist as fine as possible to prevent overwatering or leaching of the soil. Good humidity can be provided in most instances by keeping the walks and the areas beneath the benches moist at all times.

Water thoroughly when you water and then allow the soil to dry out somewhat before watering again. Avoid watering frequently with light amounts of water. It is important with foliage plants to allow the soil to dry somewhat in order that air may reach into the pockets of the soil.

When rooted cuttings are potted, be sure the moisture content of the soil is high. Then do not water again until the medium begins to dry slightly. Root growth will be retarded if heavy watering is started immediately after potting.

Once root growth has started well, feed foliage plants every 10 to 14 days, using a fertilizer which is low in or has no phosphorus. When the soil phosphorus is high and the pH is low, the minor elements are less available and this can lead to deficiency. I recommend using 25–0–25 at the rate of $1\frac{1}{2}$ to 2 pounds per 100 gallons of water, or 1 ounce to 3 gallons of water. Adjust the frequency with which you fertilize your plants during the winter months in accordance to the rate of growth.

Light Intensity and Shading for Foliage Plants

When foliage plants are grown at 70 degrees F. and above, they will use more light than plants which are grown at cooler temperatures. Those plants which are grown at temperatures of 60 degrees F. or below will do better in partial or, sometimes, heavy shade. Another quirk of foliage plants is that the young plants will utilize greater light intensities than similar plants which are mature. So the light factor is extremely important.

Some plants grown for their foliage are best liked when their coloring is intense, such as crotons, dracaenas, pothos, pandanus, and color-bromeliads. The best colors are produced when they are given as much light as they will stand. Further along in this chapter you will find a key which will supply you the information concerning light intensity, temperature, soil, and moisture for many of the most unusual and best liked of the foliage plants. To be sure you are right in judging the light intensity, use a light meter.

The best sort of shade to provide is that which can be used on the inside. Saran cloth (plastic screen) or muslin are good materials for this purpose. Either can be suspended from the rafters or wires placed above the plants and moved or removed as needed, in accordance with the outside light available. During the heat of the summer, when the sun is intense, it is a good idea to use a combination of shading compound on the glass and suspended cloth within the greenhouse. But don't rely on shading compound alone. Once again, it should be emphasized that foliage plants, as a rule, do require a greater light intensity than many seem to realize. The important thing is to supply the light in a diffused or filtered manner.

Pests and Diseases of Foliage Plants

It would be mighty nice to say that foliage plants are not afflicted by pests or diseases, but such is not the case. There are some foliage plants which are less susceptible to diseases or pests and many which, under proper growing conditions, will never show any ill effects. However, it is well to know what pests or diseases can attack foliage plants and to be prepared to handle any emergency which may occur. Keep in mind the precautions outlined in Chapter XVI on the control of pests and diseases, and remember that it is better to use preventive rather than corrective control measures in your greenhouse.

You can keep foliage plants free of insect pests in your greenhouse by establishing a once-a-month *preventive* program using Malathion or other good insecticides—thus using insecticides before infestations are noted. For instance, the two-spotted mite (the worst of several mites that attack foliage plants) can be barred with

Endrin, Kelthane, or Tedion sprays. A good specific insecticide to prevent aphids is Lindane. Several species of aphids do attack foliage plants.

Mealybugs, of which there are several kinds that dote on foliage plants, are either prevented or controlled with weekly applications of Malathion.

Perhaps the worst pest problem of foliage plants is the wicked combination of sooty mold and soft brown scale. The scale most commonly seen on foliage plants is the hard shell or armored scale, otherwise known as the ivy or oleander scale. Both soft brown and hard shell scales feed on a wide variety of foliage plants, but they can be prevented or controlled with Diazinon, Malathion, or Zectran sprays. Since sooty mold lives off secretions of scale, control of scale automatically prevents the mold.

Peperomia is hit quite often with the virus ringspot. It appears on the leaves as brown or yellow rings and in some cases leaves will show brown necrotic spots. Young leaves infected with the disease are inclined to curl, cup, or twist while not otherwise showing signs of the disease. Diseased leaves will eventually drop. Once a plant has this disease, there is no way to get rid of it. Use only healthy stock plants from which to take cuttings. And if you buy cuttings from other growers or get them from other amateur growers, be absolutely certain they are clean and healthy. Any plants which show signs of this disease should be destroyed. Check the under side of the leaves regularly for ringspots.

Phytophthora root and leaf rot is a fungus disease which attacks philodendrons when the soil is wet and humidity is high. The fungus causes circular tan or straw-colored blotches to appear. They may run up to $\frac{1}{2}$ inch in diameter. A water-soaked margin surrounds the spot as the disease progresses. If conditions are dry, the water-soaked ring disappears and in its place comes a reddish-brown margin. Diseased leaves soon become entirely yellow and fall from the plant. You can control this disease on philodendrons by keeping the plants from becoming too wet and by keeping the humidity lowered somewhat. Do not water the foliage. Good control materials for foliage and stems are Phaltan, Captan, Ferbam, Zineb, or Ziram sprays applied thoroughly to cover all the leaves and stems and in the strengths recommended by the respective manufacturers. To protect roots use Dexon soil drench.

Bacterial leaf spot is a serious bacterial disease of philodendrons which is most apt to hit the large-leaf types of philodendrons. It is introduced from the soil, and the bacteria cause small, water-soaked spots to appear beneath the leaves or on the petioles. Moderate humidity and temperature help to prevent this disease. Leaves can develop water blisters which later cause the leaf to become mushy. A spraying every 4 or 5 days with a streptomycin compound such as Agrimycin 17 also acts as a preventive. Use it at the rate of 200 parts per million of water. Any diseased leaves should be destroyed, as should badly diseased plants, to prevent further spread. Use only cuttings from disease-free plants. Sterilize the potting soil, pots, bench-covering medium, etc.

Greenhouse gardeners are often puzzled by a condition on philodendrons known as physiological leaf spot. The disease appears when temperatures are high and the growth is rapid. Sap is rapidly withdrawn from the cells beneath the leaves and this can cause pale yellow spots to appear on the leaves. The sticky sap oozes from spots which appear and the appearance of the plant is spoiled, especially when sooty mold again joins into a partnership by fastening itself to the spots. Also, the cells around the spots are often invaded by bacteria which cause dead areas to appear on the upper surface of the leaves. To prevent this disease, guard against high temperature rises when the plants are growing well. Sooty mold, which appears on the leaves as a result of the physiological problem, can be controlled with Captan 50-per-cent Wettable Powder used at the rate of $1\frac{1}{2}$ to 2 ounces per 10 gallons of water.

Propagation

You can propagate most foliage plants from tip or single-eye cuttings. A few of the others are started from runners and divisions. Coarse sand is good for propagation but one of the favorite media is that of half peatmoss and half perlite. Other good media include half peat and half sand, and sphagnum peat. The most important thing to remember, regardless of what medium you use, is to sterilize it well and be sure it is well drained.

Root-inducing hormones should be used to promote faster rooting. The propagating media and air temperature should be 70 degrees or higher. Best rooting results are received when the relative humidity is from 75 to 80 per cent. Automatic misting makes this easy to do. If you use hand syringing, be sure not to cover the cuttings.

Foliage Plant Culture

LIGHT

Complete sun—Plants in this group prefer from 4,000 to 8,000 foot-candles of light for a regular day. (A foot-candle of light is the amount of light given off by 1 candle at a distance of 1 foot.) They will tolerate from 500 to 2,000 foot-candles of artificial light if it is provided on a 16-hour basis. Artificial light is best provided by fluorescent lamps because it is cool. But incandescent or filament lamps are fine if they are set high enough above the plants to prevent a concentration of heat.

Diffused or filtered sunlight—This group of plants prefers 1,000 to 3,000 foot-candles of light for a normal day. They will tolerate from 100 to 1,000 foot-candles if given 16 hours total illumination. For the most part, they should have 100 foot-candles of light, but some will live with as little as 25 foot-candles of light, though they will fail to grow very much.

Shady situation—This group of plants prefers from 50 to 500 foot-candles of light but will do fairly well indoors with as little as 10 foot-candles. However, they should have extra high humidity.

MOISTURE

Even—Plants in this group should never be oversoaked. They prefer even moisture and being watered from below by setting the plant in a saucer.

Heavy—Keep plants of this group wet at all times, never permitting them to dry out. They are best watered from a jardiniere or saucer filled with water. Do not allow such plants to remain continuously in water but empty them at least every other day.

Alternating—Such plants need a good soaking when watered. Before watering again, permit the soil to reach the dry side. This does not mean bone dry.

SOIL

Rich—Plants of this group like a soil which has ample leafmold, well-rotted manure (rough textured), peatmoss, or humus.

Good—Good garden soil or loam which is well supplied with humus or rooted manure.

Fern fiber (*osmunda*)

TEMPERATURE RANGE

Below average—Plants in this group prefer a daytime temperature of 58 degrees F. Nighttime temperature should be around 45 degrees F.

Moderate—A moderate temperature range is the preference of this group of plants. Give them a daytime temperature of 68 degrees F. and a nighttime temperature of 55 degrees F.

Warm—This group of plants likes it warm with a daytime temperature of 80 or even up to 85 degrees F. At night they should not be in temperatures of less than 65 degrees F.

Acanthus montanus, mountain thistle or bear's breeches. Leaves 12 inches long and 6 inches wide. Lobed spiny margins and spines on leaves. Dark and light green blotches. Grows to 3 feet tall. Needs complete sun, even moisture, good soil, moderate temperature.

Aglaonema commutatum, variegated Chinese evergreen. Lustrous, beautiful foliage with interesting growth pattern. Leaves quite large, stocked with thick mid-rib. Flowers heavily, followed by lush red berries. Does well in limited light. Needs diffused sunlight, even moisture, good soil, warm temperature.

Aglaonema roebelinii, painted droptongue. Robust plant with erect stems. Leaves large and showy. Olive green, variegated silver. Needs diffused sunlight, even moisture, good soil, warm temperature.

Aglaonema simplex, Chinese evergreen. Oblong, dull green leaves, 10 inches long and 5 inches wide. Gray-green markings above. Very robust plant. Red fruit follows insignificant flowers. Needs shade, heavy moisture, rich soil, warm temperature.

Alocasia chantrieri. Intermediate-sized, arrow-shaped leaves. Deep sinuate-lobed margins. Leaves shiny metallic green above and purple beneath. Veins of light grayish green. Needs diffused sunlight, even moisture, rich soil, warm temperature.

Amomum cardamon, ginger plant. Corn-like plant with stems which become cane-like and stout. Will grow to 3 or 4 feet high. Needs ample root space, diffused sunlight, even moisture, good soil, moderate temperature.

Aphelandra aurantiaca. Rich-looking plant with elliptic, waxy leaves of dark green on top, lighter green beneath. Prominent yellowish veins. Flower: dense bracted spike of orange-yellow color. Ideal house plant. Needs complete sun, even moisture, good soil, warm temperature.

Araucaria excelsa, Norfolk Island or Australian pine. Needle-like foliage of dark green. Exotic, decorative house plant. Excellent living Christmas tree. Needs complete sun, even moisture, rich soil, moderate temperature.

Aspidistra lurida, cast iron plant. Dark green leathery foliage. Long petioles. Sturdiest of house plants. Stands darkened areas. Needs shade, even moisture, good soil, moderate temperature.

Asplenium nidus, bird's nest fern. Highly glossy foliage of yellow-green. Fronds 2 to 4 feet long, 3 to 8 inches wide. Prominent midrib on back of fronds. Nest-like center. Needs shade, heavy moisture, good soil, warm temperature.

Begonia ulmifolia. Excellent pillar plant. Rich green, typical begonia foliage. Cane-stemmed begonia. Needs diffused sunlight, even moisture, good soil, moderate temperature.

BROMELIADS:

B. Aechmea fosteriana. Lovely upright tubular plant with pale green leaves and brownish-green blotches. Native of Brazil. Needs diffused sunlight, alternating moisture, rich soil, warm temperature.

B. Aechmea ramosa. Very symmetrical plant. Dense leaves of light green coated with gray. Also a native of Brazil. Needs diffused sunlight, even moisture, rich soil, warm temperature.

B. Ananas comasus variegatus, variegated pineapple plant. Wonderful showy plant. Variegated ivory leaves with rose red edges. Produces pineapple fruit. Needs diffused light, alternating moisture, rich soil, warm temperature.

B. Billbergia nutans, queen's tears. Foliage silvery-bronze and narrow. Weeping rose-colored bracts contain greenish flowers, edged purple. Needs diffused light, alternating moisture, rich soil, warm temperature.

B. Billbergia saundersi hybrids, rainbow plant. Foliage is bayonet-like and bronzy or variegated. Crimson bracts with pendent red. Indigo flowers. Needs diffused light, alternating moisture, rich soil, warm temperature.

B. Cryptanthus zonatus zebrinus, zebra plant. Leaves of bronzy brown, and wavy. Pronounced silver cross-banding. One of the most beautiful of the bromeliads. Needs diffused light, alternating moisture, rich soil, warm temperature.

B. Nidularium innocenti straitum. Lovely rosette type of plant, with light green leaves. Leaves transversed by unequal ivory stripes. Needs diffused light, even moisture, rich soil, warm temperature.

Cissus rhombifolia, grape ivy. Bright shiny green compound leaves. Graceful trailing habit. Easily trained on pole or trellis. Rust-colored hairs beneath leaves. Needs diffused sunlight, even moisture, good soil, warm temperature.

Crotons, various. Brilliantly colored tropical shrubs. Variegated leaves of red, yellow, and green. Some with leaves that are narrow, others which are broad. Very durable plants. Need complete sun, even moisture, good soil, warm temperature.

DIEFFENBACHIA:

D. amoena. Large plant with broad leathery foliage. Dark green leaves, some white feathering. Needs diffused light, alternating moisture, good soil, moderate temperature.

D. arvida. Beautifully textured plant. Large variegated ivory-white leaves which are attractively pointed. Needs diffused light, even moisture, rich soil, warm temperature.

Dieffenbachias are among the most spectacular of foliage plants.

D. picta. Green, oval leaves are attractively blotched with white. Excellent house plant. Needs diffused light, alternating moisture, good soil, warm temperature.

D. picta roehrsi. Strong cane with large leaves. Leaf blade mostly yellow with a green border and blotched with ivory. Excellent house plant. Needs diffused light, even moisture, good soil, warm temperature.

D. picta superba. Developed from *D. picta roehrsi*. More compact plant with green and cream blotching. Needs diffused light, alternating moisture, good soil, warm temperature.

DRACAENA:

D. deremensis warneckei. Green leaves narrowly striped with white along the leaf blade. Fine house plant. Needs diffused light, even moisture, good soil, warm temperature.

D. draco, dragon's blood. Branches quite readily when terminal growth removed. Leaves occur in crowded terminal head. Reddish-colored sap. Interesting plant. Needs shade, even moisture, good soil, warm temperature.

D. godseffiana. Wiry, thin stems. Deep-green leaves, spotted white, small and leathery. Needs diffused light, heavy moisture, good soil, warm temperature.

D. sanderiana. Corn-like plant. Dwarf, gray-green with broad cream margins. Needs diffused sunlight, even moisture, good soil, warm temperature.

Episcia fulgida, flame violet. Beautiful gloxinia-like leaves of a bronzy color are centered with brilliant green veins which are somewhat iridescent. Needs shade, even moisture, rich soil, warm temperature.

Episcia lilacina viridis. Costa Rican native. Lovely emerald green foliage with faint silver center. Medium-sized plant. Needs diffused light, even moisture, rich soil, warm temperature.

Fatshedera lizei. A sub-shrub or woody vine with upright growth. Most attractive when of smaller size. Leaves leathery, dark lustrous green, and lobed. Vigorous grower. Needs complete sun, even moisture, good soil, moderate temperature.

FICUS:

F. benjamina exotica, Java or weeping fig, or weeping rubber tree. Beautiful graceful plant with very dense growth. Drooping habit. Leaves 2 to 4 inches long with short petioles. Excellent plant for Japanese effect. Needs complete sun, even moisture, good soil, warm temperature.

F. elastica, rubber tree. Traditional rubber plant with large thick glossy leaves 12 to 15 inches long on good specimens. Withstands adverse conditions. Needs complete sun, even moisture, good soil, warm temperature.

F. pandurata, fiddle leaf plant. West African plant with fiddle-shaped leaves that will sometimes grow to 18 inches long and 12 inches wide. Leaves leathery, deeply veined with wavy margins, bright fresh green, very glossy. Needs diffused light, even moisture, good soil, warm temperature.

F. radicans variegata, training rubber plant. Beautiful variegated elliptical foliage which winds rapidly. Excellent for training on "totem" pole of moss or other material. Leaves small light green and heavily variegated. Needs diffused light, even moisture, good soil, warm temperature.

F. religiosa, Bo-tree or sacred fig. Sacred plant to Buddhists. Graceful with heart-shaped pointed leaves. Bark a smooth cinnamon brown. Stocks long and slender. Leaves quiver in the slightest breeze. Needs diffused light, even moisture, good soil, warm temperature.

Fittonia vershaffelti, nerve plant. Rich dark green leaves distinctly marked with veins. Leaves light green beneath. Veins are white. White hairs cover light green stems. Excellent creeping plant. Needs diffused light, even moisture, rich soil, warm temperature.

Geogenanthus undatus, seersucker plant. Very dwarf foliage plant. Leaves ovate and petioles short. Leaf blade dark green with silver veins running lengthwise. Veins beneath are purple. Leaf surface undulating. Brown hairs cover purple stems. Ideal for dish gardens and terrariums. Needs diffused light, even moisture, rich soil, warm temperature.

Gynura aurantiaca, velvet plant. Alternate deeply toothed leaves. Stems and leaves covered with small violet hairs. Looks like purple velvet. Needs complete sun, even moisture, good soil, warm temperature.

Hedera helix variegata. Hagenburger's large-leaf variegated ivy. Beautifully variegated leaves with waxy leaf blade measuring up to 4 inches across. Excellent plant for pole or trellis. Ivies are easy to start and to grow. They are started from stem cuttings rooted preferably in sand (or in water). For best results grow under cool conditions, giving them ample moisture and an occasional feeding. This variety needs diffused sunlight, even moisture, good soil, moderate temperature.

Maranta leuconeura kerchoveana, prayer plant. Leaves often 6 inches long and 3 inches wide. Light green above and purplish or glaucous beneath. Prominent fine veins. Silken sheen beneath the foliage. Dark green markings on upper surface of leaves, reddish beneath. Leaves fold upward at night. Needs diffused light, even moisture, good soil, warm temperature.

Monstera deliciosa—Philodendron pertusum or cut-leaf philodendron. Huge rich-green leaves born on heavy vine-like stems. Tall growing. Must have pillar or pole to lean against. Excellent plant for indoor use where space is available. Needs diffused light, even moisture, good soil, warm temperature.

Neanthe bella. Compact growth with leaves of deep green. Robust plant. Ideal for indoors. Excellent dish-garden plant. Needs diffused sunlight, heavy moisture, good soil, warm temperature.

Pandanus baptisti, Baptist screwpine. Short stemmed with long narrow leaves less than 1 inch wide. Spineless leaves arch to a narrow point. Foliage of blue-green with depressed center and creamy-yellow stripes. Needs diffused light, alternating moisture, good soil, warm temperature.

Peperomia:

P. caperata, emerald gem. Rugose leaves are dark emerald green on top and light green beneath. Spikes of white flowers in sharp contrast to foliage. Dainty crinkly-leaved plant, highly popular. Needs diffused light, alternating moisture, good soil, warm temperature.

P. incana, woolly peperomia. Brazilian plant with stocky, thick, stiff stems and stiff growth habit. Silvery hairs cover entire surface of gray-green leaves. Excellent warm-room plant. Needs diffused light, alternating moisture, good soil, warm temperature.

P. minima, miniature-leaf peperomia. Bush-like plant with numerous tiny, oblong, olive-green leaves. Silver veins on leaves. Leaves bluish-red beneath. Thin red stems. Needs diffused light, alternating moisture, rich soil, warm temperature.

P. obtusifolia, green peperomia. Shiny, dark green foliage. Obovate leaves born alternately on erect stiff reddish stems. Short petioles or stems. Rugged indoor plant. Needs diffused sunlight, alternating moisture, good soil, warm temperature.

PHILODENDRON:

P. cannifolium. Procumbent stem with extremely short joints. Appears to be self-heading. Leaves large, shining, medium green, and almost lanceolate. Pronounced mid-rib. Petioles fleshy, swollen smooth, and up to a foot long. Needs diffused light, even moisture, good soil, warm temperature.

P. erubescens. Stout-stemmed climbing plant with short internodes. Leaves a foot in length, and more or less cordate in shape. Green upper surface, copper reverse. Green petiole. Good climber. Needs diffused light, even moisture, good soil, warm temperature.

P. melinoni. Self-heading type. Fleshy petiole with long sagittate leaves. Light cream mid-ribs. Short, shaggy, thick stem. Needs shade, even moisture, rich soil, warm temperature.

P. oxycardium, heartleaf philodendron. Very vigorous climbing or twining vine. Small heart-shaped leaves. Excellent for totem poles or walls. Needs diffused sunlight, even moisture, good soil, warm temperature.

P. scandens. Small-leaved, veining philodendron. Juvenile leaves reddish, mature leaves green. Heart-shaped leaves have six pairs of prominent veins, are 3 to 4 inches long. Petiole reddish and up to 4 inches long. Shiny bright green stems. Needs shade, even moisture, good soil, moderate temperature.

P. selloum. Large-leaved, self-heading type. Leaves of dark green, quite sturdy. Petiole up to 2 feet long. Leaves 18 inches long and 12 inches wide on good plants. Light green foliage becomes dark green as plants mature. Needs complete sun, even moisture, good soil, warm temperature.

P. verrucosum. Heart-shaped leaves 12 to 15 inches long and 8 inches wide. Upper surface of leaves rich, velvety, iridescent dark green with paler green veins. Underside of leaves maroon in color with bright green veins. Reddish leaf petiole 6 to 8 inches long and covered with coarse pale green hairs. Leaf bracts of new leaves pale green. Needs shade, even moisture, rich soil, warm temperature.

Phoenix roebeleni, date palm. Feather-like, shiny green foliage which droops gracefully. Flexible spines near base of mature foliage. Highly decorative and ornamental. Height 5 to 6 feet at maturity.

Slow growing. Needs diffused light, heavy moisture, good soil, warm temperature.

Pilea cadierei, aluminum plant. One foot high at maturity. Fleshy stemmed and opposite leaves. Apple green foliage with white variegation. Upright growth. Excellent dish-garden plant. Needs diffused light, even moisture, rich soil, warm temperature.

Rhoeo discolor, Moses-in-the-bulrushes or two-men-in-a-boat. Upright growth. Stem 1 foot high and leaves 12 to 15 inches long and 2 to 3 inches wide. Leaves long, narrow, and sharp tipped. Foliage dark shiny green on top and purple underneath. Upward curl of leaves makes purple coloration beneath visible on edges. Popular planter plant. Needs complete sun, even moisture, good soil, moderate temperature.

Sanchezia nobilis glaucophylla. Striking shrub with beautiful lanceolate leaves from 8 to 9 inches long. Bright green color with straw-yellow veins. Needs complete sun, even moisture, good soil, warm temperature.

Sansevieria cylindrica, Ife sansevieria. Leaves 1 inch thick, 3 to 4 feet long, cylindrical, arching, leathery, and rigid. Dark green leaves have light green bands. Stands considerable abuse. Needs complete sun, even moisture, good soil, warm temperature.

Sansevieria subspicata. Flat, broad leaves in rosette-type growth. Reddish-brown pencil line on leaf edges. Greenish-white flower spikes. Stands considerable neglect. Needs complete sun, even moisture, good soil, warm temperature.

Sansevieria trifasciata laurenti. Leaves up to 2½ feet long and as wide as several inches. Dark green leaves with transverse light green or white bands. Excellent robust plant for specimen plant or group plantings. Needs complete sun, even moisture, good soil, warm temperature.

Saxifraga sarmentosa, strawberry begonia. Roundish leaves with prominent veins. Fine hairs on leaves and petiole. New plants develop at ends of long runners. Excellent basket plant. Needs complete sun, alternating moisture, good soil, below average temperature.

Schefflera actinophylla, Australian umbrella tree. Shiny, oblong leathery leaflets measure up to 1 foot long. Greenish stem turns grayish brown at maturity. Umbrella-like appearance. Requires ample space. Needs diffused light, alternating moisture, good soil, warm temperature.

Scindapsus aureus, pothos or devil's ivy. Green glossy leaves well marked with yellow spots, blotches, or striations. Climbing plant good for poles or wall. Needs complete sun, alternating moisture, good soil, warm temperature.

SYNGONIUM:

S. albo-virens, white gold or variegated nepthytis. Whitish-colored foliage with arrow-shaped young leaves, divided older leaves. Tends to climb or vine. Slender, reddish-brown aerial shoots. Needs support. Needs diffused light, even moisture, rich soil, warm temperature.

S. auritum, five fingers. Divided rich green three-parted leaves. Thick branching stems that climb or vine. Leaves glossy and most unusual. Needs diffused light, even moisture, good soil, warm temperature.

S. podophyllum, nephthytis or arrow head. Creeping plant which can be trained well on totem pole. Leaves arrow-shaped when young, divided at maturity. Excellent house plant. Stands considerable neglect. Needs diffused light, even moisture, rich soil, warm temperature.

S. wendlandi. Creeping. Deep green leaves with broad center stripes and silver veins. Velvety appearance. Excellent plant for small planters. Needs diffused light, even moisture, rich soil, warm temperature.

Tradescantia fluminensis, wandering Jew. Narrow, pointed, white-striped, green leaves. Easily grown. Needs diffused sunlight, alternating moisture, good soil, moderate temperature.

Xanthosoma lindeni. Well-leaved plant. Very showy. Bright green leaves with white veins and mid-ribs. Sometimes taken for caladium. Needs diffused light, heavy moisture, rich soil, warm temperature.

CHAPTER XIX

Cacti and Succulents

Of all the plants which are grown in the greenhouse, I believe that cacti and succulents are the charmers of the lot—partly because of their fascinating shapes. They are easy to raise; they seldom overgrow their containers; they will stand considerable abuse, including poor soil and lack of moisture. If you have a spot in the greenhouse which can be kept drier and less humid than the rest, give yourself the treat of growing some of these daughters of the desert.

Cacti are among nature's most unusual plants. They have no permanent leaves and rarely any leaves at all. In their spongy tissue they store enough water to keep them living through almost any drought. Some are tiny, some grow to house-plant size, and still others grow almost like trees or as huge columns, 30 to 40 feet high. If you plan to grow cacti and succulents watch out for the cute little fellows known as opuntias and those which come from Australia. Most of them will quickly outgrow your greenhouse.

The beauty of cacti is four-fold: there is the beauty of the plant form; the beauty of the over-all color of the plant; the beauty of the spikes, which range from hair-like appendages, through fuzzy but prickly small stickers, to the large, wicked spikes of 4 inches or longer; and the rare beauty of the flowers. Cacti produce some of nature's gaudiest and most breathtaking flowers. If you balance your collection of cacti properly, there will rarely be a time when you will not have some plants which are flowering.

Fantastic forms of cacti are a hobby grower's dream.

Propagation

As a rule, most home greenhouse gardeners do not grow their cacti and succulents from seed or cuttings because it is a rather slow process. However, should you care to take a cutting, allow it to dry for a few days before placing it in the rooting medium. Otherwise, the wounded area will rot. Cacti and succulents' seedlings are handled in the customary manner, as discussed in Chapter XIII.

It is best to purchase rooted cuttings and small plants from California or Southern dealers. Unpack them immediately upon arrival, for plants left packed are likely to develop rot. Keep them from heat or cold. If it is not possible to pot them at once, unpack them and give them fresh air. Cacti can be left standing upright in flats for a number of days, if given plenty of light and a light sprinkling.

Lack of light in transit will sometimes cause the growing centers of cacti or succulents to be blanched. If this happens, plants so affected should be exposed to bright sunshine very gradually or they will burn.

Soil and Nutrition

Most cacti require a light soil. I recommend one consisting of 1 part coarse sand, 2 parts unscreened leafmold, and a sprinkling of old plaster, for cacti love lime. Add gravel, vermiculite, or perlite to assure good drainage. This soil is suitable for most succulents, too, although a few prefer a slightly heavier soil. Never use straight sand. It will produce unsightly plants, for there is nothing in sand upon which the plants can feed.

Though cacti and succulents do not require the amount of food that some other plants do, they do need some nutrients. I recommend that you feed them occasionally with fish emulsion or blood-meal, using either at half strength.

Watering—Ventilation—Shade—Humidity

Cacti and succulents should be kept rather dry and prefer low humidity. When the plants are actively growing, water them fairly well each time you water. Then allow them to become rather dry before watering again. During the dormant period, water sparingly.

The cooler these plants can be grown and still kept from freezing, the better. Grown in this manner, they have a more solid, natural look. When cacti and succulents are grown too warm they have a tendency to peak up and lose much of their natural beauty. Cacti normally grow only about two months out of the year. Succulents, of course, have a resting period but grow most of the time throughout the year.

Both cacti and succulents need good ventilation but avoid drafts. If you are growing other plants besides cacti and succulents in your greenhouse, you may have to do some sort of compromising on shade. During the hot, summer months, contrary to general belief, most of these plants prefer some light shade. There are some, however, that should have full sun. During the fall, winter, and spring, always give them full sun.

Varieties

Just listing the number of varieties of cacti and succulents from which you can choose plants for your own collection would take a book in itself. So in order to get the most enjoyment from such a collection, try as many species as you can. Then you will have a wide enough range of plants to assure you of fantastically beautiful blooms during every month of the year.

Aloe aristata, lace aloe. This is one of the daintiest of all the aloes. It makes a fine pot plant and blooms in small sizes. Its popular name comes from its many incurving, white-dotted gray-green leaves which are margined and tipped with hair-like teeth.

Aloe ferox, wart aloe. This one varies considerably, sometimes being copiously spiny on both sides of the leaves and again having leaves which are smooth on both sides. Dull green leaves form a rosette. Scarlet blossoms are borne on candelabra-like branches. Grows to 15 feet.

Aloe variegata, "Ausana Improved," Hummel's Improved tiger aloe. This is a hybrid developed over the years which has zones of white and green which are more uniform and distinct than some of the other aloes, which gives it a beautiful banded effect. The margin on the leaf is wider and whiter. The plant is more compact and is a strong, large-growing plant with blunter leaves. Flowers are unusually attractive. Triangular leaves borne on triangular rosettes. Grows 1 foot high.

Astrophytum myriostigma, bishop's cap. One look at this little plant quickly tells you why it received its common name, for it is an exact replica of a bishop's cap. This is a smooth, spineless, white plant, which is divided by 5 fluted ribs. It has a summertime crown of yellow flowers.

Chamaecereus silvesterii hybrid, peanut cactus. This undoubtedly, is one of the most popular of the cacti. It is often used for animal tails in pottery planters. Peanut-shaped stems branch freely from a cluster. Its flowers are a bright orange.

Cleistocactus strausii hyalacantha, white torch. This is *the* plant to grow for height and beauty. It has pure white columns bearing tubular red flowers. Its soft silkiness results from long spiny hairs.

Cotyledon undulata, silver ruffles. This is one of the most beautiful of succulents with nearly round leaves that have a crinkled edge. Its powdery white covering takes on a lavender tinge. Where the climate permits, it does well outside.

Crassula C. triebneri, St. Andrew's cross. The various jade plants are old favorites. This one has beautiful pale yellow-green leaves which are flushed and red-dotted during winter. Leaves form a perfect cross.

Echeveria jibbiflora carunculata. This is a lovely shell-pink succulent with narrow leaves that contain blister-like spots on the upper sides. It is one of the most sought-after of plants for collections. Grows 2 to 3 feet tall.

Echinocactus grusonii, golden barrel of Mexico. Even as an older plant this variety maintains its beauty. The prominent nipples borne on young spines soon turn to ribs. It is a globe-shaped, bright green plant of small size.

Euphorbia hermentiana, African milk tree. This marbled euphorbia is one of the tallest of the species. Tiny green leaves adorn mottled dark-green branches of this angular, erect plant. Spines are reddish brown.

Euphorbia splendens, crown of thorns. The religious significance of this plant makes it one of the most popular of all of the cacti. It has handsome thorns, green leaves, and lovely red flowers. It can be trained into various patterns of growth.

Fenestraria, baby toes. This lovely clustering plant comes by its name naturally, for it has glossy, window-like tips. The flowers are white or orange, depending upon variety. It is small, club-shaped, and light green.

Haworthia fasciata, zebra haworthia. There are many lovely haworthias, such as *H. chalwinii, reinwardtii, greenii, margaritifera, papillosa,* and many others. Each has its own particular beauty. *H. fasciata* is one of the loveliest and never seems to be grown in large enough supply by commercial growers. It is a select type with broad bands of white tubercles that run crosswise on dark green leaves.

Haworthia truncata. This is another of the lovely haworthias deserving special note. It has nearly black, thick, strap-shaped leaves. The tips of each leaf appear to have been cut off, leaving a window to allow light into the plant.

Hereroa dyeri, elk's horn. This one grows like a small shrub and has sickle-like, flattened, cunning leaves which resemble elk's horns. It is a very attractive plant with beautiful, small, feather flowers that open at night.

Kalanchoë beharensis, velvet elephant ear. A very striking plant which does well in a desert garden. It has huge silver to brown, velvety triangular leaves which measure up to 18 inches across. Tolerates considerable heat and drought. Grows fairly tall.

Kalanchoë tomentosa, panda plant. I think this is one of the most fascinating of all the succulents. It has silvery, plushy, soft leaves tipped with attractive brown markings. Coloring is best when it receives ample sun.

Kleinia pendula, inch worm. Another well-named plant. It is a worm-like creeper which inches its way up and down and over anything in its pathway. It has orange-red flowers which look not unlike a miniature scarlet carnation.

Lemaireocereus pruinosus, powder blue cereus. This to me is one of the most beautiful of the seedling cacti available today. In full sunshine a reddish tinge is noted through its white coating. Spines are brownish-black; flowers a powdery blue.

Mammillaria bocasana, powder puff. Everyone likes the white fuzzy balls of this plant with its reddish, hooked spines. Creamy flowers, attractive bright red fruit. Small globular plant.

Mammillaria saetigera, dumpling cactus. This medium green globular plant is another of the more than 500 mammillarias which has reached a top spot in demand. It has tubercles adorned with rosettes of attractive spines.

Notocactus pampeanus, devil's paw. A ball-shaped cactus with heavy attractive spines, it flowers with large yellow blooms in May and June.

Opuntia microdasys albistina, angora bunny ears. If ever a plant was given a proper common name, this one certainly was. Its bunny-eared leaves are covered with pure white harmless spines. The pads are 1½ inches across and the plant produces clear, yellow flowers.

Pleiospilos nelii, African split rock. You have to see this smooth-leaved plant to believe it. It actually looks like a rock split in two. It flowers well with bright bronze-orange blooms.

Rochea falcata, scarlet paintbrush. Its interesting form and its blue coloring and large heads of scarlet flowers make this one of the most popular of succulents. Thin, closely packed leaves and erect stems create the illusion of a small shrub.

Sedum adolphi hybrids, Hummel's golden sedum. This one was developed from the sedum called butter plant. These hybrids do not shatter their leaves as easily as some. Has handsome yellow, succulent leaves of medium size. White flowers.

Sedum morganianum, burro's tail. Perfectly named and perfectly suited for the purpose of adding a tail to a pottery planter or for use in hanging baskets. Its pickle-shaped leaves are of a blue color and ½ inch long.

Sedum multiceps, little Joshua tree. Looking very much like the true Joshua tree of the desert, this is one of the most demanded of all the succulents. Has small, erect branches with tight rosettes of tiny green leaves.

Stapelia variegata, star-fish or toad cactus. Although one of the more common cacti, it still starts a conversation whenever it is seen in flower. The markings and colorings of the flower vary but are usually yellow with maroon spots; flower is 2 inches in diameter, and star-like in shape. Stems are like stubby fingers.

Trichocereus spachianus, golden column. A column-shaped cactus very useful for dish gardens, it is often used as an understock for grafting of slower-growing cacti. Has large, snow-white flowers.

Zygocactus truncatus, Christmas cactus, Thanksgiving. The Christmas or crab cactus has long been a favorite house plant throughout the country. Although there is but one species, a number of varieties exist. One of the most unusual, especially from the foliage standpoint, is the variety Thanksgiving. Although its flowers are similar to the basic type of Christmas cactus (showy red blooms), the foliage has soft hooks which appear along the margin of the leaves.

Thanksgiving flowers 30 days earlier than the regular Christmas cactus. Like the others, it, too, likes to be kept reasonably moist but not wet, a fact which sets these cacti apart from the others which like it dry.

The Christmas cactus should have a soil consisting of 1 part sharp sand, 2 parts loam, 1 part leafmold or humus, and ½ part dried cow manure. To a 6-inch pot of this mixture, add a tablespoonful of bonemeal.

Give Christmas cacti good light and ordinary temperatures in the home. In the greenhouse, they can be grown from 60 to 65 degrees.

There is a trick to getting the Christmas cactus to bloom, whether it is the Thanksgiving variety or any of the others. In early fall hold back the moisture somewhat and, in the case of the greenhouse gardener, chill the plants for about 30 days by placing them in a coldframe with protection against freezing. The chilling process in a home can be accomplished by placing the plant on a porch or other place for a similar period, merely protecting it against freezing. This tends to ripen or set the buds properly so that the plant will then flower profusely when brought into the greenhouse or home and watered normally. Christmas cactus should have an occasional feeding with manure water or balanced fertilizer.

CHAPTER XX

Flowers Grown for Cutting

Many home greenhouse owners like the idea of growing flowers which can be cut for arrangements and bouquets. Here are some to be raised in ground beds, raised benches, or deep flats.

Ageratum (*Ageratum houstonianum*). When it comes to blue flowers, there is not the wide selection that there is among other colors. Ageratums are one of the loveliest of the blues. They should have a light, sandy, friable soil. Space the plants in a bench 10 by 10 inches or grow them in deep flats. Keep the plants a little on the dry side at first and then, once they have taken hold, keep them reasonably moist. Good sunlight and ventilation are necessary. Give the plants a liquid fertilizer regularly to keep the plants from becoming yellow or hard. 20–20–20 is good for these plants. Ball's Tall Blue is a good variety for cutting purposes.

Alyssum (*Lobularia maritima*). The lovely fragrance and pure white color of sweet alyssum make it a favorite for corsages or small arrangements. Follow the same cultural information outlined for ageratums.

Amazon lily (*Eucharis grandiflora*). This is a lovely cut flower grown from a bulb. Bulbs may be benched or grown in tubs or pots. Place 4 bulbs in an 8-inch pot, or 6 to a 10-inch pot. Good drainage is essential. A good soil mixture is one which contains 1 part well-rotted manure, 1 part peatmoss, 1 part sand, and 2 parts soil plus a little charcoal. You can substitute leafmold for the peatmoss. Moderate air circulation, minus drafts, is necessary. Except for the winter, some shade should be applied. Keep eucharis on the dry side as the plants are started, then apply ample water and keep the humidity high until the plants have become well established, at which time they should be kept on the dry side for 6 to 8 weeks to induce bud setting. Following the bud set, normal watering may be resumed.

Anthurium (*A. andraeanum, scherzerianum,* and Shaffer Hybrids). Among the very loveliest of flowers are the anthuriums. When cut they last for weeks. Use a rough, fibrous loam soil. They may be benched or grown in ground beds but most home greenhouse gardeners prefer to grow them in large pots. Provide excellent drainage, plenty of water, and high humidity. Shade is required during spring, summer, and fall and in winter when the days are bright. Feed with a balanced fertilizer such as 12–12–12.

Aster (*Callistephus chinensis*). Asters are light responders which can be grown at any time of the year, provided they receive daylight or sufficient artifical light for 15 hours per day. Enough light is provided by using 40-watt lights with reflectors hung 2 feet above the plants and 4 feet apart. Light must be applied from the time the seedlings have germinated until the plants have flowered.

Either the seedlings may be placed in transplant flats or pot bands at the start, or they may be placed directly into the bench where they are to be grown. Set the plants as shallowly as possible without exposing the roots. When set too deeply the plants are likely to rot. I recommend a soil mixture consisting of ¼ to ⅓ well-rotted manure and sufficient sand to be sure it is drained well. Add a little lime if the pH is low. Use 1 pound of balanced fertilizer to 35 square feet of bench. This should be sufficient to carry the plants until they flower. Feed the plants again, however, if the need is indicated. Keep asters on the moist side but not soggy. Never attempt to grow asters in soil which has not been sterilized. They need good ventilation and some shade when the sun is hot.

Asters may be grown single-stemmed or pinched to get more flowers per plant. When grown single-stemmed the flowers are larger. By this method, space them 4 by 4 inches. When the plants are to be pinched, space 8 by 8 inches. The best flowers are obtained on asters when the plants are disbudded. Remove all of the buds on each branch, leaving only the terminal buds. Greenhouse asters must have some support, such as wire and string, to insure the best quality stems and flowers.

Babysbreath (*Gypsophila elegans*). As a cut flower babysbreath is seldom used alone but it is wonderful to mix with larger flowers. It likes a soil which is well drained, but it should not be too rich or gypsophila will grow too rank. Give it plenty of air and keep it somewhat on the dry side. Plants should be spaced 3 by 4 inches. I like the varieties Paris Market and Covent Garden Market.

Blue lace flower or Didiscus (*Trachymene coerulea*). This is a dainty herbaceous plant. The flattened clusters of clear blue tubular flowers give the overall appearance of lace parasols. It is a plant which will not transplant readily and must, therefore, be sown where it is to flower. Sow sufficient seedlings to get a good stand and then thin out to 6 by 12 inches. Use a well-drained soil high in organic matter. Peatmoss up to 50 per cent can be used. The plants probably will need no feeding, but if you feed, do so very sparingly. Heavy feeding causes rank growth. Ventilate well and keep on the moist side but not overly wet. Grows 2½ feet tall.

Buddleia (*Buddleia asiatica*). This lovely native of India has long, slender spikes of sweet-scented white flowers. It is an excellent cut flower for arrangements and combines well with other flowers such as tulips, daffodils, and kalanchoës. It flowers equally well in pots, boxes, or benches. In benches it should be spaced 20 by 20 inches. Eventual pot size should be 8 to 12 inches. Give it a well-drained soil of medium texture which contains about ¼ well-rotted manure or peatmoss. Mulching is a good idea once they are established. Give buddleia plenty of water but do not keep soaked.

Good ventilation is essential. If superphosphate is used in the soil, feed every other week with ammonium sulfate.

Butterfly flower (*Schizanthus*). Schizanthus is a much overlooked flower to grow for greenhouse cutting purposes. Its dainty little flowers and wiry stems make it ideal for small arrangements and it holds up well once it has been cut. Although it can be grown in a bench or deep flats, it is usually produced in large pots. Give it a soil of 1 part each of leafmold or peatmoss and sand, and 2 parts good loam. Use a tablespoonful of bonemeal to each large pot of soil.

You must have good drainage for schizanthus and it should be started on the dry side, later on increasing the watering somewhat. Do not feed schizanthus heavily or the space between the flowers on the stem will be too great. I recommend the use of ammonium sulfate at the rate of 1 ounce to 3 gallons of water, twice monthly. You can get bushy growth by pinching schizanthus once or, possibly, twice during its early growth. Provide with plenty of ventilation, full light, and good spacing.

Calendula (*Calendula officinalis*). The calendula was once sought after more as seasoning for soups and stews than it was for its lovely flowers. Grown cool and otherwise correctly, the ball types make excellent cut flowers. Use a well-balanced soil with plenty of manure and one which is neutral. Old chrysanthemum soil will require no fertilizer if used for calendulas. When good ventilation is possible, calendulas should be well watered. If air must be restricted because of dark, winter days, run the calendula plants on the dry side. The plants take full light, except during hot summer days. Ground beds are preferred to raised beds or containers because it is easier to keep the temperatures cool in ground beds. Space the plants 12 by 12 inches. It is a good idea to pinch out the center bud of each plant to the second set of leaves below the tip in order to get good branching and more flowers. The best blooms are produced when the stems are disbudded to single flowers.

Candytuft (*Iberis*). Candytuft is available in white and in several pastel colors. There is also an *I. umbellata* group which is rather compact and has a branching habit and a hyacinth-flowered sort which blooms with spikes which resemble hyacinths. Lavender and Rose Cardinal are two of the best varieties in the *umbellata* group. Flowered Giant White is one of the best of the hyacinth-flowered sorts for forcing.

You can grow the plants in deep flats on shelves or in pots, but if you do, the quality will be reduced. It is best to grow them in ground beds or raised benches. Space the *umbellata* type 10 by 10 inches and the hyacinth-flowered 6 by 6 or 6 by 8 inches. Use a soil which consists of $\frac{1}{4}$ well-rotted manure and some sand, if needed, to improve drainage. Feed the plants well and keep them on the wet side, especially during the spring months. Supply candytuft with supports to keep them from toppling over. Full sun during the darker months is needed but shade is necessary otherwise. Provide good ventilation.

Carnation (*Dianthus caryophyllus*). A major crop for commercial cut flower growers, the carnation is also an old-time favorite of the amateur greenhouse grower. Carnations can be used in nearly every sort of manner from corsages to arrangements and their lovely fragrance and beautiful colors double their desirability. Carnations need a rich, porous soil: 1 part well-rotted cattle manure and 3 parts good, well-drained loam. Add 1 pound of 40 per cent superphosphate to 25 feet of bench space. Use only fertilized soil. The soil must be moist but not wet at the time the young plants are placed into it. Set the plants so at least ½ inch of the stem is above the soil surface to prevent rotting. I believe spacing the plants 8 by 8 inches is best, although this can be varied somewhat.

Sunny-weather temperatures for carnations should run 62 to 65 degrees and on cloudy days the temperature should be held around 58 degrees F. The best night temperature is from 48 to 50 degrees.

Keep the plants a little on the dry side when they are first benched. As they take hold, begin to keep them slightly moist. Shade is only necessary where light and heat are intense. Otherwise, carnations should have full sun. Supports are a necessity for carnations or the plants will topple over spoiling flowers and stems alike. Do not feed carnations at once. Those which are benched in August, for instance, should be fed monthly starting in September with ½ pound of 4–12–4 to 100 square feet of bench space. If your soil lacks calcium supply this with gypsum. Fish meal is often added to the soil for carnations at the time of benching.

The old-fashioned way to start carnations, following rooting of cuttings, was to place the young plants in small pots and later plant them outdoors during the summer in well-prepared beds. I prefer taking young cuttings and placing them directly into the bench where they will flower, to cut down the work and reduce the hazard from red spiders and other insects which abound outdoors.

Be very careful concerning the ventilation. They need ample air but it must be regulated to prevent condensation of moisture upon the foliage. To get the finest flowers, disbud each branch, leaving only the terminal bud.

Centaurea (*Centaurea cyanus*). Often called bachelor's button, this is an excellent flower to grow for cutting. Blue Boy is an excellent blue; Pinkie, a fine rose pink; there is also a good white. Too deep and rich a soil will cause rank growth. Consequently, grow them for best results in shallow raised beds or deep flats. Space the plants 12 by 12 inches and use a well-drained, sterilized soil which contains about ¼ well rotted manure as its only fertilizer. It is a good companion for carnations. Keep centaureas reasonably moist and provide good ventilation.

Chrysanthemum, annual. The annual chrysanthemum makes a fine cut flower for home use. It requires a moderately rich soil which should be kept on the moist side. Space plants 7 by 7 inches and give them good ventilation. Full sunshine is required most of the time although some light shading may be necessary in places. To get good flowering per plant, pinch it and be sure that supports are supplied.

Chrysanthemum, perennial (*Chrysanthemum morifolium*). Most cultural information concerning chrysanthemums is found in Chapter XVII. Although there is some lapping over of varieties grown as potted plants and those grown for cutting purposes, by and large the varieties used for cut flowers are different. A large standard mum is ideal to wear to a football game. Most types of pompon mums make excellent corsage flowers. Those grown for cut flowers are generally grown in benches but can be grown in large pots or containers. Again, I advise you to check the dealers' catalogues for variety information in response to shade-and-light treatment.

Watering benched plants is somewhat different from watering those in pots. You must be more careful at the start with benched chrysanthemums. Water them sparingly, increasing the amount of water as the plants take hold and begin to grow. Be very careful in regard to ventilation in order that condensation does not take place on the foliage. When this happens, mildew is bound to follow.

You will need crisscrossed wire-and-string supports or galvanized wire fencing to hold multi-flowered sorts upright. However, the best way to support the large-flowered chrysanthemums is with individual strings. One end of string is tied to the base of the plant and the other to a wire overhead. As the plant grows it is carefully wound around the string taking care not to damage flower or foliage. No matter what system you use, install it well ahead of benching the plants.

Whereas some varieties used for potted plants are left to grow naturally, without much disbudding, the only way you can obtain full-quality blooms of standard or other single-flowered types is by careful pinching and disbudding. Those chrysanthemums which you grow in the normal fall season will develop either a terminal bud or a crown bud by late summer or early fall. (A terminal bud is one surrounded by flowering buds and a crown bud is one which is surrounded by non-flowering vegetative shoots.) The crown bud and all but one of the vegetative shoots should be removed from each chrysanthemum plant which you wish to grow as a disbud with multiple flowers. Only the strongest shoot should be left, and if a second crown bud appears, the process should be repeated.

The most beautiful flowers of fall, however, are the single-stemmed disbudded mums. These are obtained by refraining from pinching and by leaving the center bud of the first bud cluster to develop, removing the surrounding buds. Do this as soon as possible. All other buds should be removed from chrysanthemum plants whether they are being grown by the single-stemmed or pinched method. This will require that you check the plants more frequently, inasmuch as buds appear rather quickly.

Those chrysanthemums to be pinched should be in the bench 3 to 4 weeks before that time. Pinching is done to those which are to be used as spray (cluster) type or pompon chrysanthemums. The pompon or spray types should be allowed to develop 3 or 4 stems. Disbuds which are pinched should have from 4 to 6 stems, depending upon the variety.

Clarkia (*Clarkia elegans*). These are ideal flowers for small bouquets or containers. If grown in benches using the wire-string method of support, clarkias will produce long-stemmed flowers. Grown in flats or pots, they will produce shorter-stemmed flowers. They do not require deep soil. I suggest a well-drained soil with ample humus. The plants need plenty of ventilation, good light, and should be fed only sparingly. Keep them a little on the dry side. If you plan to debranch plants in order to produce better-quality flowers, space the plants 4 by 4 inches apart. Otherwise, space them 8 by 8 inches.

Daisy, Marguerite or Boston. The Boston or Marguerite daisy is easy to grow in the greenhouse. It makes an excellent cut flower for small arrangements and holds up well in corsages. If you have old chrysanthemum soil, use it for daisies. Otherwise any good average loam that is well-drained will do. Do not feed daisies heavily, but when you do feed use a balanced fertilizer. It's a good idea to pinch the plants two or three times in order to get a good branching growth. Daisies can be grown in pots, flats, tubs, or raised benches. In the bench, space them 12 by 12 inches. Good light and ventilation and good drainage are needed. Marguerite daisies will produce more flowers if given additional light by way of 60-watt lamps placed about the plants. Use enough light to assure the plants a 14 to 16-hour day. Keep the daisies slightly moist but not wet.

Delphinium (*Delphinium belladonna* Improved and Pacific Hybrids). Both of the above-mentioned delphiniums force well in the greenhouse and make beautiful cut flowers. Belladonna is used more than the Pacific Hybrids, because the plants are free flowering and produce quantities of light blue blooms. The Pacific Hybrids are available in white, darkest blue, light blue, lavender, and mauve. Clumps may be benched, boxed, or potted in large pots early in January. They need a cold house and will not stand wet feet. Use a sterilized well-drained soil which contains ample organic matter. Water sparingly until the young plants have started to grow actively, if seedlings are used that have been started the previous August. Avoid careless watering which will splash water into the crowns or rot will occur. Depending upon the richness of the soil, probably a few feedings of well-balanced fertilizer such as 5–10–5 will be needed before the plants reach maturity. You will need supports to keep the spikes from toppling over.

Erica. There are several ericas or heaths which are commonly called heathers and which force beautifully. They can be used as potted plants or for cutting purposes. Give them good ventilation, moderate light, and a soil which is highly acid. I suggest a 50-50 combination of peatmoss and sand. Keep them somewhat on the dry side and grow them in 6-inch pots.

Euphorbia (*Euphorbia fulgens*). One of several euphorbias which can be grown in the greenhouse but it is generally considered the best. Commonly called scarlet plume, its flowering time can be regulated in the same manner as poinsettias, which are also one of the euphorbias. The poinsettia will not be discussed as a cut flower in this chapter, so if you wish to grow it as such, check its culture in Chapter XVII.

Euphorbia fulgens likes a slightly acid, heavy soil. Space the plants 10 by 10 inches, putting 2 to 3 plants in each space because they do not branch freely. Pinch in order to cause it to branch. At benching time, use 1 pound of superphosphate to 20 square feet of bench space. Wait until the plants have become well established. Then feed regularly with liquid potassium nitrate or ammonium sulfate, plus muriate of potash. These plants like a humid atmosphere but also require good fresh air, minus drafts.

Feverfew (*Chrysanthemum parthenium*). Not everyone likes the pungent fragrance of this chrysanthemum. Give it a moderately rich, well-drained soil and space the plants 12 by 12 in ground beds. They may be spaced somewhat closer on raised benches. Keep the plants on the dry side and guard against getting them overly wet, especially during the darker months of the year. To get them to flower early, provide 4 hours of extra light each night from February 5 until the buds start to develop. Full light and good ventilation are necessary. Feed feverfew occasionally with a balanced fertilizer.

Forcing branches. Forcing the branches of various flowering trees and shrubs in the greenhouse is one of the unique springtime adventures. A few are: quince, peach, apricot, cherry, prunus, forsythia, and pussywillow. The branches should be cut on days when the temperature is above freezing and after they have developed thin buds far enough that you can be reasonably sure they will continue to develop.

Place the branches into deep water in your greenhouse or in a warm room. Cover the branches with burlap or something similar which will keep them moist until the buds start to open. If you have cut the branches during freezing or severe weather start the forcing at 45 to 55 degrees. Then the temperature may be increased as the branches thaw or warm up. Remove the burlap as soon as the flowers start to open in order not to damage the blossoms.

Freesia (*Freesia hybrida*). Freesias are favorites of mine. They can be grown from seeds or corms. Avoid placing the corms too deeply. You may grow them in the bench or in large pots or deep flats. Use a light soil consisting of 3 parts of good loam, 1 part well-rotted manure or peatmoss, and sand, if needed to lighten the soil. If you use old chrysanthemum soil, leach it well before using. It may be too rich. Never allow freesias to dry out or tip burn will develop on the foliage. Grow freesias from 45 to 60 degrees and provide the plants with ample ventilation and full light. They may need a slight shading during hot summer spells. Provide supports to keep the blooms from toppling over. Freesias need moderate moisture but should never be too wet.

Gerbera. Low-growing herbaceous plant with elongated leaves. Flowers borne on long, stiff stems in colors of pinks, reds, and creams in soft shades.

Gerberas or Transvaal daisies are breathtaking when used as cut flowers or in corsages. The Duplex Hybrids are the preferred type, coming in some very unusual shades.

Gerberas may be grown from seeds, cuttings, or divisions. Strangely, when grown from seeds the fuzzy-pointed end of the seed must be protruding above the soil's surface when they are sown. Gerbera seeds are notoriously poor germinators. It is easier to grow them from divisions or started plants. The plants prefer a soil that is slightly acid and I recommend a well-composted soil that is light, with plenty of organic matter. Add a little 5–10–5, a good supply of well-rotted manure, and enough sand to insure good drainage. Although gerberas will tolerate a wide pH range, from 5.0 to 7.2, they do best when the soil is slightly acid. Be sure that the crowns of the plants are not covered when planted or the plants may rot.

After the plants reach maturity, feed regularly with liquid manure or a balanced fertilizer such as 6–8–6 or 5–10–5. Water moderately until they are well established and then increase the watering sufficiently to keep them on the moist side. Gerberas should have a temperature of 55 to 60 degrees at night. Below 55 degrees, the plants produce very few flowers. Stick closer to 55 degrees when the days are dark.

Gerberas need ample light. Inferior blooms result if the light is poor. Be sure that ventilation is good.

Greens (*Asparagus plumosus nanus* and *A. sprengeri*). There are a number of good greens plants which you can grow in order to provide greenery for the flowers that you may cut for household use. Among these plants are the various maidenhair ferns, leather fern, and others. But perhaps the most popular and certainly the most durable are *Asparagus plumosus* and *A. sprengeri*. Both of these should be kept on the moist side and grown with good ventilation and protection from the sun. In fact, they may be grown along the aisles just beneath the benches. Another good spot for fernery of this sort is in suspended pots or boxes.

Larkspur (*Delphinium ajacis*). Larkspur should be grown in a raised bench where it is easy to prevent overwatering. The latter can cause rot. Space the plants 10 by 10 inches and give them excellent drainage. Use a light, sandy loam with up to 50 per cent peatmoss in the mixture. Water only when they are well on the dry side and keep the humidity down. When you do water, however, do so well. Provide good ventilation and never allow the plants to go into the night with wet foliage. Grow larkspur on the cool side and feed the plants occasionally with 5–10–5 or a similar balanced fertilizer.

Lupine (*Lupinus hartwegi*). Annual lupines make beautiful cut flowers and are not difficult to grow in the greenhouse, if you handle them properly. The plants will not stand transplanting, so seeds should either be started in pots or in the benches where the plants are to be flowered. Lupines like a soil which is porous and well drained, preferably one which contains $\frac{1}{4}$ well-rotted manure and some sand if the soil is on the heavy side. Be sure the soil is well drained and sterilized. Avoid a soil which is too rich. Prior to blooming, lupines should have a couple of feedings of a balanced fertilizer such as 5–10–5 or 6–8–6. Keep the surface soil loose and the atmosphere dry. Foliage should be kept dry also. Plants should be spaced well—10 by 10 inches or 8 by 12 inches is good. Seedlings in a hill should be reduced to the strongest plant, once they have taken hold. Be sure to provide supports for lupines.

Marigold (*Tagetes erecta* and *T. patula*). What is so bright and cheery as a marigold? African (*T. erecta*) and French (*T. patula*) marigolds are among the best, long-lasting cut flowers. When grown in the greenhouse they take on a different texture than when grown out of doors. For greenhouse culture, I prefer the carnation-flowered and the African types, such as the All Double Strain, the Sunset Giants, the Mission Giants, and the Lieb type. All of these lend themselves to greenhouse culture. Once transplanted from the seed flats, marigolds should be grown in a cool house. Grow them in raised benches and space the carnation-flowered type 8 by 10 inches. If grown single-flowered, the Gaint African ones can be spaced 4 by 4 inches, disbudding the plants to get one perfect flower per plant. Use a fairly rich soil which has ample well-rotted manure to get the best results. Be sure they have ample water and good drainage. Use a balanced fertilizer if an extra feeding or two seems necessary.

Pinch the carnation type to get the best crop of flowers. This is also true of the French marigolds. Be sure all the plants have full sun and ample ventilation.

Mignonette (*Reseda odorata*). This rather ordinary plant transforms itself into a real beauty in the greenhouse. It has vigorous, graceful branches of rich dark green foliage, and grows 6 to 15 inches tall. The plants need a fairly rich soil, well drained. Keep them on the dry side and space the plants 10 by 12 inches apart. Mignonette does not transplant well, so it must be started where it is to flower. Give it good ventilation and avoid drafts. Just as the fragrant spikes of greenish, yellowish, or reddish flowers start to form, feed the plants with a well-balanced fertilizer.

Nemesia (*Nemesia strumosa*). This is the poor man's orchid; it produces a wealth of flowers resembling miniature snapdragons. The colors are brilliant hues of yellow, white, purple, with spotted

French marigolds can be flowered in a flat in the greenhouse.

throats. Provide the plants with good drainage and aeration, using a soil consisting of 1 part well-rotted manure, 1 part peatmoss, and 2 parts of good loam. Provide sand, if necessary. When feeding is needed, use a balanced fertilizer. Nemesias should be spaced 8 by 8 inches and grown on a raised bench or in deep flats. Supports are needed for the flowers and they need light shade from mid-spring to mid-fall.

Painted tongue (*Salpiglossis sinuata*). Salpiglossis is lovely to look at but not so pleasant to handle because of a sticky feeling. The colors are rich and unusual. Give the plants a fairly rich soil and they require little, if any, feeding thereafter. The soil should be sandy and well drained. To get good branching and additional blooms, pinch the plants while small. Provide shade in spring.

Pansy and Violet. Whereas pansies are grown from seeds, their cousins, the violets, are best started from cuttings or plant divisions. Both should be grown in benches rather than potted or in boxes or flats. Ground beds, too, are good. Set the plants firmly into the soil and space single violets and pansies 12 by 12 inches apart; double violets should be spaced 9 by 9.

Both pansies and violets should have a well-drained soil and I recommend one consisting of equal parts of loam, rotted manure, and sand, unless your soil is sufficiently light. Add a commercial fertilizer if a soil test indicates its need. Be sure the soil is deep. Best results are obtained when a mulch of peatmoss or well-rotted manure is used. Add lime if necessary to keep the soil sweet.

Never allow either pansies or violets to dry out. Keep them well watered but not overly so. During the summer and early fall syringe violets frequently. Shade is required for both these plants during the summer months, but during late fall and winter give them full sunlight. Grow them at 45 to 50 degrees night temperature. They are wonderful for corsages or small arrangements.

Phlox, annual (*Phlox drummondi*). Variety Grandiflora of the Drummond phlox is the best to grow for cut-flower forcing, producing 18 to 20-inch stems and lovely flower heads. Grandiflora Gigantea is the best of all. The colors include rose pink, chamois rose, creamy apricot, crimson, and bright scarlet. Annual phlox do not transplant well and must be seeded where they are to be grown. Space the plants 8 by 8 inches and grow them in the bench or in deep flats using a fairly rich soil. Use a fairly heavy mixture: 2 parts loam, 1 part peatmoss, and 1 part well-rotted manure. Phlox should have good light, good ventilation, good drainage, and a mulch. Keep them on the moist side but not wet.

Pincushion flower (*Scabiosa atrojurpurla*). Fascinating and very unusual are good descriptive terms for the scabiosa or mourning bride. Annual scabiosas do best in the greenhouse and should have a non-acid soil mixture with a good percentage of non-acid peatmoss or leafmold. If you must use the acid sort, correct it with lime. Give these plants good ventilation, plenty of sunlight, and grow them on the dry side. Grow them cool or the stems will be weak. Pinch back the young plants to make them stocky. Feed occasionally with a balanced fertilizer.

Primrose (*Primula malacoides*). This is probably one that you would not have thought of as a cut flower. However, the dainty, delicate flowers hold up very well, indeed. For its culture check Chapter XVII.

Scarlet plume. See *Euphorbia fulgens* in this chapter.

Scarlet sage (*Salvia splendens*). Seldom considered a cut flower, it really should be. It does well in the greenhouse and is easy to grow. Plants can be started from cuttings taken outside in the fall or from seeds. Give salvias full sunlight, good ventilation, and a rich loamy soil. Be sure to guard against drafts.

Snapdragon (*Antirrhinum majus*). There are few flowers which are as interesting as snapdragon. If you are interested in growing cut flowers, devote considerable space to snapdragons. They are inexpensive to grow and make excellent cut flowers for the home. Also, snapdragons can be started at various times during the year, giving you lovely blooms any time you like.

Snapdragons are grown from seed and should be started in either of two ways: by transplanting the seedlings into flats, then to plant bands, and finally into the bench; or by transplanting them directly from the seedling flats into the bench. If you use the former method, exercise care to prevent the young plants in pots, bands, or transplant flats from becoming root-bound or hardened. Also, they should not be allowed to start stretching upward before benching.

Sterilized soil is a real must with snapdragons, inasmuch as they are very susceptible to rot and other diseases. Snapdragons do well either in raised beds or ground beds. If the plants are to be pinched, thereby producing more flowers but of lesser quality, they should be spaced 7 by 8 inches on raised benches or 8 by 8 inches on ground beds. If you grow them single-stemmed, allow 3 by 6 inches for plants grown during the winter, and 3 by 5 inches for plants growing during the spring.

Contrary to reputation, snapdragons do not thrive in poor soil. Use a mixture consisting of 1 part of well-rotted cow manure and 3 parts of good soil. Use 1 pound of 40 per cent superphosphate to 25 square feet of bench. Check your drainage to make sure that it is excellent. The natural habitat of snapdragons is on the Cliffs of Dover in England, an indication of the sort of well-drained situation they prefer. During bright weather snapdragons need plenty of water to keep them moving along without a check in growth. But when the weather is dark, reduce the water to match the growing. Shade the plants when the sun is hot. Otherwise they should have full sun. If watering has been heavy, feed the plants accordingly. Avoid cold drafts over the plants but provide good ventilation on bright days and some ventilation even during dark weather. You will need supports to keep the stems from becoming crooked.

Cut snapdragons with care in order to have them flower a second time. Leave from 3 to 4 sets of leaves on each branch you cut.

Statice (*Statice sinuata, S. suworowi*). The name statice is really a misnomer, for the various species are now classified under either the genus Armeria or Limonium. But like so many names, the word is likely to stick with the flower. Some of the best varieties of *S. sinuata* are Market Grower's Blue, Lavender Queen, Snow Witch, Rosea Superba, and Bonduelli Superba. *S. sinuata* is suitable for drying but not *S. suworowi* or rat-tail statice. Both are good as fresh cut flowers. Both statices like a medium light soil which is well drained. Keep the soil moist but not wet and remember that statices thrive in a cool temperature. Give the plants full sunlight and good ventilation. An occasional feeding with a balanced liquid fertilizer is a good idea.

Stevia (*Stevia ivaefolia*). This fragrant, tiny-flowered plant is not generally thought of as one to use alone as a cut flower. But it is beautifully adapted to use as a filler with larger flowers. Although it can be grown in benches, you can start the young plants in small pots and gradually work them up to 6-inch pots in which they may be flowered. The usual procedure is to place the potted plants outdoors in frames or some other semi-protected area during the summer. Then bring them in before frost and force them in the greenhouse. Pinch the plants once a month during their outdoor stay, or should you grow them straight through in the greenhouse, also pinch them, to get good branching. I suggest a soil which consists of at least ¼ well-rotted manure. The plants will need full light, good ventilation, ample water, and supports to keep the flowers from toppling over.

Stock (*Mathiola incana*). Column stock is another one of those fine quality flowers which you should grow for cutting. Its lovely fragrance and beautiful colors make it a favorite of almost everyone who sees and grows it.

It requires care to guard against some of the soil-borne diseases that attack it. But using sterilized soil and good cultural practices enable you to grow it well.

Started from seeds, stock can be transplanted from the flats into various sized pots and finally into the bench itself. But I see no reason why you should not bench it directly or ground-bed it from the seed flat. Space the plants 3 by 6, 3 by 8, or 4 by 6 inches. The plants will flower more rapidly if grown on raised benches than in ground beds. To flower stocks on ground beds in January, seeds should be sown 6½ months earlier; on raised benches 5½ months earlier. This difference in timing exists at all times of the year.

Stock prefers a well-aerated, porous soil. If you are starting with a soil built up with cover crops, add about 25 per cent peatmoss. Soil which has not had this advantage should be enriched with a generous portion of well-rotted cow manure. Also, add 1 pound of superphosphate to each 20 square feet of bench space.

Keep stock slightly on the dry side during the winter and give additional water as the weather brightens. On the average, stock may be given a good soaking every 5 to 7 days in raised beds. Be sure the foliage is dry before night. Ample ventilation is important with stock. Control ventilation carefully to prevent condensation in the evening. Temperatures should be below 60 degrees to set buds. Once set, temperatures may be increased somewhat.

Feed stock with a balanced but weak liquid fertilizer solution every 10 days to 2 weeks. Provide supports for stock. Remove some of the lower leaves from the plants to increase the air circulation and thereby reduce the possibility of disease.

Strelitzia. Strelitzia, or bird-of-paradise, produces strikingly beautiful flowers. They are popular in corsages and for tall arrangements. Rigid boat-like bracts bear the showy blooms, part of which is a tongue formed by several petals. Yellow flowers combine with dark blue tongues and purple canoe-like bracts in one of nature's masterpieces. Although the plants can be started from divisions, suckers, or seeds, I advise buying started plants. If you start your own, it will be several years before you can enjoy flowers. Grow the plants in ground beds or in large pots or tubs. They need a deep, well-drained, rich soil.

Although they can be grown as cool as 50 degrees, you obtain more flowers at 55 to 60 degrees during the night. The soil should be enriched by frequent feedings. During the warmer months give some shade, but during the fall, winter, and early spring the plants should have full light.

Sweet pea (*Lathyrus odoratus*). Unless you have ample head room in your greenhouse, it is not a good idea to try sweet peas, however beautiful and lovely they are. Give sweet peas a loose, rich soil which is nearly neutral. The soil must be deep and well worked and the seeds planted directly where they are to grow. Work in an ample supply of cow manure into the row area before planting. Don't forget that sweet peas must have A-1 drainage. Good ventilation and careful application of air is necessary to prevent condensation on the vines, which could cause mildew. Copious amounts of water and regular feedings with a balanced fertilizer are necessary. Guard against sudden temperature changes, for sweet peas are temperamental and when this occurs they drop their buds.

Tithonia or Mexican sunflower (*Tithonia rotundifolia.*) This charmer produces rich-colored, orange-scarlet, daisy-like flowers. It does well in the greenhouse if grown around 52 to 58 degrees. To curb its rank growth, use shallow, well-drained soil that is not too rich. Give the plants full sunlight and plenty of ventilation. Grow on the dry side.

Venidium (*V. fastuosum*, Ball Hybrids). *V. fastuosum* is bright orange and the Ball Hybrids come in tones of salmon, buff, and bright orange. Also daisy-like flowers, venidiums differ from tithonias in that they require a rich, well-drained soil. Allow them 12 by 12-inch spacing. A raised bench is best and the plants should be kept a little on the dry side. An ideal temperature is 48 to 50 degrees. The plants should have plenty of ventilation and full sunlight. Give them support and feed sparingly, as needed, with a balanced fertilizer.

Wallflower (*Cheiranthus cheiri*). The wallflower is another almost overlooked flower which should be grown for cutting in the greenhouse. I particularly like the annual, Gold Standard. There is no orange quite like this one. Growth is not unlike that of stock and the plant has a lovely fragrance. Give wallflowers a moderately rich, well-drained and aerated soil. The plants should have good ventilation and plenty of water. They need full sunlight when they are growing and flowering. Use a balanced fertilizer on a regular schedule.

Zinnia. Almost all zinnias do well in the greenhouse. Their color and texture seems enhanced and they flower quite rapidly. Space the plants 4 by 5 or 4 by 6 inches, depending upon the variety, in a light, rich soil well supplied with organic matter and well drained. Give plenty of fresh air and full sunlight. Keep on the dry side and fertilize lightly every 2 to 3 weeks for best flower production. If you disbud the larger types to a single flower, you will be amazed at the size and quality blooms you will get.

Cut-flower Tips

Much can be done to keep cut flowers longer by handling them properly. Always remove them from the plants with a sharp knife, never shears which pinch the stems. Roses and many other hard-stemmed flowers will have longer vase life if the lower portion of the stems are scraped and thorns carefully removed.

Recut stems, remove lower foliage, and change the water frequently on flowers in the house. Clean out the vase or other container periodically with a good disinfectant. If you have a refrigerator in which you keep flowers, remove diseased blooms, petals, and leaves before storing. Always keep the refrigerator clean of plant debris. Never store fruits such as apples, bananas, avocados, lemons, etc., in the same refrigerator. Such fruits give off ethylene gas which adversely affects many cut flowers. Also, never store calla lilies, peonies, and hollyhocks in the same box with carnations and snapdragons. If you do, the carnations will go to sleep and the snapdragons will drop their florets.

Generally speaking, freshly cut flowers will do their best if the stems are first placed in pails of warm water (80 to 100 degrees) and then set in a cool place. When changing the water, however, use cool water.

There are some excellent flower preservatives on the market which you can use to add life to the cut flowers once they are placed in water. The cost is little and the results wonderful.

CHAPTER XXI

Growing Plants
for Outdoors

Almost all of us have our pet economies or, to put it another way, economical excuses for spending money in another way. I must confess that one of my biggest alibis for owning a home greenhouse was that it afforded me a means of growing annuals and bedding plants for my garden so I did not have to buy any. Imaginary savings or real, anyone who starts annuals in his own greenhouse always has the satisfaction of looking over his landscape and knowing that each annual he sees he started from a "pup."

Nothing stands still. Everything evolves and changes as progress is made. This is no less true with the procedures of growing plants in a greenhouse. Even the matter of what containers are used changes from time to time. Greenhouse flats are still the favored container for growing young bedding plants. I like the small insert flats developed the past few years. They make it possible to grow a dozen or so plants of a given variety, placing four or more of these midget flats in one large flat for easy handling. Commercial growers use these, too, as well as the traditional greenhouse size.

Tiny annual seedlings which are overcrowded require special attention in watering and feeding them, especially if they are left in the flats longer than they should be. It is best to move the plants from the flats as early as possible consistent with outdoor weather and the readiness of your flower beds. Extra feeding to hold them over in the flats a bit longer only results in making the plants taller than is desirable for safe transplanting into flower beds.

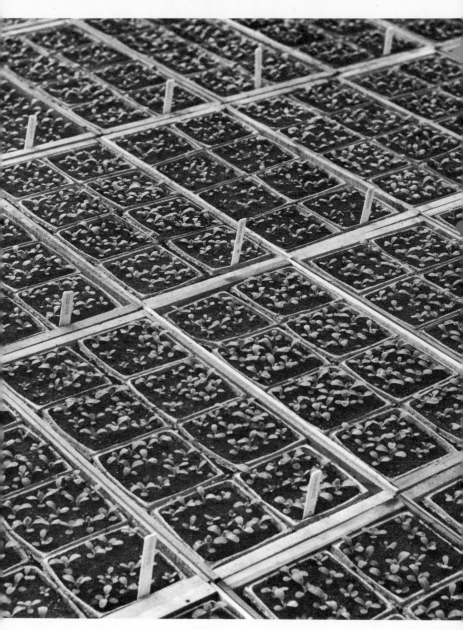

Bedding plants shown are planted 12 to a
"pony" flat, eight small flats to a regular flat.

Whatever way you use to provide additional room for your annuals is a good idea, since space is quite an acute problem at times. Some extra space can be provided by using shelves in the greenhouse. Don't overdo this, however, or too much shade will fall on the plants below.

The small "pony" flats are ideal inasmuch as they make it possible to plant smaller amounts of the individual annuals you wish to grow. In this way you are able to give them more individual care than you could otherwise. Even better than using small flats for your annuals is the idea of using pots of one sort or another.

Using a pot for each of the bedding plants you are growing assures them of ample room and the safest of transplanting conditions. When a plant is dug from a transplant flat, it is inevitable that some roots are injured. Also, soil falls from the root ball and this can create a hazard for the tiny plant. But any plant knocked out of a pot arrives in the flower bed outside with its roots undamaged and its root ball intact. I am not too much in favor of using small clay pots for bedding plants because they dry out rapidly and a tiny plant, once dehydrated, will quite likely not return to its former vigor. You can offset some of this danger from dehydration by placing your small pots in flats which have a layer of moss in the bottom. Some of this danger is also reduced by using plastic pots.

Plant bands are excellent for bedding plants. They supply the individual plants with more soil and their band-to-band placement assures the plants of greater moisture retention. There are plant bands made of various materials, such as veneer, tarpaper, etc. Some of these materials do not disintegrate rapidly in the soil and it is much better to remove them from the plant ball before setting your plants into flower beds. Those which are made of compressed manure or other materials need not be removed before planting.

My favorites are the peat pots. Peat pots assure your plants of even moisture at all times and when it comes to placing the plants in flower beds, the chore couldn't be simpler. You simply plant pot and all.

Just one more thing in regard to keeping your bedding plants in the greenhouse moist enough. Be sure to give extra attention to the plants which are closest to the edge of your benches and those which are on shelves. And make certain that flats and pots set level so that each and every one gets its just share of water.

Perhaps we'd better say a little more about soil and soil sterilization. Bedding plants are highly susceptible to damp-off and other soil-borne diseases. If you sterilize your soil, not only will you prevent some of the diseases such as damp-off from taking place, but you will also get rid of weed seed. If you have ever weeded many flats of annuals in the spring, you know what a chore this can be.

If your greenhouse is sizable enough to grow quite a few flats of bedding plants, you will certainly appreciate having a soil shredder. It can reduce hours of labor to minutes and the results of preparing and mixing the soil are much better than by hand. I have already mentioned the use of shelves to give you additional space for bedding plants in the spring. By looking around your greenhouse you can undoubtedly find other places which will serve as extra room on a temporary basis. Try using some of the aisle space next to the walls. You might even find it possible to place shelves beneath the benches, provided you can give the plants supplementary lighting.

Birds and rodents probably cause more trouble to bedding plants grown in greenhouses than you might imagine. You can screen the birds out. And be sure to keep an eye open for rodents which might tunnel in. Trap or otherwise rid the greenhouse of them immediately.

Use your coldframes and hotbeds in every way possible to relieve the space pressure in your greenhouse. If you followed the advice given in Chapter VIII, you have your coldframes placed so that there is little danger due to poor drainage or other matters. Be sure to keep the weeds and grass down around your coldframes to help control pests and diseases as well as eliminate unsightliness. Use every care as you water your bedding plants in the frames so that they do not suffer damage. For one thing, use an extension nozzle to gently apply the water close to the plants. Use rollers or a piece of pipe at each corner of the frame past which you pull the hose.

Timing Annuals

You may have wondered how it is possible for commercial greenhouse growers to bring in their spring plants at the right time each year. First of all, the commercial grower knows how long it takes to germinate each and every one of the flowers or vegetables that he grows and how long it will take to get them to the right size for planting outdoors.

You, too, should have a fairly good idea of when to start the various things you wish to grow. The chart in this chapter will help you with much of this information, but you should also keep your own records, for individual growing conditions produce individual results. Your preferences when it comes to the time for moving plants outdoors may also be different from those preferred by others. In order to know when to start your seedlings, it is necessary to know how long it takes to mature your various kinds of flowers and vegetable plants to the proper stage for transplanting outdoors. The most desirable plants for this purpose are those which are short, stocky, and ready to plant out while growing vigorously. The secret of producing these kinds is to grow plants cool and give them ample sunlight. As soon as the seeds have germinated, bedding plants should be moved to a cooler place (but where the temperature is not too cold). Then they should go into the coldframe as they reach the setting-out stage to harden them off before exposure to the outdoor temperatures.

From 4 to 5 weeks are required to produce flatted marigolds, calendulas, and zinnias of the proper size to set out. From 6 to 8 weeks are required for celosia, cleome, balsam, *Phlox drummondi,* portulaca, torenia, Unwin dahlias, verbenas, eggplants, peppers, and tomato plants. Allow 7 to 9 weeks for ageratum, nicotiana, snapdragons, petunia, salvia, *Vinca rosea,* and sweet alyssum.

Why Annuals?

If you need any convincing, here are a dozen mighty good reasons why you should consider annuals for your yard: (1) They flower profusely. Many annuals produce a blaze of color throughout the summer. (2) Annuals are less costly than other plants. A few dozen annuals represent only a small cost when you can grow them yourself from seed. (3) Most annuals bloom for a longer period than shrubs, perennials, or trees. (4) There is an annual for every garden purpose. (5) You can teach junior a lesson in neatness, persistence, and beauty by letting him plant and care for some annuals all his own. (6) For cutting, annuals are superb. (7) Whether you live in a castle or a cottage, annuals are appropriate. (8) Spaces emptied by plants which have been winter-killed are quickly filled with annuals. (9) If you have some unsightly objects in your yard, hide them with tall, rapid-growing annuals. (10) Some such as African marigolds make wonderful summer hedges.

(11) Places calling for climbers or vines can be filled beautifully with annuals. (12) If you like everlastings or strawflowers, you will find them among annuals.

Among the annuals which are preferred by most people are these: Candytuft (*Iberis*); flossflower (*Ageratum*); heliotrope (*Heliotropium*)—not an annual but often treated as one; geranium (*Pelargonium*)—also not an annual; marigold, French and African (*Tagetes*); mignonette (*Reseda*); nasturtium (*Tropaeolum*); pansy (*Viola tricolor*); petunia (*Petunia*); pot marigold (*Calendula*); scabious (*Scabiosa*); snapdragon (*Antirrhinum*). Among perennials treated as annuals are: stock (*Mathiola*); sweet alyssum (*Lobularia*); sweet sultan (*Centaurea moschata*); tobacco, ornamental (*Nicotiana*); verbena (*Verbena*).

Hints To Heed

Perhaps a few reminders or additional thoughts might be well on certain plants which you will be interested in as bedding plants.

Begonias were pretty well covered in Chapter XVII. My favorite way of starting the tubers is in flats or waxed cartons which are half-filled with peatmoss. Once again, let me emphasize that they must be kept moist. Here is my favorite soil mixture for tuberous begonias and fuchsias: 1 part each of good loam and sand and 2 parts each of well-rotted manure and compost or oak leafmold.

Cannas are old-fashioned favorites from grandma's day. My favorite way of starting the tuberous roots is in flats filled with a 50–50 mixture of soil and sand (you can use straight sand). As soon as rooting has started well, pot the tubers in 4 or 5-inch pots. Some gardeners prefer to start them directly in the pots. This is all right, too. At the start, water cannas carefully, increasing the water as they begin to grow.

Coltness and Unwin **dahlias** are perky little plants which bloom throughout the entire summer outdoors. Check Chapter XVII for their culture. You can grow them in pots or plant bands and those tubers planted outdoors may be dug in the fall and used again the following year.

Fuchsias are wonderful plants for shady areas, producing an abundance of flowers. There have been many wonderful new varieties developed during the past years and their culture has been much encouraged and emphasized by fuchsia societies which exist throughout the United States. Start fuchsias from terminal cuttings, which can be taken from fall until spring. Use a sharp, sterile knife for the purpose, never shears. Root fuchsia cuttings with 60-degree bottom heat and then grow them at 50 to 55 degrees. Keep the plants moist but not overly wet. Pay especially close attention to fuchsias grown as hanging baskets so that they do not dry out.

Geraniums are another one of those old-time favorites that grandma liked so well. Though they are not annuals, they are treated as such. Geraniums need plenty of fresh air, the more the better. Grow them at 50 to 55 degrees and give them full light. It is a fallacy to believe that geraniums do not like good watering. The trick is to water them well when they need it and then allow them to approach the dry side before watering them again. They prefer low humidity. A good soil mixture for geraniums consists of 1 part well-rotted manure to 3 parts of sandy loam. Add some superphosphate to the soil. Be sure that ample drainage material is used in the bottom of the pot. Geraniums do their best when fed monthly with superphosphate.

Both **marigolds** and **zinnias** are discussed in Chapter XX. They are among the most colorful of annuals which you can use in your yard. Tall African marigolds and the giant zinnias make a beautiful background to intermingle with perennials and shrubs in your borders. Dwarf French marigolds and the dwarf zinnias are lovely edging flowers. The large marigolds and zinnias can be used in hedge-like fashion. Provide both marigolds and zinnias with full sun and give them a fairly rich, well-drained soil. Both marigolds and zinnias respond well to pinching to provide greater branching of the plants. A common mistake is to start French marigolds and zinnias too early. The seeds germinate quite rapidly and before you realize it, they are ready to transplant into your flower beds.

Pansies are dealt with under Chapter XX, insofar as greenhouse culture is concerned. But the pansies which you produce for outdoor use are generally sown outside in late July or early August. They can be sown in some areas in open beds if there is no danger of them becoming too dry. Usually, however, they are sown in coldframes. Then the plants are transplanted and spaced properly in the beds where they are to be grown. I like to hurry them a bit by planting the seedlings in plant bands or peat pots and then taking them into a cool greenhouse where they will develop into good, full-fledged plants, complete with blooms, and ready to set out in the yard in early spring.

Petunias rank high on a list, if not at the top, of those annuals which are used to brighten the landscape. There are so many lovely varieties now, especially those of the F_1 type. Petunia breeders over the years have developed plants which grow to a modest height and which produce a continuous abundance of flowers throughout the summer until frost cuts them down. Petunia seed is extra fine. Check Chapter XIII for the best methods of sowing fine seed.

Petunia seed should be germinated at 65 degrees and the plants grown at 45 to 50 degrees. You may grow petunias in flats, of course, but it is best to grow them in pots, plant bands, or peat pots. I prefer the latter. Give the plants a loamy well-drained soil. A good mixture is 1 part each of sand, peatmoss, and well-rotted manure and 2 parts of loam. To a bushel of this mixture, add a 3-inch potful of superphosphate and mix the ingredients thoroughly.

Snapdragon culture is covered quite thoroughly in Chapter XX. They are a wonderful flower for the garden. Actually, snapdragons are tender perennials but they are always used as annuals in the garden. Inside and outside be sure to give them good drainage and a near-neutral soil.

There are also some fine **vines** which you can start in the greenhouse for outdoor use. These include the green and variegated ivies and these are covered in Chapter XVIII on foliage plants, and then there are others such as trailing lobelias, Mexican ivy (*Cobaea scandens*), and German or parlor ivy. Southerners are very familiar with German ivy. Start this from cuttings for the quickest results. Plants which you have outside should be brought in before frost hits them to serve as stock plants. Preferred temperature for German ivy is 50 to 55 degrees.

Fragrant plants are always a hit in the garden. They are always something to which you can point with pride and suggest that visitors test with a sniff. Among the best of the fragrant plants you can start are scented-leaf geraniums, heliotropes, and lemon verbenas.

There are a good many other annuals, of course, which will provide an abundance of color and interest to your garden. Coleus, impatiens, ageratum, and verbena will splash the garden with color. The same thing can be said of mesembryanthemums, abutilons, echeverias, salpiglossis, pennisetums, schizanthus, campanulas, astilbes, alternantheras, and many others. Give a thought to growing gourds as something unusual that you can carry over into fall and winter by way of the fruit which you may harvest and prepare for indoor display. Most of the plants recommended in this paragraph are best started in plant bands or peat pots.

And don't forget the many wonderful vegetable plants which you can grow for your vegetable garden. Start early in the spring with head lettuce, cabbage, cauliflower, and Brussels sprouts. These can be followed by the more tender plants such as tomatoes, eggplants, peppers, and others. The early vegetables should be grown at 50 to 55 degrees and the more tender ones grown at 58 to 60 degrees. Choose good, up-to-date varieties and buy the best of seed.

Greenhouse Bedding-plant Sowings

Probably more home greenhouse owners are interested in starting bedding plants from seed than any other plants. With that in mind the following chart was devised for quick reference.

The best average germinating temperatures for bedding-plant seeds are 65 to 75 degrees. Optimum night growing temperature for annuals while in the greenhouse are 45 to 50 degrees.

Principal plants grown from seed for cut flowers and potted plants are not found in the chart below. They are listed in a chart found in Chapter XIII.

KEY TO BEDDING PLANT SOWINGS

SOWING TIME: 3—Sow indoors 3 months before time to plant outdoors; 2—2 months; 1—1 month.

COLORS: W—white. Y—yellow. O—orange. P—pink. Ro—rose. R—red. B—blue. L—lavender. V—violet. Cr—crimson. Co—copper. S—salmon. Sc—scarlet. Bu—buff. M—maroon. Mah—mahogany.

DAYS TO GERMINATE: Number of days required for seeds to germinate under good growing conditions.

SEED LONGEVITY: The number of years seeds may be kept under good storage conditions and still give fair germination.

SUN OR SHADE: S—Full sun. PSh—Partial shade; needs shade in heat of day to do well. Sh—No full sun, shade.

HEIGHT: All heights given in inches. Wide range in height indicates dwarf and large forms.

OUTDOOR BLOOM TIME: 5—May; 6—June; 7—July; 8—August; 9—September; 10—October. First bloom given as if planted at earliest possible date. Period of bloom often covers a succession of plantings.

USES: Extra uses or special uses: E—edging. R—rock garden. C—cut flowers. Cor—corsage flower. Ev—everlasting, good for winter bouquets. Comb—combination pots. P—good as pot plant. V—annual vine.

PROPER NAME OF FLOWER / COMMON NAME	SOWING TIME	COLORS	DAYS TO GERMINATE	SEED LONGEVITY	SUN OR SHADE	HEIGHT INCHES	OUTDOOR BLOOM TIME	USES
Ageratum houstonianum Flossflower	3	LBWP	14	4	S	8–12	7–8–9–10	**ECombP**
Anchusa capensis Cape bugloss	2	B	—	—	S-PSh	18	7–8–9–10	C
Antirrhinum majus Snapdragon	3	WYPCoCr	10–14	3–4	S-PSh	12–36	7–8–9–10	C
Arctotis stoechadifolia African daisy	3	WYPML CrO	21	—	S	10–12	7–8–9–10	C
Brachycome iberidifolia Swan River daisy	2	BRoWV	10	3–4	S	9–12	7–8–9	E
Browallia speciosa Amethyst	2	BW	28–40	2–3	S	10–18	6–7–8–9–10	CPV
Calendula officinalis Pot marigold	1	BuYORo	14	**5–6**	S-PSh	15–24	7–8–9–10	C
Callistephus chinensis China aster	2	WPRoLV	8–12	1–2	S-PSh	18–36	7–8–9–10	—
Celosia argentea cristata Crested cockscomb	2	YOCrVR	6–10	4	S	10–18	7–8–9	CComb
Celosia argentea plumosa Feather cockscomb	2	YORCr	6–10	4	S	12–36	7–8–9	CComb
Centaurea americana Basket flower	2	WLP	20–30	1–2	S-PSh	36	7–8–9	C
Centaurea cyanus Cornflower	2	WBVCrMP	15	3	S-PSh	24–30	6–7–8–9	CCor
Centaurea imperialis Sweet sultan	2	WPYRoL	15	1–2	S-PSh	18–30	7–8–9	CCor

PROPER NAME OF FLOWER COMMON NAME	SOWING TIME	COLORS	DAYS TO GERMINATE	SEED LONGEVITY	SUN OR SHADE	HEIGHT INCHES	OUTDOOR BLOOM TIME	USES
Chrysanthemum coronarium Crown daisy	2	WPYCr	11–18	4–5	S	18	7-8-9	C
Cleome spinosa Spiderflower	2	PY	21	—	S	36–48	7-8-9	—
Cobaea scandens Purplebell	2	BV	15–20	2	S	Vine	7-8-9	V
Coreopsis drummondi Calliopsis	1	YMah	14	2–3	S	9–36	6-7-8-9-10	C
Cosmos bipinnatus Cosmos	1	RoPW	10–14	3–4	S	36–60	7-8-9-10	C
Cosmos sulphureus Yellow cosmos	2	YO	14	—	S	36–48	8-9-10	C
Cynoglossum amabile Chinese forget-me-not	2	BW	10	2–3	S-PSh	30	6-7-8	—
Dianthus caryophyllus Carnation	3	PRWYS	10	4–5	S	15–18	6-7-8-9-10	CCor
Dimorphotheca aurantiaca Cape marigold	2	WYOS	15–21	1	S	12	7-8-9	—
Erysimum perofskianum Annual wallflower	2	YMah	10–14	5	S	12–24	8-9-10	—
Gaillardia pulchella Rosering gaillardia	2	YOM	15–20	2	S	15–24	6-7-8-9-10	C
Godetia grandiflora Satinflower	2	RoLWPCr	15	3	PSh	12–20	6-7-8-9-10	EC
Gomphrena globosa Globe amaranth	2	WPCr	15	2–3	S	18–24	7-8-9	CEv

PROPER NAME OF FLOWER / COMMON NAME	SOWING TIME	COLORS	DAYS TO GERMINATE	SEED LONGEVITY	SUN OR SHADE	HEIGHT INCHES	OUTDOOR BLOOM TIME	USES
Gypsophila elegans Baby's breath	Succ.	WPRo	10–14	2	S–PSh	12–15	7–8–9	EC
Helichrysum bracteatum Strawflower	2	WPYOCrRo	14	1–2	S	30	8–9	CEvCor
Helipterum roseum Rose sunray	2	WPRo	14	3	S	15	7–8	CEv
Hunnemannia fumariaefolia Santa Barbara poppy	2	Y	14	2	S	24	7–8–9–10	C
Iberis umbellata Globe candytuft	Succ.	WPLRo	14	2–3	S–PSh	12–18	6–7–8–9–10	C
Impatiens balsamina Garden balsam	2	WLPR	15	2	PSh	8–30	8–9	CombP
Lavatera trimestris Herb tree mallow	2	PW	14–35	4–5	PSh–Sh	24–36	7–8–9–10	C
Limonium sinuatum Notchleaf sea lavender	2	WYRoBL	14–21	2–3	S	24–30	7–8–9	CEvCor
Linum grandiflorum Flowering flax	2	Cr	14	5	S	15–18	5–6–7–8–9–10	C
Lobelia erinus Edging lobelia	3	BW	10–15	3–4	S–PSh	4–10	7–8–9–10	ECombP
Lobularia maritima Sweet alyssum	2–Succ.	WV	10–20	4	S–PSh–Sh	4–8	5–6–7–8–9–10	ECombP
Lupinus pubescens Annual lupine	2	BRoW	10	2	PSh	12–24	7–8	C
Mathiola incana Annual stock	2	WPLC	6–10	5–6	S	15–30	7–8–9	C

191

PROPER NAME OF FLOWER / COMMON NAME	SOWING TIME	COLORS	DAYS TO GERMINATE	SEED LONGEVITY	SUN OR SHADE	HEIGHT INCHES	OUTDOOR BLOOM TIME	USES
Myosotis alpestris Forget-me-not	3	WRoB	14	2	PSh	12	5–6–7–8–9–10	REC
Nicotiana alata Winged tobacco	3	WPCr	10	3–4	S–PSh	15–30	6–7–8–9–10	—
Nierembergia hippomanica Dwarf cupflower	3	LBV	—	—	S	6	7–8–9–10	REP
Petunia hybrida Common petunia	3	PSRoWLV	10	2–3	S–PSh	10–18	7–8–9–10	CCombP
Phaseolus coccineus Scarlet runner bean	3	Sc	7–10	—	S–PSh	Vine	7–8–9	C
Phlox drummondi Drummond phlox	2	WYBuSCrVP	10–15	1–2	S	10–20	7–8–9	C
Portulaca grandiflora Rose moss	2	PRSCrWYO	14	3	S	4–6	7–8–9–10	RE
Reseda odorata Mignonette	2	YCoCrW	11–14	2–4	PSh	12–18	7–8–9–10	C
Salpiglossis sinuata Painted tongue	3	YVLCrW	14	6–7	S–PSh	30	7–8–9–10	C
Salvia farinacea Mealycup sage	3	B	15–20	—	S	30	7–8–9–10	C
Salvia splendens Scarlet sage	3	Sc	14	1	S	10–24	8–9–10	—
Sanvitalia procumbens Creeping zinnia	2	Y	10	4–5	S	6–10	6–7–8–9–10	E
Scabiosa atropurpurea Pincushion flower	2	WLPMRo	14–21	2–3	S	24–36	7–8–9–10	C

PROPER NAME OF FLOWER / COMMON NAME	SOWING TIME	COLORS	DAYS TO GERMINATE	SEED LONGEVITY	SUN OR SHADE	HEIGHT INCHES	OUTDOOR BLOOM TIME	USES
Tagetes erecta African marigold	1	YO	8	2–3	S	24–36	7–8–9–10	C
Tagetes patula French marigold	1	YOMah	8	2–3	S	8–15	6–7–8–9–10	ECComb
Thunbergia alata Black-eyed clockvine	2	WYBuO	21	2	S	Vine	7–8–9	V
Tithonia rotundifolia Mexican sunflower	3	Ro	25	2	S	72	9–10	—
Trachymene caerulea Blue lace flower	2	LB	12–14	2–3	PSh	18–30	7–8–9–10	CCor
Verbena hortensis Garden verbena	2	WPRoSLV	14	1	S–PSh	8–18	7–8–9–10	CCombP
Zinnia elegans Common zinnia	1	WYOPRo	5–10	6–7	S	12–36	7–8–9–10	C

Hanging Baskets

Among the most fascinating plants which you can grow in your greenhouse are the drooping or hanging sorts that you can use in hanging pots or baskets. Hanging baskets are used both outdoors and indoors: the outdoor ones in shaded parts of the yard; the indoor baskets on porches, in sun rooms, as well as in the greenhouse itself.

Fuchsia Pink Galore, lovely hanging basket variety.

Once your cuttings are rooted and the young plants are set into the hanging baskets there is no bench space used. The suspended baskets add nothing more to the cost of heating your greenhouse, merely using space that otherwise is not used for growing purposes. Be careful, however, not to overdo the idea lest you throw too much shade on the other plants.

CHOOSING THE RIGHT PLANTS

The species and varieties which you choose for hanging baskets, pots, or boxes are largely a matter of personal taste. But you must consider how plants are to be used. Some plants are interchangeable. They can be used indoors or outdoors. But, by and large, those which do best outdoors will not do as well indoors and vice versa. You must also consider the room you have available. If your space is considerable, the larger hanging plants such as fuchsias, tuberous begonias, and petunias are ideal. If the space is restricted, stick to smaller and daintier things such as ivy geraniums, and ivy.

Use good judgment as you select plants for various spots. Don't expect fuchsias, begonias, or foliage plants to thrive in the sun—or for geraniums, lantanas, petunias, and most annuals to do well on a shaded porch or beneath a large shade tree.

Here are the plants which are the most popular and easy to train for hanging basket use:

Achimene. There are a number of varieties which do well in hanging baskets. They like the shady areas which are more or less draft free. For cultural information check Chapter XVII.

Begonia, tuberous. There are some gorgeous tuberous begonias which may be used for hanging baskets. They are also ideal for semi-shaded garden houses or for hanging anywhere the hot afternoon sun is avoided. Check Chapter XVII for culture.

Campanula. One of the best of the campanulas for trailing effects is *Campanula isophylla,* the star-of-Bethlehem. This plant requires considerable pinching during early growth to cause it to branch freely and produce an effective, breathtaking plant. This species can be started from divisions, spring cuttings or seed. They do best in a rich soil. Feed them in spring with well-rotted manure and bonemeal. Feed two or three times during growing season with a balanced fertilizer. Never crowd campanulas. Keep moist.

Episcia cupreata. This is one of the loveliest plants to use in hanging pots or baskets in semi-shaded areas indoors or out. Plants are best started by leaf cuttings or runners. Once the runners are rooted properly, they may be placed directly into a hanging basket. Use two or three plants. These plants like a temperature of 65 to 75 degrees. Do not place them outdoors until temperatures have moderated in late spring or early summer. Use the same soil as recommended for African violets in Chapter XVII. The episcia should be kept on the moist side at all times. Feed as recommended for other foliage plants in Chapter XVIII.

Fuchsia. The trailing fuchsias make some of the most spectacular of all the hanging baskets. Be sure you do not try to use the upright sorts for this purpose. The trailing ones should be pinched in the center to get the lateral shots started well. These laterals will quickly begin their trailing. For complete information see pages 185–186.

Ivy. There are a number of ivies which do well in either sun or shade. See Chapter XVIII for their culture.

Ivy geranium. The ivy geranium is a natural for hanging pots and baskets and it likes full sun. It will generally survive in areas where other plants will not. Check Chapter XXI for geranium culture.

Lantana, drooping. The drooping lantanas make excellent hanging plants. As with fuchsias, pinch out the center tip to get good lateral growth started. It likes full sun. Check page 199.

Petunia. For a blaze of color in the full sun it is very hard to beat certain varieties of petunias for hanging basket use. Try the Cascade varieties or others recommended for balcony or bedding use. Check Chapter XXI for growing preferences.

Piper ornatum. Commonly called Celebes pepper, this attractive plant has heart-shaped short, pointed leaves which run from 2 to 4 inches wide and from 2½ to 5 inches long. The foliage is shiny, bright green, and new growth has pinkish white spots on it. It must have a well-drained soil and one which is high in organic matter. Grow it at a temperature of 50 degrees. You can propagate it from half-ripened wood using bottom heat. It is a beautiful hanging basket or bowl plant for shady areas.

Thunbergia. Thunbergia belong to the acanthus family and are tender climbing plants from tropical regions. Propagated by seeds, cuttings or layers. Although other species of thunbergia can be used in baskets, the best one for this purpose is *T. grandiflora* or skyflower, the most common of the blue kinds. It has large heart-shaped leaves and bell-shaped flowers. It makes a fine plant for full sun.

Wandering Jew. This is probably the best known of all vining plants, having been grown for generations. There are some excellent varieties available. Its common name of spiderwort is probably just as well forgotten but don't be fooled by the name. Some of these plants have spectacular variations in foliage color. Wandering Jew also flowers, although the flowers are not too significant. It makes an excellent hanging basket for sun or shade. Check Chapter XVIII for further information.

CONTAINERS

There are many different sizes and shapes of containers used for hanging baskets. There are clay baskets, redwood ones, and the traditional wire baskets lined with sphagnum or green tree moss. Be sure there are adequate drainage holes in the solid type such as clay pots or plastic containers.

It is very important, too, to provide hanging baskets with a well-prepared soil which drains. It is also important that the soil contain ample humus so that it will retain enough moisture to hold the plant over for several hours at a time. Baskets may be planted singly or you may choose combinations of the same type of plants or various types of plants. The important thing to remember is to place plants together which are compatible, especially in light preference.

While the young plants are growing to the size you want, before hanging them in their showplace, continue a liquid feeding with a balanced fertilizer. Liquid fish fertilizer is often preferred for this purpose, especially for tuberous begonias, fuchsias, and the like. The liquid fertilizing should continue through the summer.

Never allow a hanging basket to dry out completely. Keep it on the moist side, insofar as possible. This may mean that the basket hanging outside may require more than one watering on some days.

PLANTING A WIRE BASKET. When planting a wire basket line it with sphagnum or green tree moss. If the latter is used, place the more attractive side out. Next, place 3 or 4 inches of well-prepared potting soil in the bottom and firm it slightly.

Now you are ready for placement of the plants. Choose only thrifty ones which offer the promise of an attractive hanging basket. Set one or more of the plants on the soil in the bottom of the basket and fill more soil around each plant, firming it as you go. If the plants have been started in peat pots, plant pots and all.

Following the planting, soak the basket thoroughly. In order to get sufficient water at the top of your basket without run-off be sure that sufficient space is left when planting. Both soil and moss should be moist at the time of planting. If at any time water does not seem to be penetrating all parts of the basket, lower it into a shallow pan of water and allow it to draw moisture from below.

Perennials and Shrubs To Force

There are a good many beautiful perennials and shrubs which can be forced in the greenhouse and the plants then used in your home or elsewhere. You can start many different perennials from seed and some from cuttings in a cool greenhouse. Check Chapter XIII to get complete information. If you force perennials inside, do this by using clumps or divisions of clumps which are brought into the greenhouse for this purpose. Divisions may include chunks cut from or broken from the original clumps or they may refer to suckers or stolons divided from the main plant.

Generally speaking, the shrubs you start in your greenhouse for landscape use require a very cool temperature. In fact, propagation in many instances calls only for bottom heat and enough air temperature to prevent severe freezing. However, if you are forcing various shrubs as potted or tubbed plants or for cut-flower purposes, use mature plants and warmer temperatures. Here are some of the unusual shrubs you might consider for this purpose:

Acacia. Among the acacias are various ones which do well when forced. Cuttings of half-ripened wood with a heel are rooted in a cool temperature. Use a medium of sand and peatmoss. Grow acacias at 45 to 50 degrees and do not attempt to force them with higher temperatures. Give them a soil which contains ample leaf-mold and is sandy enough to provide good drainage. Plants must be well watered but never overwet. Give them good sunlight and moderate ventilation. After flowering cut the plants back.

Acalypha (*A. hispida*). This is the lovely chenille plant described in Chapter XVII.

African hemp (*Sparmannia*). This is a most unusual plant with dense, hairy foliage and heavy-bloom heads. It is a member of the linden family. Propagated from cuttings made in April which should be kept well shaded, then grow in a rich soil consisting of loam, peat, and sand. Give it full sunlight, good ventilation and a 45 to 55 degree temperature.

Centropogon. *C. lucyanus* is a lovely variety of this plant which has tubular flowers of a rosy-carmine hue and shiny green foliage which is saw-edged. The plants are started from cuttings and then grown in well-drained, fibrous loam. Grow the plant at 60 to 65 degrees F.

Hebe. *Hebe speciosa* and *H. traversi* are most frequently grown. The former has reddish-purple flowers and growth of about 5 feet. The latter has smaller white flowers and the same height. Start the plants from either cuttings or seeds. They should have a well-drained soil which is moderately fertile, good air circulation, and a temperature of 50 to 55 degrees.

Lantana. The lantanas are old-time bedding plant favorites which are often grown, especially in the far South, as large shrubs. They have handsome foliage and lovely clusters of brilliant orange, yellow, pink, or red flowers. They should be started from seeds or cuttings and grown at 60 to 65 degrees F. Give them a well-drained, moderately rich soil and keep them moist but not wet. They require good ventilation and should be pruned back severely in late spring. Such carry-over plants should then be repotted into fresh soil.

Mexican orange (*Choisya ternata*). This a lovely plant which will bloom for several months with white flowers like orange blossoms. Its handsome foliage is leathery and bright green. Give it a well-drained, light soil. Keep it on the dry side and give it good ventilation. It does best at 50 to 55 degrees.

Oleander (*Nerium oleander*). There probably is no one in the South who does not know and admire the oleander. It is a handsome evergreen which produces large clusters of beautiful flowers. It should be started from cuttings of mature wood and plants grown in a good loam soil. Feed the plants well during their growing period and always give them ample fresh air and sunlight.

Yellow or East Indian flax (*Reinwardtia*). This handsome shrubby plant has flowers of a beautiful bright yellow. It is grown from cuttings taken from basal shoots. The young plants should be pinched back to promote good branching and a more compact growth. Grow them at 50 to 65 degrees and use a sandy loam soil which contains a good quantity of leafmold and some well-rotted manure. They can be grown in 5-inch or 6-inch pots. Guard against red spiders.

CHAPTER XXII

Orchids Deserve a Chapter of Their Own

Beware! Never buy a single orchid plant—unless you have plans to expand the growing of orchids a great deal or are strong enough to resist the temptation. Orchids have a way of "getting" to anyone with a home greenhouse. Perhaps it is the exotic nature of orchids or, on the other hand, it could be the recollection of the cost of the last orchid corsage purchased at a florist shop that tempts many to grow their own.

Generally speaking, orchids are not the kind of plants which you mix with others in a home greenhouse. There are some exceptions, however, such as the terrestrial orchids—cymbidiums and cypripediums. Even so, their companion plants should be well chosen.

It is a bit costly to get started with the growing of orchids. One does not sow a few seeds or take some cuttings as a starting point. Instead, unless you are someone with infinite patience, the correct way to get started is by purchasing mature plants. True, orchid hybridists start their orchid seed in flasks of agar. Then, under conditions of sanitation that would do justice to a modern hospital, the young seedlings are nursed through multiple and finally singular pottings until a total of about seven years has elapsed, in the case of cattleya orchid, before flowers are received and the grower knows just what he has achieved with this new hybrid plant. The result may be something outstanding or it may be worthless. The very fact that orchid hybridists and commercial growers are always seeking larger, more substantial, and richer-colored flowers makes it possible for amateur growers to buy plants at reduced prices quite often. If you have become bitten by the orchid bug, contact some of the commercial growers to see if they have such plants available. Regardless of whether you buy new or old varieties, however, buy from reliable dealers and have some idea of what sort of plants you are obtaining and what kind of flowers the varieties you buy will produce.

Although I certainly wouldn't advise that you buy orchid seedlings in a flask, unless you have some previous experience in handling these tiny and delicate young plants, you can buy them in community pots for growing them on to maturity. This also requires some basic understanding of young orchids and, as mentioned before, considerable patience to grow them to maturity. My suggestion is to start with a few mature plants, according to what the budget allows. Then, perhaps, supplement your stock of orchids with young plants in 1½, 2, 3, or 4-inch pots. Or you can buy the semi-dormant root-like bulbs called "back" bulbs which have been cut from established plants or divisions of established plants. Again, I want to caution you to buy from a reliable person who will be sure to see that you receive divisions which have healthy pseudo-bulbs.

If you should ask a commercial grower which types are the most popular, besides the cattleyas, he would undoubtedly name the cymbidiums and cypripediums. Both of these belong in the semi-terrestrial group and have rather fleshy root systems. They will grow quite well in a porous soil. Most popular of the terrestrial group are the calanthes. With almost any good soil, you can produce good calanthes.

Baskets, Pots, and Other Containers

There probably never existed a gardener, either the outdoor variety or one with a greenhouse, who did not possess some of the venturesome spirit which makes him want to try new and "unheard of" ideas once in a while. My only advice where orchids are concerned is to remind you that orchids are costly and time-consuming to raise and it might be well to restrict your experimental thoughts somewhat. But perhaps as you hear of things that others have tried and you get the feel of growing orchids, you will learn that orchids, like most other flowers, are subject to cultural practices not always found in books.

Perhaps the most unusual idea I ever noticed was that used by a commercial orchid grower. In his houses he built tents of overlapping rough cedar planks. At the peak of each tent he ran a perforated water line. Through this line each day was pumped a weak nutrient solution that trickled through the holes and spread over the planks. The roots of his semi-epiphytes (mostly cattleyas) picked up food from the saturated boards. Overflow nutrient water was collected in troughs at the bottom and pumped back to the central tank. This grower had the system hooked up with a timing device so that the nutrient water was pumped over the tents for a given period each day.

It seems wisest, however, for most amateurs to stick with conventional containers. Wooden baskets, boxes, or clay pots are popular. Some orchids, such as cypripediums, cymbidiums, and calanthes, can be grown in benches. I know one grower who goes out into the woods where pine and fir needles have dropped and decayed by the millions, scoops up the top layer of soil which contains needles in all degrees of decay and rotting wood, and grows terrestrial and semi-terrestrial orchids in this. What's more, he does an excellent job.

My preference is for a tier of shelves, four high, in step fashion which allows each shelf of plants to have full exposure to light and air circulation. The shelves should be built of sturdy, long-lasting material such as redwood or treated cedar slats. Allow an inch between each slat. Galvanized hardware cloth is an excellent substitute for the slats.

Potting Orchids

Potting terrestrial or semi-terrestrial orchids is similar to potting other plants. Be sure the soil is tucked firmly about the roots and do everything possible to avoid damaging them.

Potting with osmunda fiber, the roots of *Osmunda cinnamomea* fern, is quite another story. The main thing to remember is that great care must be used in packing this fiber in tightly against the plant roots. If you want to learn the intricacies of handling osmunda fiber, consult a book on orchids or a commercial orchid grower. Shredded cedar or redwood tree bark, haydite, silica, gravel, and various other inert materials are also being used by orchid growers today for non-terrestrial orchids. However, it is hard to beat osmunda fiber, once you know how to use it. No matter what medium is used, seek one which supplies good drainage, aeration, and support for your plant.

Too much moisture about the roots of an orchid creates an intolerable condition. Give only as much water as the plant can properly absorb. More orchid growers get into trouble with their plants through overpotting than any other way, simply because too much medium creates too great a reservoir of moisture.

A community pot of orchid seedlings usually contains from 5 to 25 tiny plants. The next step in the potting is to place each individual plant into a 1½-inch pot. Be extremely careful with the root system so that it will not be damaged. To learn the technique of potting visit an experienced commercial or amateur orchid grower. You will note they never hurry when potting. If it takes you a half hour or longer to pot a single large plant, compliment yourself for doing the job carefully.

About a year and a half is the usual length of time for keeping a young orchid plant in a 1½-inch pot. From then on until the plant has reached maturity, repot every two years. (Check the portions of this chapter dealing with specific genera for special information about timing and repotting.)

Here is the way to pot a mature orchid: Fill the bottom third or half of the pot, basket, or box with broken crock (pieces of flower pot). Over this place a layer of moist shredded osmunda, gravel, or other inert material. Spread the roots of the plant evenly over the osmunda as you place the plant in the pot. If you are using osmunda, shredded bark, gravel, perlite, or other such material, compress the medium about the roots very tightly using the rounded end of a dibble stick or fingers to do so. If you use vermiculite, however, do not compress it. Be sure the osmunda fibers run parallel. Another "must" is placing the oldest pseudo-bulb close to the side of the pot (no more than ¼ inch, in fact). This allows ample growing space for the plant. There are two other important matters you must consider when using osmunda for orchids. Be sure that the fiber is evenly placed in the pot to insure even water distribution and an equalized breakdown of the osmunda fiber. All excess osmunda should be trimmed off flush with the pot.

Humidity and Ventilation

Orchids are quite fussy about humidity even though the humidity needed varies with the genus of orchid. Those which require lower light intensity need lower humidity than other orchids. Higher relative humidity is necessary for those orchids which require high light intensity. The temperature must also be considered in regard to humidity. When temperatures decrease the humidity requirement is less; when the temperature increases, greater humidity is necessary. When light intensity is high, it takes higher relative humidity to prevent burning of orchid plants.

Proper control of ventilation ties in with moisture. Except under very dire weather conditions, orchids should have some ventilation every day. This is the only way that supplies of carbon dioxide and oxygen can be assured.

Controlling Diseases and Pests

Like all other plants, the enemies of orchids are many. None can be more disconcerting than snails and slugs which attack your flowers after you have waited so patiently for them. Examine new plants introduced into your greenhouse for any evidence of slugs or snails before the plants are placed on your shelves. Isolated benches which do not touch the sides of the greenhouse and which have legs that are surrounded by small reservoirs of water are a good means of keeping slugs, snails, and other crawling insects from getting to your orchid plants. Slugs and snails can be controlled with metaldehyde bait or Slugit or Zectran sprays. Aphids, mealybugs, thrips, and scale are also destructive pests of orchids. Check Chapter XVI for the best controls of these pests.

If you note a silver coloring or later a rusty brown on the upper surface of the leaves of your plants, it is quite likely a sign that they are being attacked by mites. Some good miticides are described in Chapter XVI.

Cattleya flies are a special pest of cattleyas and they, along with weevils, ants, roaches, and springtails, can be controlled with methods recommended for rose midge, etc.

Always examine any new plants very carefully for signs of disease. Those which show signs of incurable diseases should be isolated at once and discarded. Leaf scorch or pseudo-bulb rot is a disease which causes a tip blight or scorch of the leaves and oblique mark or a water-soaked streak running from the pseudo-bulb to the base of a leaf. This disease is frequently found on miltonias. You can control it by soaking or drenching infected plants in a solution consisting of 1 part of 8-quinolinol benzoate or Natriphene to 2,000 parts of water. Follow the manufacturer's recommendations carefully.

Cypripediums often get brown rot. Circular or oval-shaped spots which become necrotic are symptoms of this. To control it, keep temperatures beneath 65 degrees F. and provide good aeration. Do not syringe the plants. The same chemical controls as outlined for leaf scorch will also help to control brown rot. Drench the seedlings by submerging them for about an hour, but older plants will need to be submerged for several hours to ensure control.

Phalaenopsis are often affected with brown spot which may occur on seedlings or older plants. Water-soaked dark green spots occur which turn brown and then black. Use the same control methods outlined for brown rot on cypripediums. If the disease appears on cattleyas, daub the affected places with a swab which has been soaked with a 1-to-1,000 solution of corrosive sublimate. Pythium black rot and other fungus diseases also hit orchids. Cattleyas are especially susceptible to pythium black rot. It can be controlled by keeping temperatures no more than 60 degrees F. and by reducing humidity and being careful not to overwater the plants.

Practice strict sanitation as a means of keeping vectors or insect carriers away from orchids which will transmit virus diseases to them. There are a number of symptoms which indicate that a plant is infected with a virus. Stunted plants, dying or dead leaves, lesions of dead or dying tissue, rings or partial rings of tissue that are abnormally lighter or darker in color, imperfectly formed leaves or flowers, leaves which are streaked or molded, and breaking of the flower colors are all indications of virus problems. Once plants are infected with a virus, there is no chance of ridding them of it. Discard such plants.

Important Growing Pointers for the Most Popular Orchids

EPIPHYTIC

Cattleya. Pay close attention to the watering of cattleyas. Fresh root activity is a sign for repotting. Immediately after repotting, omit watering for 2 weeks but keep humidity up by fogging so that the foliage will not become dehydrated. Normal watering should consist of soaking the medium thoroughly each time and then re-

White cattleya orchids.

fraining from additional watering until the medium has become quite dry. When the plants are dormant, even less water is given them. Provide good light, but guard against burning especially where the white-flowered varieties are concerned. Young seedlings also need additional shade. Daytime temperatures should run from 60 to 75 degrees and at night give them 55 to 65 degrees.

Coelogyne. This one is fussy about repotting, which shouldn't be done except when really necessary. Pot the plants immediately following flowering in a basket or box which has very good drainage. For the potting medium, use a combination of live sphagnum and osmunda. The plants will use a large amount of water during their growing period but should be kept on the dry side after they have matured. Keep them somewhat dry until flower spikes show. Then increase the watering a little. These orchids need as much light as possible during the darker winter months but shade should be given them during the summer. During the winter provide them with a 55 to 60 degree night temperature and 60 to 65 degrees in the daytime. In the summertime temperatures can be increased to 60 to 65 degrees nights and to 65 to 70 degrees days.

Dendrobium. Like coelogyne, repotting this orchid too frequently causes trouble. Confine its root system to the smallest pot possible and repot only when absolutely necessary. Water sparingly at the start and increase the amount of water to a heavy amount when the plants are growing well. There are both deciduous and evergreen species of dendrobiums. The evergreen sort rests only a short time, but the deciduous type requires a longer rest period. During this rest the deciduous species should receive no water at all in the case of mature plants. Evergreen dendrobiums should receive a minimum of 60 degrees during the winter months, slightly higher during the day. While growing, the deciduous types should have 55 to 60 degrees. Reduce this to 50 degrees when the plants are dormant. Shade these orchids until they have reached maturity and then give them as much light as possible, short of burning them.

Epidendrum (See also **Epidendrum** under Terrestrial Orchids). Repot after flowering. Give the plants maximum light, and water carefully immediately after potting. Increase watering to copious amounts when the growth has become lush. During the winter give epidendrums a night temperature of 55 to 60 degrees and a daytime temperature of 60 to 65 degrees. Summertime temperatures should be 60 to 65 degrees at night and 65 to 70 degrees days.

Laelia. Drainage for the laelias must be well-nigh perfect. When new growth starts, following dormancy, repot. Immediately after potting, water the plants thoroughly and then refrain from watering until the medium has become dry. The only moisture given the plants during the rest period should be by way of a syringing of the foliage. These plants need plenty of air and light, but provide enough shade to prevent burning of plants. Give them winter temperatures of 55 degrees at nights and 60 degrees during the day. Summertime temperature should be 60 and 65 degrees. The alpine sorts of the laelias should be grown at 45 degrees.

Miltonia. Pot miltonias in brown or black osmunda, chopped osmunda with a little sand and some half-decayed oak leaves and charcoal, or shredded bark. Repotting should take place when 4 to 5 inches of new growth is showing. Syringe the foliage and water very cautiously after repotting until the plants are well established; then water heavily. It is necessary to shade miltonias whenever the sun is bright. Both winter and summer temperatures should run from 50 degrees night to 60 degrees daytimes.

Odontoglossum. Pot odontoglossums in a mixture of half-decayed oak leaves, finely chopped osmunda, a little sand, and some charcoal. Although firming the medium is required, do not overdo it. Ample drainage material is necessary. Potting of this genus should take place in March or September. Water sparingly after repotting and fog the plants several times each day when the weather is bright. Once good root growth has started, the plants can be kept quite moist. The spread between daytime temperatures is considerable (45 to 70 degrees). Don't run the temperature higher than 70. Give this genus good air circulation and plenty of light during the winter. During the summer, heavy shading is necessary. Odontoglossums will tell you when the light is too great by a pink tint to the foliage.

Oncidium. Good drainage is absolutely essential. After flowering, repot oncidiums and water very carefully at first. Increase watering until full growth has been reached. Then water heavily. When growth has ceased, reduce watering to a minimum and fog-spray the foliage until flowering spikes appear. Oncidiums require full light and no shading. Give them winter temperatures of 55 to 60 degrees at night and 60 to 65 degrees during the day. In the summer temperatures should be around 60 to 65 degrees during the night and 65 to 75 degrees during the day.

Phalaenopsis. This genus needs plenty of drainage material, up to ½ potful in a deep pot. Add charcoal to the potting medium. Repot only when the root medium has broken down enough to require it. Repotting should take place after flowering and after drying the plants somewhat to make the roots more pliable. If too many roots are injured, the plant suffers drastically. After the plant has started to grow, water it well and keep it moist at all times. Supply ample humidity. Both inside and outside shade is necessary to protect phalaenopsis orchids and they should have plenty of fresh air, but no drafts. Run the plants 65 degrees at night and 75 degrees by day.

Vanda. The delightful little orchids which you receive at supermarket or other open-house celebrations are likely to be vandas which are grown in Hawaii. Add charcoal to the osmunda or other medium which you use for potting the plants. The medium should not be firmed too much. Water sparingly until the plants are established and then water them well. Vandas like full light (unless the sun is quite bright), plenty of fresh air, and regular feedings of a dilute manure water. Sudden temperature changes affect vandas drastically. Keep them at 58 to 65 degrees nights and from 70 to 80 degrees days.

TERRESTRIAL

Cymbidium. Never repot cymbidiums until absolutely necessary. When repotted, the plants show their resentment for a considerable period before flourishing again. Pot in a medium consisting of equal quantities of coarse osmunda, leafmold, cow manure, and sand. Add to this some charcoal, granite chips, and a small amount of bonemeal. Regular forest duff will also make a good potting medium, as will shredded bark. Right after repotting and during their resting period, be very careful with the amount of water supplied. During the active growing period, however, give cymbidiums a heavy amount of water. Cymbidiums should have full light, plenty of air, and a growing temperature, night and day, of 45 degrees.

Cypripedium. The cypripedium is another one which is quite fussy about having plenty of drainage and restricted watering until freshly potted plants have begun to show new root activity. These orchids should be potted in a medium of equal parts of osmunda, leafmold, and sand. Once the plants have started to grow well, keep them moist constantly. No shade is required during the winter, but they need shading when the sun is bright. The regular or plain-leaved cypripediums should have a winter night temperature of 45 degrees and a summertime night temperature of as close to 55 degrees as possible.

The mottled cypripediums have different temperature likes. They prefer winter temperatures of 55 to 60 degrees at nights and 60 to 65 degrees during the day. During the summer they should receive 60 to 65 degrees nights and 65 to 70 degrees during the day.

Epidendrum. Some of the epidendrum are terrestrials. Check epidendrum under Epiphytic for most of the information concerning epidendrum culture. The terrestrial epidendrums like a potting soil consisting of equal amounts of leafmold, well-rotted cow manure, coarse osmunda, and sand, with some charcoal, granite chips, and bonemeal added.

CHAPTER XXIII
Potted Roses

If you have thought that growing roses in your yard was a thrill, you will find that growing them in your greenhouse doubles that thrill by way of improved foliage and higher-quality blooms with fewer imperfections. Most home greenhouses do not afford enough room for the grower to produce a bench of roses, but almost any home greenhouse has enough room for a few pots of roses. The cultural information contained in this chapter applies to either potted or benched rose plants.

If you decide to force roses in your greenhouse, keep two things in mind. One, buy your dormant rosebushes from a reliable dealer who will give you high-quality stock which will force well. Two, choose varieties which are known to be good forcing stock. Not all roses will force properly in the greenhouse, especially those to be grown in pots or tubs.

Among the floribundas, my favorite is still Garnette, a small-flowering sweetheart type of rose which produces rich, dark red blooms. It is long-lasting on the plant or when cut. Another Garnette-type floribunda is Tommy Bright, which produces bright red flowers with stiff petals. Golden Garnette is a clear golden yellow floribunda of good quality. Sonora is a deep, multi-colored pink floribunda which is long-lasting and disease-resistant.

Red is still the most popular color of roses with most people. And still among the favorites for red roses to be forced are Better Times, Red Delight, and Happiness. A newer and very good-looking hybrid tea red rose is Red American Beauty. It is a dark red with fragrance galore. Pink roses run a close second to red and high on the list of pink roses is Rose Elf (Rosenelfe), a pink floribunda which lasts and lasts and lasts. Rapture is an old-time pink tea rose which is still quite popular, and Sonnet, a large pink hybrid tea, has a nice long bud and rich fragrance.

Tropicana is a brilliant orange-red hybrid tea rose which is currently riding the crest of popularity. It has large flowers which keep quite well. Among the yellows are two lovely hybrid teas which I

The exotic Tropicana, a hybrid tea rose. Its flowers are orange-red.

like very much. One is Golden Chalice. The other is Amber Gold, a clear yellow with pointed buds that open quite large. If you like white roses, and I certainly do, try Starbright.

Order your rosebushes to arrive in the latter part of November— be sure to order them far enough ahead of time to be sure of getting them. Either potted or in the bench, each rosebush should be given about 2 square feet for the tea roses and 1½ square feet for the smaller sorts. Only dormant budded stock should be used for forcing in the greenhouse.

Check Bushes

Frost injury to roses, often occurring during shipment, is difficult to determine upon receipt of the plants, and subsequent growth alone cannot be relied upon to determine the full extent of the injury because that growth depends upon so many other factors. If there is a possibility that your bushes might have been received frost-damaged there are a couple of good tests which were devised at Cornell University to determine whether or not your bushes are alive. One test consists of cutting sample canes from each of your bushes and soaking them for 24 hours in a solution of 1-per-cent 2,3,5-triphenyltetrazolium chloride. This will give an indication if actual killing of the tissue has taken place. Living tissue is stained but no stain can be detected in dead tissue, even though death has just occurred. Injury not resulting in death of the stems cannot, however, be detected by this method.

For less severe injury it is suggested that stem sections be soaked in distilled water for 24 hours and the conductivity of the water be tested. Any injured cell tends to lose its mineral salts to the distilled water and an increase in conductivity resulting from increase in mineral content is an indication of severity of injury. This test, while giving evidence of injury, is most reliable when correlated with later failure of normal growth.

After examination, if the bushes are not to be potted at once, keep them covered with moist burlap in a cool, moist location until you are ready.

Pruning and Potting

Baby ramblers, hybrid perpetuals, and hybrid teas should be

pruned to within 8 or 10 inches of the crown at the time they are potted. As for the climbers, the only pruning necessary is that required to remove any dead wood which may exist. With all the bushes, however, remove any dead or damaged wood and any injured roots. Remove any diseased portion of canes below the diseased area. Also remove all weak and spindling growth. If the roots are dry upon arrival, immerse them before potting in a bucket of water and allow them to soak for several hours.

Pot each plant so that the graft or bud union is just a little beneath the soil surface. I suggest that you use a heavy soil, preferably one of 3 parts good garden loam and 1 part well-rotted manure. Roses prefer a pH of 6.0 to 6.5. Sterilized soil is best. To each wheelbarrow load add a 4-inch potful of superphosphate. Soil should be packed about the roots very firmly, removing all air pockets. Following potting, the bushes may be placed in a cool place until you are ready to force them. It takes about 8 to 10 weeks to force the average rosebush. Before placing your potted rose either outdoors for storage or in the greenhouse, however, water the plants well.

Moisture

It is important to maintain high humidity around the plants until the buds start to grow when you force them. Lightly mist the plants frequently to encourage them to "break." I prefer to cover the tops of the plants with burlap, Visqueen plastic, or polyethylene film. Should you use something like this, be sure to remove it long enough to give the plants frequent syringing. Then remove the covering just as soon as the buds begin to show development.

Relative humidity is necessarily rather high during this period of getting the plants to break. Once the growth has started, a relative humidity of less than 75 per cent should be kept; less than 70 per cent is even better. This calls for close control of both temperature and ventilation. Actual watering of the plants, until the leaves have started to show, should be somewhat restricted. After the leaves have started to show, keep the plants on the moist side.

Shade and Ventilation

It is more fun to force rosebushes during the fall, winter, and spring months before they are in flower outdoors than during the late spring or summer months. If you force them before late spring, you will probably not need to put any shade on the glass. But if you are producing them during the warmer times of the year or if your home is in the South, you likely will need some shade on the glass.

Give the plants plenty of air, even if this means running the heat more than for other flowers and plants. In fact, if good circulation of warm air from heating pipes through the ventilators is not maintained, especially toward evening, condensation of moisture can occur on the foliage which will encourage the development of mildew.

Feeding and Mulching

Once your roses have started to grow well, apply a light feeding of a liquid fertilizer every 2 weeks. I recommend ammonium sulfate or a balanced fertilizer. If the original condition of the soil is quite rich, the feeding program should be modified. Be careful not to overfeed roses. Be sure that the plants are moist before the feeding is done each time. Usually, a feeding every 3 to 4 weeks is sufficient.

Try using a mulch around your rosebushes. This is always done when rosebushes are benched, and I think it is a good idea to do so with potted roses, too. Use a thin mulch of manure, sawdust, corn cobs, vermiculite, or other material and apply it to the soil around the bushes about a month or two after planting. Then, gradually increase its depth until it has reached a depth of about 4 inches. As the mulch decomposes, add to it from time to time, keeping it about 4 inches thick. It is much more necessary to keep a close tab on the nutrient level when material such as corn cobs or sawdust are used. Such materials have a tendency to temporarily rob the soil of its fertility as they decompose. Vermiculite, of course, has no nutrients in it and thus requires that more attention be paid to the application of fertilizer from time to time. Good mulching increases both stem length and the production of flowers on the bushes. A word of warning: Because some mulches harbor harmful insects, it is necessary to exercise greater precaution against pest and disease problems.

Temperature

Good temperature control is very important to the forcing of rosebushes. Say you bring your potted roses in from the coldframe about the 1st to 15th of January. Then start them at 45 degrees, raise it to 50 degrees within 10 days or so, and as the growth gets under way, move it up to 55 degrees. About 6 weeks after you have brought in your roses for forcing, move the temperature up to 60. If you are trying to force roses for a specific date, you can increase the temperature to as high as 62 degrees. However, such a temperature tends to soften the flowers and the stems somewhat.

Pinching Roses

One of the most difficult things for the amateur grower to learn about producing roses is pinching. It is mainly learned from experience but here are a few pointers for the neophyte to consider: When the plants have reached the height of about 2 feet (shorter, for some varieties), soft-pinch them. A soft pinch is that which can be snipped out with a fingernail or snapped off at the end of the branch without benefit of a cutting tool. Make a soft pinch when the flower buds become visible above the foliage. The earlier flowers are usually not too desirable and this soft pinch will force growth from breaks lower on the bushes.

A big advantage of a soft pinch is that the new growth blends with the old stem, thus giving additional stem length to the rose, if you intend to cut it. Soft pinches, therefore, produce the longer-stemmed, larger-budded roses. It is well to remember, however, when the stem diameter is less than $5/32$ of an inch, a soft pinch probably will fail to work; blind growth may result, and those breaks that do develop will produce poor-quality blooms.

Pests and Diseases

Undoubtedly, the biggest problem most greenhouse gardeners have is mildew. Good, carefully controlled ventilation is still the most important factor in its control. This fungus spreads rapidly when condensation occurs on the foliage. Always allow plenty of air to circulate about the bushes to remove excessive moisture, especially in the evening when the ventilators are being closed. Closing of the ventilators should be done gradually, and the extra heat used will be worth far more than the cost of a little fuel consumed; the heat will pick up the excessive moisture, preventing it from being deposited on the plants. The greatest trouble from mildew is experienced in the spring and fall. Omazene and Mildex are good control materials, as well as ordinary sulfur. Sulfur can be vaporized with vaporizers which are made for this purpose.

Cane cankers can cause considerable trouble. There are three different fungi which can cause this disease, but one, *Leptosphaeria coniothyrium,* is the most severe in the greenhouse. It causes pale yellow or reddish spots to appear on the canes. These gradually become brown or black and enlarge. As the bark cracks, sunken cankers appear. Such cankers can grow and kill a cane and may affect the grafted area, making the plant useless. The disease is spread by spores. To help control canker, leave as short a stub as possible when the flower is cut from the plant. Any infected cane should be removed and burned. When a cane is removed, cut 3 or 4 inches beneath the infected area and leave the shortest possible stub where a stub is necessary. Use denatured alcohol or mercuric chloride solution at the rate of 1-to-1,000 to sterilize the shears between cuts.

Crown gall is another disease which sometimes affects greenhouse roses. It occurs on the crowns, canes, or roots of the plant and the galls are usually quite numerous on the soil line or just beneath it. Wounds are another place where the disease can get started. To control crown gall, remove the old, diseased plants and destroy them. Be sure to use sterilized soil and disease-free plants when planting new beds.

There are various virus diseases of roses which can be troublesome. Virus may cause small chlorotic spots on the foliage and sometimes distortion of the leaf blade takes place. If yellow mosaic occurs, the spots will be brighter yellow and markings will be quite conspicuous. When streak virus occurs, brown or yellow vein banding occurs, or yellowish-green banding or dull brownish rings show up on the canes. The answer to virus problems is, first, buy only virus-free stock, and, two, use sterilized soil.

The worst pest to attack roses in the greenhouse is the red spider. Two things thwart one's efforts to control red spiders. One is incomplete coverage of all the plant surfaces with a miticide. Two is the ability of red spiders to immunize themselves against miticides. Many different materials are used to fight this pest, but none of them will do any good unless coverage is thorough. Sloppy coverage will serve only to build up resistant strains of mites. It is a good idea to use more than one miticide, alternating from one to the other. If you begin to suspect that one material is not working well, switch to another immediately.

Aphids can be a problem on roses, but they are easily controlled, as outlined in Chapter XVI.

Neither root nematodes nor root lesion nematodes are always easily detected. One of the reasons that nematodes are such a problem is because all too many greenhouse growers do not seem to realize how easily nematode infection is spread. For instance, even though the soil in raised benches may be free of nematodes, if they exist in the aisles, merely the raising of one's foot from the aisle to the bench may be the means of starting an infestation of the pests in the bench. Nematodes are often indicated if the roots are short and there are numerous white roots only $\frac{1}{8}$ inch long. Root knot nematodes cause root galls that can easily be seen. There is no known way to get at nematodes already in the roots, short of destroying the plants. There are soil drenches which are fairly effective as a means of control for nematodes in the soil. And, of course, where soil sterilization is possible, nematodes can be eliminated.

CHAPTER XXIV

Overhead and in the Corners

Nothing makes the greenhouse more cozy than vines. There are some mighty handsome twiners and climbers, most of which flower. You can grow them in pots or tubs placed in the corners or on shelves and the vines can be strung overhead. Avoid too much overhead growth, however, for that causes too great an amount of shade beneath. A better idea is to grow them in pots equipped with 4 to 5-foot trellises.

When you check on some of these vines, don't let the fact that their normal growth is 20 feet or more stop you from growing them in your greenhouse. By growing them in pots or tubs, the root area is restricted and, consequently, vine growth is also restricted. Also, you can prune any of the vines which tend to get out of bounds to keep them restricted to the area where you want them.

You will have to "educate" your vines by training them the way you want them to grow. If you intend to have them hanging from the braces or rafters, guide them in that direction with florist's green wire, string, or raffia. Tie each branch of the vine singly, never group them. Be sure that the loop around the branch allows plenty of growth room and fasten it securely to the greenhouse.

Feed your vines regularly during their growing periods and avoid feeding them when dormant. By paying attention to the feeding of your plants and adding fresh soil each spring or fall to the tops of the pots or tubs, you can keep vines growing in the same containers for quite long periods. But when your vines begin to look

Vining plants can be hung from the rafters.

leggy and coarse and fail to provide your greenhouse with the original beauty that they gave to it, it is time to get rid of them. Don't hesitate to do so, for you can start new vines from cuttings and have replacements in a relatively short time.

Here are some of my favorites:

Allamanda. Allamandas are Brazilian natives which produce spectacular yellow or purplish flowers which are followed by prickly fruits. They should be grown at 60 to 65 degrees.

During their growing season, allamandas should have plenty of water and be fed with a balanced fertilizer regularly. They are somewhat dormant in January and early February, at which time they should be run quite dry. In late February, cut the plants back and start watering them more heavily to start new growth. Should you repot the plants, do so before new growth has commenced. Either new or old wood can be used to propagate allamandas.

Bignonia. You may have heard of this plant under the name of Trumpet-flower or Cross-vine. It has lovely yellowish-red tubular flowers, stiff leaves, and branched tendrils. This evergreen climber likes a light, well-drained soil and moderate feeding. It does best at 45 to 50 degrees. To train or restrict it, prune bignonia after it has flowered.

Clematis. Clematis plants produce some of the most spectacular flowers of all the viny plants. The large, flowering sorts have starry-like flowers of purple and white. You might prefer *C. paniculata,* which is a species with feathery-like flowers.

Clematis vines should have a cool temperature (45 to 50) and they prefer a loose, rich soil which is well drained. These vines do very well when trellised and excite many oh's and ah's whenever visitors see the vines in bloom. Clematis cannot stand soil which is strongly acid. To alleviate this, add lime to acid soils. Mulching the plants each year with well-rotted manure promotes better growth. Pruning should be done immediately after flowering.

Clerodendron. *C. thomsonae,* commonly called glorybower, has lovely crimson flowers with white calyxes, the flowers turning purplish as they age. Grow clerodendron in a well-drained soil at 60 to 65. The plant should always be on the moist side, but not wet, and it requires some shade. Propagate it from cuttings or seed.

Ficeus Pumila (*F. repens*). This is a lovely, neat little climbing plant which is ideally suited against a brick or concrete wall. Grow it on a trellis. It likes a warm temperature, preferably 65 degrees nights and up to 80 degrees days. Give it a filtered or diffused light and a soil rich with rotted manure and humus. Keep it moist but do not let the soil become water-soaked. It is grown from cuttings.

Hoya. There are several hoyas, but perhaps the best known and most popular is *H. carnosa.* There is also a variegated form. This native of Queensland and China was first recommended as a house plant as early as 1824. It is a lush climbing vine that produces large, thick leathery leaves that look as though they are wax-covered. Its pinkish-white waxy flowers are ideal for corsage use. Grow hoya on the dry side and use a soil which is half sand and half peatmoss. Provide excellent drainage and always allow the plant to dry out sufficiently between waterings. It should have filtered sunlight. It is an excellent trellis plant. Propagate from petiole and leaf-bud cuttings.

H. australis is another fine hoya. It flowers well and the blooms have the fragrance of honeysuckle. This one grows more vigorously than *H. carnosa.*

Passiflora. The passion flower excites the imagination of Christians who point out the interesting flowers whose parts are emblematic of the Crucifixion. The flowers, about 4 inches across, are intricate in detail. The outer edges of the petals are white, shading to soft mauve and blue near the crown. Give the plants a good rich soil containing plenty of humus, such as leafmold and well-rotted manure. They should be kept on the moist side (not wet) and given a temperature of 55 to 60 degrees. Give them moderate ventilation and feed them regularly with a balanced fertilizer or liquid manure. Omit the feeding and reduce watering when the plants are dormant. You can propagate them from cuttings or seeds.

Plumbago. Few seem to know this plant by its common name, leadwort. Grow the plants in a turfy, moderately rich, well-drained soil. *P. capensis* can be trained well as a climber. Plumbago has phlox-like flowers of blue, purplish-red, and white. Grow them at 45 to 50 degrees. To get good branching and well-shaped plants, pinch them 2 or 3 times. Each spring the old plants should be cut back closely to allow for new growth. The plants may be started from cuttings of mature wood, seeds, or by plant division.

Rhaphieophora celatocaulis. This very unusual climber is called the shingle plant because its leaves cling closely together in shingle-like fashion. It makes an excellent totem plant against a wall. It has lovely semi-heart-shaped leaves of medium green with pronounced veins. Give it a soil mixture containing ample humus, such as 2 parts loam or sandy loam and 1 part peatmoss. It needs good drainage and should be grown at temperatures of 65 degrees nights and 80 days. Keep the plant moist at all times. Feed it with a balanced fertilizer regularly and protect it from direct rays of the sun.

Solanum jasminoides. If not restricted, this lovely little climber will grow to a length of about 10 feet. It has starry, bluish-white flowers and attractive foliage. It belongs to the nightshade family and is related to the ornamental pepper and Jerusalem cherry. Usually started from seed in a medium greenhouse temperature. Grown under glass in the north, but outside in the south and California.

Stephanotis floribunda. Stephanotis is definitely one vine which will need some restriction when grown under ideal conditions. It produces a lovely flower for corsages. Give it a turfy, fiberous loam which contains peatmoss or leafmold. Provide good drainage and ample water during the growing season. Decrease water and keep the plant a little on the dry side during the winter months. Stephanotis needs good air circulation to harden and mature the wood. Give it full light. A 65-degree night temperature is ideal for stephanotis and it grows very well if trained up near the glass. Its lovely waxy white, tubular-shaped flowers have a wonderful fragrance that is never forgotten.

Mulching is a good idea and stephanotis should be fed regularly with a balanced fertilizer. Propagate the plants by cuttings or layers.

Streptosolen jamesoni. A native of Ecuador, this tropical shrub has small, oval, wrinkled leaves and flowers of orange-red. It likes a warm greenhouse, 65 degrees nights and 80 days; a rich loamy soil containing rotted manure and humus, and filtered or diffused sunlight. Keep it moist but do not let the soil become water-soaked. It is grown from cuttings.

Swainsona. Anyone not familiar with this plant might at first mistake the flowers for miniature, white sweet peas, to which swainsona is related. *S. galegifolia* also comes with varieties that flower with rosy-violet, red, and pink flowers. Swainsona is an excellent corsage flower.

The plants should have a deep, rich, well-drained soil. Once the plants are well established, feed regularly with a balanced fertilizer or liquid manure. Full sunlight, good ventilation, and a 50-degree night temperature is best for swainsonas which may be strung in the manner of sweet peas or may be grown on a trellis. The plants flower over a considerable period, and following one flowering, the plants may be cut back and new growth started for a second flowering. Plants are best started from cuttings, although they can also be propagated from seeds. Make cuttings in January. Guard against mildew.

Tecomaria. *T. capensis,* commonly known as Cape honeysuckle, is the one most often grown in greenhouses. It has lovely clusters of showy orange-red flowers and fascinating feathery foliage. Grow it at 45 to 50 degrees nights and give it a well-drained, light soil. The plants should be fed moderately with a balanced fertilizer. It is started from cuttings.

Trachelospermum jasminoides. *T. jasminoides* is known by most gardeners as star jasmine or star jessamine. It has flat-topped clusters of fragrant tubular white flowers and foliage with opposite leaves.

Although it grows quite slowly, it makes a fine, trellised plant for growing in large pots or tubs in a corner or against a wall in the greenhouse. Give jasmines a cool temperature (45 to 50 degrees nights) and good ventilation. The plants should have a well-drained soil of fibrous nature. Start from cuttings.

CHAPTER XXV

Bulbs Are
Quickies to Force

Mention bulbs to the average gardener and his mind's eye will quickly bring forth Technicolor pictures of bright, spring-flowering bulbs—tulips, hyacinths, daffodils, miscellaneous narcissi, scillas, etc. When you own a home greenhouse, you can move up the spring season to mid-winter if you so desire, by forcing spring bulbs indoors.

But don't be fooled into believing that just any old bulb will do for forcing. Only top quality bulbs should be used. Large-sized ones usually produce the choicest and earliest blooms. Smaller bulbs do not stand so much forcing, and often will not bloom satisfactorily, if at all. However, you can bring some of these smaller, less than top-grade bulbs into flower provided you use more moderate temperatures and let them flower in more normal fashion. The best hyacinth bulbs to use are 18 to 19 centimeters and up. The earliest and best iris blooms are from 10 cm. or larger bulbs. To get the finest tulip flowers use bulbs 12 cm. and up. With daffodils, number one, double-nosed bulbs are the very best for heavy-flowering, high-quality blooms.

Before you order any bulbs for forcing, read up on the latest information contained in catalogues and bulb books about varieties which are good for forcing. There are new varieties and it pays to know about them. On the other hand, some of the older varieties, such as King Alfred daffodils, are still among the best forcing bulbs. But you should know the various storage requirements, earliness factors, and growing habits, including height, foliage, flower substance, color, and response to forcing.

Even though you will learn a great deal from the catalogues and books, you will still have to learn much about forcing bulbs by personal experience, because each one's individual growing conditions are different. The spring-flowering bulbs were once known as Dutch bulbs. However, since the development of the bulb-growing industry in the Pacific Northwest, U.S. bulbs have gained a world-wide reputation for reliability in forcing. This is particularly true of Northwest bulbous iris, which are now sold to forcers in the European market. But both Northwest and Holland-grown spring bulbs are highly reliable for forcing purposes.

Don't just go to the corner dealer and buy ordinary spring bulbs for forcing. Buy those bulbs which have been especially prepared for forcing purposes by the bulb growers themselves. Such growers practice rigid disease controls. They also grade and otherwise handle bulbs carefully, but they go even beyond that. For instance, iris growers give early-dug forcing bulbs a heat-curing treatment of 90 degrees for 10 days. What this does is provide a curing process which sometimes does not occur naturally from the heat of the sun. When iris bulbs are not sufficiently cured, they do not force properly. Iris bulb growers, too, in some instances precool bulbs, but this is of no advantage to you unless you plant the bulbs immediately or continue to keep them cool until you plant them.

"Prepared" hyacinth bulbs now make it much easier to force hyacinths. Heating pipes are used beneath the bulb beds by hyacinth bulb producers and this extra heat treatment enables the forcer (commercial or amateur) to produce hyacinth flowers much earlier than would otherwise be possible.

Precooling

Immediately when your bulbs arrive, place them in a cool place until time to force them. The ideal precooling temperature for iris, hyacinths, tulips, and daffodil bulbs is 50 degrees. To be ideal, the precooling room or cellar should have a relative humidity of 70 per cent or more.

Timing Blooms

After precooling, it takes from 4 to 6 weeks to force tulip bulbs. Temperature requirements are different for various varieties and whether or not the bulbs have been precooled also makes a difference. The size of the bulb is a third factor in the variance of time for forcing tulips.

Iris bulbs that have been precooled starting in the latter part of August or early part of September can be forced into bloom for Thanksgiving (using Wedgewood iris). I think it is fun to have iris flowers start blooming in December, shortly before Christmas, continuing with blooms until March, using the later varieties and by using non-precooled bulbs, which will flower later. Iris bulbs which have not been precooled should not be forced to bloom before January 15.

It takes 4 weeks of forcing to flower most daffodil varieties. Precooled daffodils can be forced beginning the end of November, while bulbs not precooled should usually not be forced before December 15.

As for hyacinths, it takes about 4 weeks to force the bulbs during the winter and early spring. It requires only about 3 weeks to force them for Easter.

Before you do any bulb forcing, procure from your supplier a schedule showing the length of time required for forcing each variety of hyacinth, tulp, daffodil, and iris which you intend to grow. You can save yourself a lot of headaches if you do.

Bulbs which are not to be precooled should be flatted, potted, or benched immediately upon arrival. If you find this impossible at the moment, place the bulbs in cool, well-aired storage until they can be potted or benched. If the bulbs are allowed to become warm before potting, blooming dates will be delayed. If you do your own precooling be sure all get equal treatment of temperature and air. To do this, keep them just safely above freezing temperature (35 to 40 degrees) and move and turn them at least once each week for 6 weeks or more. Shallow trays with screen bottoms are best for precooling storage. After precooling, do not place the bulbs in a warm place. Such cured bulbs should not be chosen for late plantings and should not be planted in warm soil. Although you do not have to precool bulbs, it does give you a 2 to 3 weeks' advantage in forcing time.

Soil

Except where differences are noted, the best soil for forcing bulbs discussed in this chapter is one which is loose, well-drained, and sterilized. If you have good field soil nearby, use this and add a little sand and peatmoss to it, if it is a little on the heavy side.

If the field soil has been properly built up, you should not need to add fertilizer to it when you force the bulbs. Although I have seen some commercial as well as amateur growers add a little commercial fertilizer to their bulb soil, research has shown that there is usually little to be gained by adding fertilizer to soil being used for the forcing of bulbs. The bulbs themselves carry an ample food supply for a single forcing. Unless you know your soil to be of rather poor quality, I would not add fertilizer to it.

Diseases and Pests of Spring Bulbs

If you use a bulb storage house be sure to fumigate it thoroughly between usage. The worst pest which you can probably expect on bulb stock is aphids, and they are commonly carried over in a bulb storage house. Good aphid control is described in Chapter XVI.

The forcing period for spring bulbs is quite short. This means that there is little chance of any fungus or virus disease injuring your plants, if your purchased clean stock from a reliable dealer in the first place. Pay close attention to temperatures, watering, and ventilation to further insure yourself good plants and flowers.

Any problem which might occur from nematodes or fungi will be largely controlled by using sterilized soil. I doubt that you will ever require it, but if you do, Systox can be used as a soil drench or spray to help control fungi or nematodes.

Don't worry about narcissus bulb fly, if you bought good bulbs from a reliable dealer. This is a problem with which the bulb producer must contend. Don't blame the blindness or blasting which may occur on bulbous plants on the bulb producer. It very likely is the result of some variation made in correct forcing procedures.

Daffodils

Unpack immediately and place your daffodil bulbs in precooling storage. If they are not to be precooled, flat or pot them immediately. Daffodil bulbs do best in deep flats, bulb to bulb. You can force them, however, in pots. Daffodils (tulips and hyacinths, too), after flatting or potting, should go into a coldframe, bulb storage house, or cellar, or be buried in a pit for rooting. The best idea is to place them in a bulb storage house where a constant temperature of 48 degrees may be maintained. The daffodil bulbs can also be stored in a greenhouse bench if a 48-degree temperature can be maintained.

Wherever they are placed for the rooting process, a good drainage is essential. During the rooting process, it is a good idea to run them a little on the dry side. As soon as the shoots have grown 3 to 4 inches long, the plants are ready to be removed to the greenhouse for forcing. If you plan on leaving the bulbs for a longer period, the temperature should not be over 40 degrees.

Start forcing daffodils at 60 degrees. After 3 weeks raise the temperature to 65 or 70 degrees for the balance of the forcing. There is an exception to this recommendation, however, and this has to do with the outdoor temperature at the time of forcing. If the outdoor temperature is at 0, daffodils and other spring bulbs should be started in the greenhouse at 40 degrees; if the outdoor temperature is 50 degrees, the bulbs should be started at 60 degrees. If you follow this rule, quality will be increased in your blooms. Also, you will avoid much grassy foliage and produce better stems on bulbous flowers by not forcing the plants at more than 65 degrees.

Most of these recommendations for daffodils also apply to other narcissi which you can force. However, to determine variations in my recommendations with respect to various varieties, I suggest you get exact information from the grower or supplier from whom you purchase your bulbs.

Tulips

Like daffodils, tulip bulbs should be potted, flatted, or benched with the tips of the bulbs barely above the surface of the soil. Be careful to insure that each pot or flat receives an equal amount of water by making sure that the flats or pots are uniformly filled with soil and are placed level.

Although you may root tulip bulbs outdoors or in coldframes, I recommend, wherever possible, the rooting be done in a bulb storage house or building where the temperature can be kept at a constant 48 to 50 degrees. Potted or flatted bulbs have a tendency to dry out around the edges in particular and you should check them frequently while they are in storage to make sure that this does not happen. Good ventilation as well as a constant temperature is important to the proper rooting of tulip bulbs.

When the tulips are brought into the greenhouse for forcing, if you want longer stems, shade the plants heavily at first. This is important with the earlier, shorter-stemmed varieties. As soon as the plants have started to grow well, place them in full light.

Follow the temperature-relationship recommendations made under daffodils in this chapter. Under normal conditions, tulip forcing should start at 55 degrees and then be raised to a maximum of 60 degrees for the balance of the forcing. Although you can force them at higher temperatures, quality will be sacrificed. Forcing temperatures should be uniform day and night and remember that tulips must have plenty of ventilation and water. To prevent fungus disease problems, avoid splashing water on the foliage.

Irises

The most difficult of the spring bulbs to force are the bulbous irises. Once planted, the pots or flats should be placed where they are to be forced and not moved again. For once iris roots have protruded through the bottom of the flats or pots, the protruding roots will be damaged if they are moved, and this will check the development of the plants. It may even keep them from blooming.

As soon as iris bulbs are removed from cold storage they should be planted in a cool soil and forced at 50 to 55 degrees for 10 days to 2 weeks. Space the bulbs 3 by 3 inches when planting.

If you grow irises in pots, be sure that the pots are well soaked before using them—any moisture drawn from the bulbs during the forcing will injure them. I dislike the idea of using new pots, too, unless they have been presoaked and rinsed thoroughly to remove some of the salts which might injure the iris bulbs. One reason for preferring flats over pots is that it is much easier accidently to move a pot than a flat.

It is better to grow irises in the bench, for they form a heavier root system and produce superior stems, foliage, and flowers than do those grown in flats. If you prefer to flat or pot your iris bulbs ahead of time and remove them to a bulb storage house for rooting, you may, provided that you move them into the greenhouse for forcing before any roots begin to appear at the bottom of the pots or flats.

Cover iris bulbs entirely. An easy way to plant iris bulbs, is to soak the bench or flat soil thoroughly and then merely push the bulbs into the soil, covering them with a ½ to 1-inch layer of peatmoss. Then soak the soil again so that it is thoroughly wet. Never allow iris

soil to dry or root development will be sorely arrested. Keep iris plantings moist at all times. The safest idea is to use water which is as
near the temperature of the air as possible. Cold water can sometimes cause trouble when forcing iris.

Wedgwood iris should be forced at 55 degrees, night and day,
and Emperor, another good reliable variety, forces best at 40 degrees. If you are growing various varieties of iris, forcing temperatures from 50 to 56 degrees are fine. Some varieties force well up to
60 degrees, but do not go over 60. Too high a temperature will
cause bud blasting. I suggest that you start forcing at a little lower
temperature until you can see the buds or feel them, at which time
you can give them the maximum forcing temperature recommended.
Bulb size and maximum temperature which will work properly are in
direct relationship. The larger the bulb, the greater the forcing temperature it will take. You must carry smaller bulbs cooler to get
consistent blooming.

Irises need ample ventilation but no drafts. Be sure they have full
light at all times. I don't believe, if your soil is of fair to good quality,
that you need to feed the bulbs during forcing. But should this seem
necessary, use a mild solution of nitrate of soda or one of magnesium
sulfate, either of which may help to produce better foliage color.
But be sure you need this feeding before you apply it.

Hyacinths

Hyacinths are almost as touchy as iris but in a different way.
You can root your hyacinth bulbs outdoors but be sure that you protect the bulbs from any surplus water or freezing during this early
stage. If you choose to root them in beds outdoors, cover them 4 to
6 inches deep. You can grow your hyacinths in flats, if they are to
be used for cutting, but I always like growing them in pots so that
they can be toted into the house when they are in flower. Again, if
you have it, a bulb house or cellar is the ideal place to root hyacinths. If you do put them into such a place, make sure that water
will not drip upon them from above. Hyacinths should be potted so
that the tips are covered to about ½ inch. Keep the bulbs moist but
not wet while they are in the bulb house. An ideal temperature during the rooting stage is 48 to 50 degrees. Leave them there until a
good root system has been established.

When moved into the greenhouse for forcing, keep them more or less dark to "pull out" the bud and develop the foliage. You can do this by placing the pots beneath the bench and darkening the area with shade cloth around the legs. While in the dark, the plants should be kept at 65 to 75 degrees. As soon as the buds are showing properly and the foliage has developed, place the plants in full light and give them a forcing temperature of 60 degrees. It will take about 10 days to 2 weeks to flower them once they have been removed from the dark.

Supply the hyacinths with good ventilation and water well. However, avoid splashing water on them at all times. You can force hyacinths a little faster by using a higher temperature but, if you do, quality will be sacrificed.

Squills and Grape Hyacinths

Some of the fun received from producing bulbous flowers comes from growing the lesser-known things, such as squills or scillas. You can grow either squills or grape hyacinths in flats or pots and they force easily. Place them outdoors or in a bulb house for rooting and give them protection in the very cold areas.

Force squills or scillas at 50 degrees and grape hyacinths will take a range of 45 to 52 degrees. *S. hisfanica* (*campanulata*) is the best scilla for forcing as a cut flower. Begin in February. You can start forcing grape hyacinths in late January. Both grape hyacinths and squills should be given good ventilation, full light and constant moisture.

Anemones and Ixias

Anemones have always been among my favorite flowers, perhaps because they remind me of the wild anemones we had growing in the foothills of my home state of Colorado. The French anemones which you want for forcing have bright, cheerful flowers, borne on wiry stems. You can grow them in flats or pots, starting them in September or October. Start them right in the greenhouse, preferably giving them a night temperature of 40. They will force fairly well at 50, but some quality is sacrificed.

Bulbs may be planted almost touching and you should use soil as recommended earlier in this chapter for general bulbous plants. I have seen attempts made to plant anemones and irises together, but

I do not recommend this. Anemones are highly susceptible to crown rot and this is brought on through careless or over-watering.

Another disease which hits anemones is mildew. To prevent or help control this, be sure the relative humidity is watched carefully. Pay close attention to ventilation so that condensation of water on the plants is prevented.

To give ixias a good start, flat or pot them in September and then place them in a dark storage at 45 degrees for rooting. Remove them in early December into a 50-degree temperature for forcing. They like good light, ample ventilation, and even moisture. You will need to support them in some manner to prevent crooked stems.

Callas

There are two kinds of calla lilies which are very delightful for forcing in the greenhouse. Neither sort is a lily; both are grown from rhizomes. Callas belong to the aurm family. White callas can be grown in benches, large pots, or beds. A common resting time of the rhizomes is during the month of July and early August, which means that August, then, is a good time to start the plants. Be sure to get disease-free rhizomes. When replanting rhizomes, if diseased areas are noted, use a sterile knife to remove the infected areas. Disinfect the knife between cuts and cut into healthy tissue far enough to in-sure removal of all diseased tissue. The rhizomes can then be treated with Fermate, Semesan, Ceresan, formaldehyde, or Spergon. I pre-fer the latter used at the rate of 2 ounces to 1 gallon of water. Soak the rhizomes in this mixture for 1 hour.

Plant in a mixture of half sand and half peatmoss at the start. Or, if you prefer, plant them, at the start, in sterilized soil. Be sure the rhizomes are potted or benched while they are still wet from the soak-ing. It is preferable to plant callas in pots, I believe, inasmuch as it is easier to control disease on them and there is the added advantage of moving them from one spot to another as space needs dictate. However, I must agree that better-quality flowers are produced when callas are grown in raised benches or ground beds. When potting use 1 rhizome to a 5, 6, or 7-inch pot, according to rhizome size, or 3 rhizomes in an 8 or 9-inch pot.

Use a rich soil that is well drained and a little on the acid side. Add superphosphate and a good supply of well-rotted manure. I also like the idea of applying a mulch of manure to the top of the soil for callas. This will help retain moisture as well as add some fertility to the soil. Start the callas a little on the dry side and then increase the water until they receive copious amounts at maturity. Be sure drainage is good.

Grow white callas at 50 to 60 degrees and provide them with good air circulation. Give the plants full light from September until June and then provide them with some shade from June until September— about 2,000 foot-candles is ideal.

Callas are heavy feeders, especially when grown in pots. If you add bonemeal or superphosphate to the original soil, this should be enough phosphorus to carry them through. You should feed thereafter with a complete fertilizer which contains a higher percentage of nitrogen and potassium. Liquid manure is also a good feed for calla lilies. Too much nitrogen, however, will restrict flowering and overproduce foliage. When this happens, some foliage can be removed to encourage heavier flowering, but don't overdo it.

The culture and care of yellow callas is a little different from that of white callas. One important matter is to preheat the rhizomes at 85 to 90 degrees for 2 to 3 weeks before planting them. I suggest that you place the rhizomes in flats, the bottoms of which are covered with sphagnum or peatmoss. Keep the moss moist and soon roots will begin to appear. You can vary this treatment by giving them the heat treatment and then covering them with sphagnum or peatmoss after reducing the temperature to 60 to 65 degrees until the roots have developed. The rhizomes are then taken from the flats and planted in large pots, using a good, rich soil which contains from $\frac{1}{4}$ to $\frac{1}{3}$ part of well-rotted manure. For each bushel of this soil, add one 3-inch potful of bonemeal or superphosphate.

Yellow callas respond well to regular feedings of ammonium sulfate, at the rate of 1 ounce to 2 gallons of water. The best temperature for yellow callas is 65 degrees. Time the arrival of yellow calla rhizomes for November in order to treat them and then pot them into 5 or 6-inch pots in December. This will give you blooms in April or May.

For those who wish, there are also miniature white, pink, and so-called black callas to experiment with.

If root rot develops with callas, remove the old rhizomes, dry and scrub them thoroughly, and then remove the rot spots as recommended earlier. Soak the rhizomes in formaldehyde or Spergon. Soft-rot control is much the same. Use no manure or other organic fertilizer where soft rot is concerned. Any virus-infected plants should be destroyed.

Thrips, red spiders, and mealybugs are the worst pests. For their control see Chapter XVI.

Easter Lilies

Who can think of Easter without visioning the Easter lily? There are several varieties of Easter lilies grown which claim the Croft lily as their ancestor. Also grown to some extent are the Georgia and Creole lilies. The latter two grow somewhat taller than the others and are less desirable for pot-plant purposes. A basic rule to consider concerning the timing of Easter lilies is that it requires 120 days from potting to flowering to force them in the Northern states. In the South, Easter lilies require 112 days.

Easter lilies for forcing should be ordered for arrival in October. Immediately after arrival of the bulbs, store in trays or in pots for 4 to 6 weeks, depending upon the timing and the bulb's arrival, at a temperature of 45 to 50 degrees. Croft-type lilies to be flowered later than Easter should be stored at 33 or 34 degrees. Georgia and Creole lilies should be stored at 45 degrees for Easter. If not potted prior to storing, I suggest the bulbs be placed in moist peatmoss for storage.

Bulb size has a relationship to the number of flowers and buds you may expect. Ten-centimeter and larger bulbs produce 6 or more blooms; 9 to 10-centimeter bulbs, 5 blooms; 8 to 9-centimeter bulbs, 4 blooms; and 7 to 8-centimeter bulbs, 3 blooms.

The first 2 to 6 inches of an Easter lily's growth appears to govern flowering. Hence, exact care at that time is important. Perhaps the most critical time for an Easter lily occurs during the last 2 or 3 weeks. If the weather is dark at that time, you can partly offset the situation by a slight increase in temperature. The normal forcing temperatures for Easter lilies are 60 degrees at nights, with daytime temperatures of 70 to 75. If you find your Easter lilies are behind schedule, as long as 80 days before Easter, you can increase the night temperature to 65 to 70 degrees.

If the plants are too far advanced, you can grow them at 55 degrees (nights). Easter lilies which flower too early may be stored successfully for up to 2 weeks in a refrigerated room without lights.

The plants should be watered well just before they go into storage, and stored just as the first flower on each plant is ready to crack open. Store them at 38 to 40 degrees F.

Easter lilies need a soil which contains ample humus which can be supplied with peatmoss or well-rotted manure. I suggest an average greenhouse soil with about ⅓ peatmoss and some fine sand added to help insure good drainage. Plant the bulbs in 5½ or 6-inch three-quarter pots. To provide good drainage, use ½ inch of pea gravel or its equivalent in the bottom of the pots. Place the bulbs squarely in the pot so that the flowering stem will protrude from the center of the soil. The bulbs should be covered with at least 2 inches of soil. This will give the stem roots, which occur a few inches above the bulb, a chance to accomplish their function of providing additional moisture and root to the plant. Be sure the depth of the bulb and the soil level in the pot are uniform. This will insure uniform watering and feeding of the plants. Be sure they set level on the bench. Easter lilies must not be crowded or they will suffer in quality and be more susceptible to disease. Soil, pots, benches, and bench-covering medium must be sterilized. Croft-type lilies sometimes suffer from a physiological ailment known as scorch. This is caused from improper pH. The pH for Easter lilies should be 6.5 to 7.0. Calcium sulfate (gypsum) or agricultural lime can be used to raise the pH level where necessary. Be sure to test the soil you use for Easter lilies before planting your bulbs. The addition of a 2-inch potful of bloodmeal to a bushel of soil mixture is a good idea. The bloodmeal and later feedings of nitrogen will help counteract the scorch. Avoid fertilizers that are quickly available at the start or the root system will not develop properly.

Immediately after potting the bulbs, water Easter lilies. Then allow the plants to approach the dry side until the tops are out of the pots and the plants are well rooted. After the plants have reached 4 inches in height, you may increase the moisture level to a moderate degree; this prevents bud blasting. When the plants have reached about 6 inches, reduce the moisture again so the plants are on the dry side.

Fairly high humidity is important for lilies. This is especially true when they are behind schedule. To add humidity, syringe the plants, but do not overdo it or they will stretch too much. Syringing with water of 70 to 80 degrees temperature will hasten their flowering. Using warm water will also do this. It is important to give

Easter lilies full light to get good bud production. To keep plants from growing toward the sun, rotate from time to time.

The bud count is increased by feeding throughout the forcing period but, strangely, the plants are not stretched by regular feeding. The size of blooms depends jointly upon correct watering and good fertilizing practices.

Other than scorch, previously mentioned, mosaic, a virus disease spread by aphids, is apt to be the only one which will affect your plants during the relatively short forcing period. Keeping aphids under control in accordance with the methods recommended in Chapter XVI should assure you of no problems from this, provided you purchased your bulbs from reliable dealers. Plants affected badly with mosaic should be destroyed.

Botrytis is another disease which can trouble Easter lilies, provided ventilation and humidity are not correct. Provide good ventilation and lower the humidity (also avoid overhead syringing for a while) to help correct botrytis. Again, check control methods in Chapter XVI.

Album, Auratum, and Rubrum Lilies

Three of the loveliest lilies I know for good forcing are album, auratum, and rubrum. They are lovely for corsages and bouquets. Their delicious fragrance makes them a favorite with most who know of them. By keeping the bulbs in cold storage, at 33 to 34 degrees, the bulbs can be held and started at most any time of the year. Those planted in February will flower in July or August. If planted in December or January, they will flower in May or June. The forcing time required decreases as the season advances into spring. Use a soil consisting of 4 parts loam, 1 part manure, and a 4-inch potful of either calcium sulfate (gypsum) or agricultural lime added to each wheelbarrow load. Also add a small amount of bloodmeal.

Best results are obtained by using bulbs of 8 to 9-inch circumference. Grow the bulbs in pots at temperatures of 50 to 60 degrees. Pots can be set outdoors in coldframes when warm weather arrives. Be sure the pots always set where drainage is good.

Other Lilies

Coral lily. The coral lily (*L. pumilum*) is known by many as

Jamboree strain of *L. speciosum rubrum*
lily forces beautifully. (*Herman V. Wall*)

L. tenuifolium. It is a lovely little plant, growing from 18 to 24 inches in height and produces from 4 to 15 flowers on a stem. When bulbs which have been stored at 33 to 34 degrees are brought in for forcing, they will flower in 8 to 12 weeks at a temperature of 60 degrees. They can also be grown from seeds but this is a long-drawn-out process.

For coral lilies use only sterilized soil, plant them in well-drained soil, avoid the splashing of water on the foliage, and provide good temperature and ventilation control to prevent condensation of moisture on the foliage. Bud count can be increased by feeding the plants regularly with a dilute fertilizer.

Erabu lily. If you like a pure-white lily, the erabu is hard to beat. Use the same soil mixture as recommended for album and rubrum lilies and plant erabu bulbs in 5½ or 6-inch pots. Start forcing at 50 to 55 degrees, until the roots are well formed, and then increase the temperature to 68 degrees for best forcing. Water the plants well each time and then allow them to reach the dry side before watering again. Never allow them to dry out, however.

Formosanum lily. *Lilium formosanum* lily is a variation of the Philippine lily which has blooms with white throats and purplish-colored reverses on the petals. Check the paragraph on Philippine lily for cultural information.

Glory lily. The glory lily, or gloriosa, is not a true lily. It has lovely, colorful blooms usually of red and yellow with a curious form. Its flowers have wavy, reflexed segments and the stamens are long and spreading. They are grown from tubers, tuber divisions, or from offsets.

Start tubers in early spring in pots. Give them a rough, turfy loam which contains plenty of leafmold. Feed the plants regularly and liberally, once growth is well established.

Guernsey lily. The Guernsey lily (*Nerine sarniensis*) is not a lily. Rather, it belongs to the amaryllis family. Its flowers run from pink to scarlet and produce lovely recurved petals. See amaryllis for culture information.

Lily-of-the-Nile. Lily-of-the-Nile (*Agapanthus africanus*) is a member of the lily family with blue flowers. Give it the same sort of soil recommended for album and rubrum lilies and grow it in a cool greenhouse. It needs ample water during spring and summer when it is growing, but water must be restricted during fall and early winter.

Philippine and White Queen lilies. These produce pure white, bell-shaped flowers, similar to Easter lilies, and they can be grown from seeds. It takes 12 to 14 months to produce the Philippine lily and 14 to 16 months to grow the White Queen lily. The White Queen lily is generally considered superior to the Philippine, producing more flowers per plant.

Sow seeds in January on leafmold, covering them lightly with finer leafmold for best germination. Leafmold should be barely moist but not wet. Germinate the seeds at 40 degrees. If watering is necessary, do so with tepid water. Provide bottom heat to get good germination.

These lilies like a fairly rich sandy soil. Space the plants well.

Grow them in the greenhouse at 52 to 54 degrees. The temperature may be raised slightly as flowering approaches. These lilies do best when grown in beds, rather than pots.

Miscellaneous Bulbous Plants

Amaryllis. There are many plants which belong to this large plant family. A number of them are called "amaryllis." Some are true amaryllis and others are not. The genus *Hippeastrum* is the one generally grown. This one has huge lily-bell flowers which come in red, white, and shades of pink.

Bulbs are best started in November or December, using a good turfy loam. To a bushel of such soil, add a 4-inch potful of balanced fertilizer such as 2–10–10. The bulbs should be only ⅓ buried and the soil should be kept moist once growth has started. Continue to water the bulb after flowering, for the foliage does not appear until then. This will enable it to store up food for another year. In early fall discontinue watering and rest for 6 to 8 or more weeks as desired.

Blood lily. The haemanthus also belongs to the amaryllis family. (Check amaryllis for its culture.) Its flower heads contain dozens of star-shaped florets on a fleshy stem. Grow it at 50 to 60 degrees F.

Cape cowslip. This one is probably best known by its scientific name, *Lachenalia*. It can be used for potted plants or hanging baskets, inasmuch as there are both pendulous and erect varieties. Pot the bulbs during August or September in a good turfy soil, bringing them in from the coldframe in late November or early December. Force them at 50 degrees F. and give them good ventilation, minus drafts.

Crocus. One of the bravest of early spring flowers is the crocus. We know that spring is on the way when the crocus appear. Use a soil similar to that used for tulips and force the corms in 4 or 5-inch shallow pots at 45 to 50 degrees F.

Gladiolus. Gladiolus corms are not forced as much in the greenhouses as they once were. But their quality is increased and their beauty enhanced when they are. You can plant the corms as close as 2 by 6 or 4 by 6 inches, using a light soil of only moderate fertility. The corm will supply all the food you need in a normal soil to force the plants into flower.

Grow gladiolus at 50 degrees. Provide supports of some sort as the plants begin to stretch upward. Thrips are a principal enemy of gladiolus. Check Chapter XVI for their control.

Lily-of-the-valley. True lily-of-the-valley is *Convallaria majalis*. This lovely flower and its wonderful fragrance always seem to spell "wedding." However, it is equally lovely for small arrangements, corsages, and just for "sniffing." For forcing, purchase pips which have received a freezing treatment. Pips which have not been frozen will not force properly. The loveliest of flowers are produced when the pips are forced at the high temperature of 80 degrees. At this temperature, they force in 3 weeks. However, you can force them at cooler temperatures, too, taking from 4 to 5 weeks for flowering. Plant the pips in equal parts of sand and peat or sphagnum moss. Start the forcing in a dark place. Once the pips have emerged, finish the forcing in full light.

Ornithogalum. Use *O. arabicum*. It produces heavy, fragrant clusters of flowers which are borne on heavy, fleshy stems. Commonly called star-of-Bethlehem, it produces flowers before the foliage appears. Keep the plants moist and force them at 55 to 65 degrees.

Oxalis. Use a light soil and an intermediate forcing temperature for this little fellow. It is grown from button-like tubers and produces flowers of white, yellow, or pink. Feed the plants now and then with ammonium sulfate or liquid manure.

Ranunculus. *R. asiaticus* is grown from tubers and requires a rich, well-drained soil. Force them at 50 degrees and follow the cultural procedures recommended for anemones.

Scarborough lily. Scarborough lily, *Vallota speciosa,* needs 50 to 55 degrees for forcing. Soil must be well drained and kept moist. It will reward you with lily-like flowers of scarlet during the spring and summer.

Tritonia. *T. crocosmaeflora* should be potted in October for flowers in April. There are reds, yellows, and oranges with a dozen or so cup-shaped blooms to each branch. Grow them at 45 to 50 degrees.

Tuberose. *Polianthes tuberosa* has lovely, white, fragrant flowers. Force it at 55 to 60 degrees and water it heavily after good growth has started. It requires a coarse loam which is well drained.

Veltheimia. *V. virdifolia* produces an unusual, tritonia-like flower. Its yellow blossoms, tinged with red, are borne on medium-sized spikes. It has beautiful sword-shaped foliage. Bulbs should be started in November or December. Force them at 50 degrees and keep them moist through flowering. Then run on the dry side.

CHAPTER XXVI

A Word About Maintenance

I would be remiss if I did not put full emphasis upon the importance of good maintenance of a greenhouse. It does cost money to do maintenance work on a greenhouse but it is a lot more costly if you neglect it. Neglect also breeds disinterest, for when you fail to produce the quality blooms and plants you hoped for, your interest is bound to wane.

On the market today are many fine construction materials and operating equipment such as were not available just a few years ago. Most of these materials and equipment are designed to do a longer-lasting job than ever before with less cost of upkeep. But, even so, there are certain maintenance problems from time to time when you own a greenhouse.

The most intelligent approach to greenhouse maintenance is to foresee things well enough so that as few emergencies occur as possible. This means doing various maintenance jobs on schedule and anticipating the wear and tear that takes place with equipment, replacing it when necessary, thereby preventing many emergencies in the first place.

The natural time to handle most of the maintenance work around the greenhouse is during the summer. This is the time of year when there is a minimum of growing activity, and the time you normally would spend with crops can be, instead, turned toward repair and upkeep. But in addition to this summertime maintenance work, you should have regular inspection dates throughout the year when you take time to inspect everything from machinery and heating and ventilating equipment to the greenhouse itself.

Maintenance Pointers

Every part of the greenhouse needs inspection and attention from time to time. Here are the things to look for:

(1) The foundation can, and often does, need attention. The masonry type of foundation requires the least upkeep of all, but even it can be subject to damage from alternate freezing and thawing which can work small cracks into sizable ones. Usually this is something which can wait until summer rolls around, but any places which are letting in the cold can be patched up temporarily. Wooden foundations or side walls, of course, take an awful beating from within and without and are in need of constant attention. That is the reason why wood is not so desirable here. Maintenance is too costly. The normal maintenance of the wood side wall or foundation amounts to regular painting and treatment with wood preservatives to increase the life of the wood.

The greenhouse owner with wooden foundations or side walls would do well to consider replacing them with masonry during the summer as a means of eliminating considerable maintenance. Cracks which come in a masonry foundation due to settling of the foundation or other causes should be repaired by filling in the cracks or replacing those portions which are too badly damaged. If settling has been the cause of the damage, check the reason and correct it by extending the foundation further beneath the soil surface or by stabilizing the footing with rocks, etc.

(2) What needs to be done to the greenhouse, itself, to maintain it properly? Look the glass over well. The obviously cracked and broken panes are easy to spot and must be replaced. Not so easily spotted but equally necessary to replace are the "worn" panes of glass, those which are scratched and weathered, for they are not capable of transmitting the amount of light which you need. If the need is great, consider a complete reglazing job. Don't put any glass back that is beginning to show signs of weathering.

Whether or not you reglaze doesn't depend entirely upon the condition of the glass; the condition of the glazing compound which holds the glass is of equal importance. If the compound is missing in only a few places, these can be replaced with putty or glazing compound. But if the putty shows the need of general replacement, think about reglazing. Whether patching or doing an entire reglazing job, use one of the newer, better glazing compounds instead of common putty. They are simple to apply and have a longer life.

Push any slipped panes back into place and refasten them with glazing points. (If reglazing is to be done, all glass must be removed and thoroughly cleaned.) Discard the "worn" panes.

Rafters must have all nails, screws, etc., removed and the same sort of inspection and removal is necessary on the ridge cap. All putty must be cleaned from the bars; for this job there are bar cleaners available which will make the task considerably easier. A bar cleaner will remove rust, spots, paint flakes, splinters, and rough spots. Once the glass has been removed each bar should be thoroughly inspected. Those showing deterioration to any degree which makes them unsound should be replaced with new ones.

Both new and badly weathered rafters or other wood members of the greenhouse should, first of all, receive a priming coat of paint which contains white lead and raw linseed oil. This will give the wood a good foundation for the finish coats. The wood is penetrated by the primer, giving it a moisture-resisting quality that is necessary in a greenhouse. Then give the wood two coats of a high-grade greenhouse paint, making sure there is ample time between coats for the paint to dry. A good greenhouse paint is not a house paint. It is a multi-pigment paint and should have a fungicide added.

If painting is done without removal of the glass, the task becomes much simpler. There are bar painters available which apply greenhouse paints to the bars in rapid order. However, the bars must be in fairly good condition. All cracked and damaged glass must still be replaced before the painting job is done, for the weight of the bar painter may break through cracked panes.

If the job of reglazing is any size at all, by all means use a glazing gun for applying the compound. First, make sure that the panes are securely in place and will not slip. Then, using a good grade of glazing compound that won't harden and crack, as putty does in time, use the gun to do a speedy, even job. Although glazing compounds form a tough skin on the surface, they remain soft beneath. Learn the trick of applying just the right amount. You don't want to have to go along afterwards and remove excess glazing compound, but neither should you be stingy with it. After a little practice, it will become simple to use the glazing gun and thereby to lay a ribbon of glazing compound on that is just the right thickness.

Do a neat, thorough job as you replace the glass on the rafters. The overlapping should be uniform and each pane should line up with those on either side. At the bottom corners of each pane, place a greenhouse tack to hold the pane in place and place another tack on each side about halfway up the pane. Be careful, however, that it is snug enough, but not too snug against the pane. If the pane is bent by the pressure of the tack, the glass may break. Even though it may not crack at once, the alternating temperatures and storms which occur will be bound to cause cracking later. Once the glass is in place, the glazing compound is ready to go on. Even though you may only be replacing a few panes here and there, do the job well. Should a poorly installed pane become dislodged during a storm, it could be the cause for a "chain reaction" that could cost you a large number of panes. Also, remember, every loose-fitting pane of glass constitutes a heat loss and heat is money.

If you have never used bar caps and your rafters are in good condition, consider installing bar caps when reglazing and painting. Although the bar caps represent an additional cost, I am firmly convinced that bar caps will more than pay for themselves in a relatively short period. First of all, bar caps tighten up older greenhouses and prevent glass slippage, frequent reglazing, and painting. I have heard commercial growers state that the cost of bar caps' installation is entirely paid for in six years or less, simply because of the savings realized on maintenance. This doesn't recognize the saving on heat, too, which is bound to occur by having a tighter greenhouse.

Painting the greenhouse rafters on the inside presents another problem, unless the house is being reglazed. In that case the rafters are bare and much easier to paint and, more than likely, the greenhouse is free of plants. If you can possibly arrange to have your greenhouse empty before doing any painting on the inside, you will find the task shortened considerably, for it takes almost as long to cover the plants to protect them from paint as it does to paint the greenhouse. Painting on the inside must be done when the greenhouse can be aired well to rid the house of fumes.

Where plants are in the greenhouse at the time of painting the inside, do not cover too large an area at one time, and be sure to start early enough in the day to allow most of the paint fumes to dissipate before it is necessary to lower ventilators at night. An ideal time to paint the inside is when ventilators can be left open all night.

Don't fail to give the gutters on the inside and the drip grooves proper attention. Gutters should be thoroughly cleaned and repaired, removing all grit and scum. The gutters should have a heavy coating of tar-base gutter paint which is necessary to resist the extra moisture present in these parts.

The steel-rafter greenhouse doesn't require the maintenance that a wooden greenhouse does, but don't be lulled into thinking that it is maintenance-free. The steel house should also have a thorough checking and reglazing. And, at frequent intervals, it should be repainted with aluminum paint to protect the metal from rust. The all-aluminum greenhouse, of course, has far fewer maintenance problems. In the main, only an occasional inspection of glass is needed.

As you paint your greenhouse, don't make the mistake of painting the metal parts with the same paint you use on the wooden ones. The metal parts need special attention. Although the deterioration is not as rapid on metal as it is on wood, rust can consume the iron or steel parts of a greenhouse in time. Oftentimes, the damage occurs at a much faster rate than one would think possible, especially when rust has a good foothold. Hinges, purlins, posts, fittings, and all other metal parts (except aluminum) should, first of all, have the rust removed with a wire brush. Remove and replace those parts which are badly rusted. Then use a good clear corrosion-resistant paint which will penetrate the pitted and damp areas of the metal. This should be followed with a good coat (two, if needed) of high-quality rust-preventive paint for best results.

Ventilating Equipment

If you have been successfully growing plants in your greenhouse for a while, you know the importance of having ventilating equipment which works well at all times. Whether automatic or manual, the ventilation equipment must be checked periodically, kept properly lubricated, and otherwise maintained at all times. Most greenhouses are equipped with arm-and-rod or rack-and-pinion apparatus. Check each part of the apparatus carefully, replacing badly worn parts and repairing minor defects. The gears will be greatly reduced in their efficiency once they begin to wear considerably. Do not allow them to approach the danger point. Ventilating equipment must be inspected more often than just each summer. Be sure to use the type of oil or grease recommended by the manufacturer.

Check the arm-and-rod of each sash, making sure that the adjustment screws are holding firmly and determining whether or not each sash is being raised in perfect alignment with the other sash on the same apparatus. With the rack-and-pinion type of apparatus it is necessary to regularly inspect the teeth and bearings to see if they are in good working order and the chain drive should have no broken links which are bound to cause real trouble sooner or later. All joints, universal joints, etc., of either type of apparatus should be inspected carefully, for there is considerable wear and tear on these parts. Replace those which appear weakened.

One point is often overlooked which every year brings damage to greenhouses and grief to the owners. This is the matter of sash which are not securely fastened to the ventilating apparatus. In a storm considerable strain is placed at this point and loose screws or bolts often pull loose, causing considerable damage as sash go flying against the greenhouse.

To properly maintain the ventilating equipment, as well as the heating system, wiring, etc., keep on hand at all times a reasonable supply of spare parts. If your greenhouse is of fairly good size and even, perhaps, in the semi-commercial bracket, it is wise to have a complete set of major parts as well as minor.

The automatic ventilating system requires some specialized maintenance not needed with the manual apparatus. Keep the regular check on the motor-driven power unit and the thermostatic controls. They must be in perfect condition at all times. Follow the manufacturer's recommendations and inspect the full unit regularly. Of course, in case of a breakdown of automatic equipment, there is always the manual system to fall back on.

Cooling System

If you have a cooling system in your greenhouse, make a thorough check of exhaust fans, louvers, evaporative coolers, and whatever other parts go with the particular cooling device used. A critical examination of the entire system should be given prior to the time it receives heavy usage. Thereafter, it should be given almost daily attention.

Heating System

If there is any place where the most exacting attention must be given at all times, it is in connection with the heating system. In addition to a summer inspection and renovation, a fall check should be made before the system becomes used again. Search for possible weaknesses. Constant vigilance must be used to catch any troubles which appear.

If you have a boiler in your greenhouse, have it drained and given a thorough cleaning in the summer. If it is necessary to have heat most of the summer, use auxiliary heat while the cleaning is going on.

If you have a cast iron boiler, flush it out well to remove sediment. Then refill with clean water and let the boiler stand filled until fall. Then drain the boiler again, flush it out once more, and refill it. During the summer leave the manhole open at the top of steel tubular boilers so the boilers can air out and dry properly. All exposed metal should be kept either oiled or painted during the summer to prevent rusting. A good maintenance idea is to start a little wood fire from time to time to keep the boiler dried out.

Grates should be shaken thoroughly to clean them of ashes and to do a good job (especially in the corners) of cleaning out the ash pit. This latter suggestion, of course, applies to greenhouses which burn coal, wood, coke, or briquettes. Daily maintenance in the greenhouse heated with coal is that of removing the ashes or clinkers. Often disastrous fires are started by careless handling of ashes. Never place them against a wall or other inflammable materials.

Whether you use coal, oil, or other fuel, it is necessary to clean all the soot from the flue or tube surfaces. Small stacks should be taken down and cleaned. Large ones have clean-out doors through which the stack can be thoroughly cleaned of all soot. Keep a wary eye on the stack at all times and replace it promptly when it shows signs of wearing thin. As a matter of safety plus heat conservation, keep the furnace well insulated. Replace or replenish insulating material as needed.

The brick-set or horizontal tubular boiler requires that mud or scale in the belly of the boiler directly over the fire box must be removed. The brick work should be dried out by lighting a slow wood fire in the boiler and letting it burn several hours.

Check all the valves, stems, and fittings to make sure there are no leaks. Clean and oil all pumps and motors. Be sure that traps are working perfectly. For almost all of these items, it is not merely a matter of summertime inspection but also of daily routine inspection.

All lines on hot water or steam should be thoroughly checked. Be sure there are no sags or leaks. In a hot water gravity system, if the pipes slope improperly, the water movement is impaired. Steam lines must be properly vented. Be sure the vents are working correctly. Automatic water feeders should be carefully checked. Many greenhouses have pneumatically operated control systems on thermostats and valves and these should be checked to make sure they are in first-rate condition. In the fall check the lines to be sure that there is no water standing in them. Water in the lines can damage thermostats.

All condensation should be drained from air lines. Make sure that you also drain the lines at regular intervals during the firing season. Do it at least once a week. Condensation is a big problem in some greenhouses. If this is a problem in yours, put the air storage tanks in a cold location such as a refrigerator. This helps prevent an accumulation of condensation in the lines.

Occasionally a greenhouse which is heated with oil will have trouble with an exposed feed line when weather becomes too cold to permit the oil to run freely. This can be rectified by wrapping lead-covered heating cable around the line and plugging it in when the weather is cold. Keep either X-liquid or Smooth-on handy in case of a cracked boiler section. This will temporarily plug up a crack unless it is too large. You can also use water glass for this purpose, too, on cast iron boilers which, of course, are the longest-lasting boilers anyway.

Electric Wiring and Outlets

A breakdown in the electrical system in a greenhouse can be just as disastrous as a heating breakdown and quite often greenhouse fires come as a result of faulty wiring or overloaded systems. All such important equipment as pumps, refrigerators, stokers, etc., should be on individual circuits.

There is usually more carelessness shown in a greenhouse around the electrical system than anywhere else. Circuits are often loaded to capacity and beyond. Yet the owner adds still more load to the existing circuit with the result that a breakdown occurs or, perhaps, even a fire.

Each summer check your system for obvious defects such as worn wiring, improperly installed lighting, etc. If in doubt, have a good electrician check your system to make sure that you are not overloading the outlets at any point. Never add an additional load to an outlet unless you are certain it will not overload the line.

Propagating Equipment

One of the most important items in connection with propagation is the propagating cable which you use. Be sure that it is working correctly. Regularly check the thermostat to make sure it is accurate. Only a few degrees off in temperature, one way or the other, can quickly ruin a lot of cuttings. The cable itself should be inspected at least once each year to determine that no damage has come to it as cuttings were inserted or removed.

The propagating bench should be inspected for proper drainage and general condition of the bench itself. It is a costly and annoying thing to have a propagating bench collapse. If you happen to have an intermittent misting system, this delicate apparatus should have a regular and thorough examination to be sure it is in correct operation. It is of utmost importance that the length of time and the frequency of mist application fits exactly to specifications. Check this often and also go over the system for leaks and dripping. Be sure that each nozzle is functioning correctly. Remove and clean those which are not. An important maintenance point in connection with the misting system is protection for the "brain." Use polyethylene for this job.

Watering and Fertilizing Equipment

Each summer thoroughly examine the watering system. Repair and replace leaky pipes, faucets, and nozzles. Undue moisture from leaky conditions can be the cause of diseases getting a head start. Never allow such conditions to go without repair at once. When replacements of faucets, etc., are made, get the best equipment possible. It proves cheaper in the long run.

If you have been using your regular water system as a means

of transferring liquid fertilizers from a central point to the plants for feeding, be sure that your water system receives extra attention, for the fertilizing materials can cause corrosion of the pipes, faucets, etc. After fertilizer applications, always flush out the line with clear water. It is better to use a separate line for transferring the fertilizer. This, too, should be flushed after use.

Be sure to check the tank in which you mix fertilizer and clean it periodically. A metal tank should be coated in some manner to prevent corrosion. Check the agitator to be sure that it is working properly and make certain that the motor which operates the agitator and pump, and the pump itself, are working correctly. If you use a fertilizer proportioner, check its accuracy once in a while.

A constant water-level system needs systematic checking. Float valves and other regulating devices can get out of order, which will result in the crops receiving an improper amount of water.

Automatic watering devices of many sorts are becoming more and more popular. However, they can get out of order just as can anything else. Check any such devices quite often. Nozzles along the bench and holes in the plastic-hole waterers become plugged, causing uneven watering. Keep the orifices clean. Guard against any leaks or drippage which may occur and cause undue soaking of a portion of the bench. Check the scales and electrical implementers which regulate automatic pot-plant watering devices.

Automatic Controls and Thermometers

Check the "brains" which operate the thermostats, humidistats, aquastats, etc., in your greenhouse regularly. Repair or replace any which are faulty at once.

Use low-voltage thermostats operated by storage batteries instead of those operated from the electrical system as a protection against power failure. This means that the batteries which operate the thermostats, etc., must be checked and replaced before there is any danger of failure in them. Check alarm systems frequently. Check batteries, wiring, and bell. Do this by having a "false alarm" every once in a while.

Check the low-water, cut-off switch, the water-line regulator, aquastat, and automatic stack switch. Any irregularities with these devices can cause serious trouble. Be sure the pop-off safety valve and the pressure gauge on the furnace are working okay. Keep fuses, fustats, etc., so that everyone knows where they are in case of an emergency.

Often overlooked is the fact that the ordinary greenhouse thermometer can become inaccurate. Check it at least once each year and be sure it is checked against a thermometer which is known to be correct. Here, again, use a good greenhouse thermometer, not a home thermometer. Only a degree or two of inaccuracy can hurt many plants.

Benches and Aisles

Wooden benches deteriorate at a rapid rate and need yearly inspections. After some experience with wooden benches, you may desire to switch to one of the asbestos or other permanent materials. Wooden benches should receive regular treatment with a good wood preservative. Pipe legs and braces should have rust removed and be repainted. Check Chapter VII for other ideas on bench construction which will apply to replacement and repair.

Aisles should always be properly maintained. This means keeping them clean and, for that matter, keeping it clean and neat beneath the benches. You are working at cross purposes when you fumigate and spray the greenhouse regularly, only to provide ideal spots for insects and diseases to hide in debris along the aisles or beneath the benches.

Miscellaneous Maintenance

Among the auxiliary areas which need maintenance are the potting shed, soil shed, bulb house or cellar, lath houses, etc. Coldframes must have attention to keep them in prime condition. The frames themselves need repainting and reputtying and the foundations upon which they rest must be kept in good repair as protection from cold and rodents. Use the same high-quality materials on coldframes you use in the greenhouse itself to keep them in the best of condition.

Check regularly all portable equipment such as high-pressure spray equipment, soil shredder, sterilizing equipment, and other items. Each should be maintained well and be in usable condition at all times. Nothing is more aggravating than to prepare to do a job which requires a piece of equipment only to find it is not in working order. Sprayers should be properly cleaned and rinsed after each spraying. Hand tools should be cleaned and put away in good order. Keep everything in a regular place and ready to go at all times.

Check the black shade cloth regularly to be sure that there are no tears or worn spots that would affect your plants adversely. Do all of these things as a matter of regular maintenance and you will find yourself happily growing better plants and flowers and enjoying your wonderful hobby more and more each day.

Index

(Illustrations are designated by italic numbers.
See under Flowers and Plants for alphabetical listing.
See under Greenhouse for greenhouse listings in order of appearance.)